This edition published in Great Britain in 2013 by Soundcheck Books LLP, 88 Northchurch Road, London, N1 3NY, under licence from Helter Skelter Publishing Limited of PO Box 50497, London, W8 9FA

Copyright © Brian Rabey 2013

ISBN: 978-0-9571442-4-8

A CIP record for this book is available from the British Library

Book design: Benn Linfield (www.bennlinfield.com)
Printed by Bell & Bain Ltd, Glasgow

A Passion Play

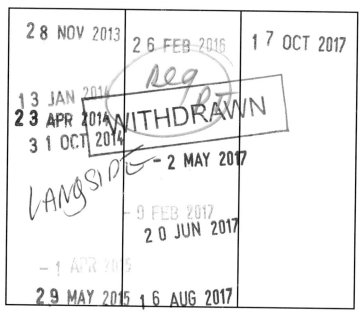

A Passion Play

The Story Of Ian Anderson And Jethro Tull

by Brian Rabey

soundcheck books
the stories behind the sounds

To my parents: wish they were here

Contents

Part 2: The Thoughts Of Ian Anderson

Special Thanks

Shona Anderson, Sam Emerson, Karen Fraser, Martyn Goddard,
Claire Grimley, Anne Leighton, Cindy Redmond, Chris Riley,
Martin Webb, Kenneth Wylie.

Also, many thanks to Ian Anderson and Glenn Cornick for
providing photographs from their personal collections.

Forewords

ANNE LEIGHTON

In 1995, I started working with Jethro Tull, firstly doing publicity for Martin Barre then, the following year, Ian was looking for someone outside of EMI to promote the band to journalists. It's always been pretty exciting to work with Ian and the gang.

Out of the gate, on the first tour, Martin gave me half a dozen names of journalists throughout North America, and one of them was Brian Rabey. Brian is a passionate writer who wishes the whole world would be into musician-based artists, such as the members of Jethro Tull. 60 million Jethro Tull fans agree with him. I see Brian's *A Passion Play* book as a unifier for the Tull fans, who respect studied work and writers who care about what they're creating.

My own history with Tull first started as a fan in high school, when I would hear those songs like 'Aqualung' and 'Bungle In The Jungle' on the radio. I thought, 'This guy has a cool voice, and this is the only thing I like on FM radio.' 'Bungle In The Jungle' was a favourite song, 'cause I knew – from the lion's growl and the pouncing chorus – that it had cats in it. I used the rhythm of 'Teacher' as a metre for lots of my protest poems.

When I finally got into the music business, working as an editor at *Hit Parader* magazine, the publicists sent me an array of albums including new ones from Jethro Tull (*Crest Of A Knave*) and Bob Dylan. So many of the other albums that I got were average with one to three songs that were good, and the rest not so good. Every song by Tull and Dylan was great. So when Tull beat Metallica for the best Hard Rock/Heavy Metal album at the Grammys, I thought they deserved it.

In 1995, when I was doing publicity at Imago Records, the product manager wanted to know what I thought of the band Jethro Tull, and I told him that I loved them, so I publicised Martin's album *The Meeting* in conjunction with the band's North American tour. Martin was getting interviews, internet chats, and loving the attention. Brian was one of the writers. I met Martin face-to-face at a gig in New Jersey, and he mentioned that Ian was a fan of my work. It made me feel good.

Two weeks before the 1996 tour, my phone rang, 'Hi Anne, this is Ian Anderson ...' and I jumped to the phone, and we started laughing and talking. And suddenly, I was hired to drum up interviews for the band, which I did. So much has happened since then, and I've learned a lot and rubbed elbows with folks in an array of worlds beyond just the music industry. Ian's got supporters in health industries, politics, and even the cat world.

A Passion Play – The Story Of Ian Anderson And Jethro Tull offers insight that I never knew, because Brian has studied them in the same way a scholar would. I think it's worth discovering Jethro Tull. This band, and Brian, continue to pave their own paths.

MICK ABRAHAMS

I'm probably the least qualified person to write about Jethro Tull on an overall basis, except to say that my time with the band was the starting block for Tull's future progression. You remember initially we were a unique rock/jazz/blues outfit approaching the music from a different direction to most of our contemporaries? Personally, I was sad – to some small degree – to leave the band when things were happening for us, but Ian's creative processes were working in a different mode to mine and I felt antagonistic towards the management, which sadly caused conflict between Ian and myself.

All that, of course, is ancient history. I'm glad to say those rifts have long since healed and it's a real pleasure to occasionally share a stage with Ian and blow a few of the old tunes that started the legend that is Tull. I haven't read the book yet, but I'm sure you'll enjoy reading this account of the life and times of one of the all time greats of rock music, headed by one of the most talented musicians ever to grace our planet.

CLIVE BUNKER

I was sitting on the tour bus the other day and jotted this down. Please edit or correct spelling or disregard completely if you wish, but if you can use any of this note or not ... I tried.

Having left the band so long ago, I can look back and see that we did get a bit of a name for ourselves. And that name has lasted, so we didn't waste our youth after all. It is also a testament to Ian that he keeps the standards high enough for the band to last. I must say I'm one of his biggest fans.

Short and sweet – but there you go. Take care everybody.

Cheers!

ANDY GIDDINGS

I often scare myself with the thought of how things might have been so different. Until around 1991, I was a 'jobbing muso' who wandered, as we do, from studio to studio, tour to tour and, in between, club gig to club gig.

A member of the 50 or 60 strong audience, for posterity, recorded one such club gig on a cassette recorder. Months later, and without my knowledge, the recording somehow fell into the hands of J.T. Production Manager Kenny Wylie, and was eventually passed on to Ian Anderson. Tull's keyboard player at the time was the mighty Maartin Allcock who, coincidentally, was looking to increase his commitments with the fab Fairport Convention. So contact was made with the sender of the cassette to obtain the identity of the keyboard player on the recording.

Getting the picture? Well this is the scary part:

The sender of the tape just happened to call me ...

... I just happened to be home at the time ...

... Kenny Wylie just happened to be a top man ...

... Jethro Tull just happened to be a splendid bunch of chaps who just happened to be looking for a keyboard player.

Phew! See what I mean?

The rest, as they say, is not so much history, more a fantastic journey through rock, jazz, folk and classical music, and around the world – a few times! I'm proud to appear on several Tull records, and lucky enough to have worked alongside Ian on the *Divinities* project, *The Secret Life Of Birds* and *Rupi's Dance*.

Even if you're not completely up to date with your J.T. record collection, that's O.K., because I know how great all the albums are. Jethro Tull is indeed a formidable musical force. You can count on one foot the number of bands who are celebrating their 40th Anniversary. Looking down at my own foot, I make that six.

In closing, I would like to extend my sincere thanks to some of the nicest people I have had the pleasure of meeting, namely the fans. You have been both kind and accepting over the years.

If we've met, I hope I was courteous and generous at the bar.

If we haven't ... see you soon.

JEFFREY HAMMOND-HAMMOND

To Ena Sanderone (As Ian found himself being addressed by an effervescent stewardess on boarding a United Airlines flight from Asheville, NC to Atlanta in January 1975):

Despite his dislike of being Ian Tull/Jethro Anderson and his persistent protestations to the contrary, there is only one person responsible for the continuous stream of creativity that I've known for the last 45 years. Perhaps, though, the Ian Anderson/Jethro Tull dichotomy emphasises the fact that knowing the music is not necessarily knowing the man. What I do know is that, both musically and personally, he still has the capacity to surprise.

It may disappoint some to learn that this brief foreword contains no embellished anecdotes, no wry comments, or previously unknown band trivia – simply an expression of gratitude to the man who for many and, for me, *is* Jethro Tull.

DOANE PERRY — SOMEWHERE OVER GREENLAND

It seems, somehow, that this is where a good deal of my entire musical life has been spent and although I have been playing for considerably longer than that, I suppose that feeling arises because it seems that some of my most significant musical experiences have occurred within the context of this band.

When I consider the vast panorama of gigs we have done all over the globe in that time it is mind boggling, and yet that probably totals less than half the total number of concerts the band has performed in its very colourful career.

Writing from my own perspective about the years I have spent in the band is a greater challenge than imagined, if only because the broadness of the experience does not fit easily into such a small space. I am sure some of you who know me will recognise, and quickly acknowledge, that brevity is not the strongest of my suits!

When I was 14 years old, I saw Jethro Tull for the first time and I thought they were the best band I had ever seen. I even got to meet the remarkable Clive Bunker two years later at the Fillmore East in New York City, sneaking out for the late show on two consecutive school nights. My parents were blissfully unaware of these nocturnal rendezvous with my friends in the East Village, where we would often meet to go to the Fillmore, Electric Circus or other area jazz and rock clubs. They probably just thought I was a bit bleary-eyed from staying up all night studying. In a sense, I was. Ahh … what trusting folk these parents be!

I saw the band many times over the next few years. They grew in popularity and musical intensity and I often imagined what it would be like to drive such a powerful engine. Would you come nearly unglued, holding on at the absolute precipice of your abilities, or would it be like driving a very finely tuned racing car with plenty of extra muscle in reserve under the hood? As it turns out it has, at times, been a mixture of both, sometimes vacillating wildly between extremes like the needle on a VU meter, all in one evening's performance. It can be a scary, exhilarating and extremely satisfying roller coaster ride, presuming we don't have any train wrecks, although we've had a few of those on stage over the years.

It's funny how, after all this time, the imminent threat of one still lurks with a subtle power around the corner from tricky transitions, extreme dynamic changes, odd time signatures, visual cues, last minute arrangement changes and beginning, middle and ends of songs! It's an oddly exciting adrenalin rush of these possibilities, and maybe the singular one, of playing it correctly and possibly even *very* well, that is part of the nightly fuel that keeps it interesting and us on our toes. I can never recall feeling a sense of complacency when we have performed, and I believe that is one of the intangible, yet clearly perceived, elements felt by the audience that keeps them with us – even if we're having an off night.

I know that maybe it is considered unfashionable to say how you feel – particularly when it comes to your own work – but it makes me immensely proud to have been a part of this wonderfully unique band that has contributed so much to my own life. I feel truly blessed to be able to say that I loved my work and the people with whom I got to share it every night on stage.

So a sincere, heartfelt thanks to all members of Jethro and of course to all of you for listening.

Preface

Where do you begin with the story of an institution that remains as enigmatic 45 years on as it was when it first surfaced, when the individuals who made up, or continue to make up, that group first got together? And how many Jethro Tulls are there, have there been, or still exist?

It's all in the perspective you take, the one you've had for x amount of years and it's also the one you take the closer you get to the origins. It's all about angles and perspective. The book I have written is worlds apart from the book Ian Anderson, or his production manager of many years, Kenneth Wylie, would write ... and so on.

The public at large would argue that Jethro Tull is Ian Anderson and ... friends. Fans have a better idea of the truth. But I see there having been four Jethro Tulls (not counting the original agriculturist who invented the seed drill, whose name was plucked from the pages of a book when the then John Evan Band had run out of names to get re-bookings):

1. The original decision to form a group by school friends Ian Anderson, Jeffrey Hammond and John Evans, better known then as The Blades (named after a private club featured in Ian Fleming's James Bond novel *Moonraker*).
2. The band that had metamorphosed into what became the first Jethro Tull proper with Anderson, Mick Abrahams on guitar, Glenn Cornick on bass and Clive Bunker on drums.
3. The Jethro Tull that emerged as a result of the departure of Abrahams, Cornick and Bunker, which was almost the identical lineup of the original Blades, plus Martin Barre on guitar (who replaced Abrahams after the group's first album, *This Was*) and Barrie Barlow, who had been involved in two versions of the band pre Jethro Tull and post The Blades. This was the lineup, ironically and coincidentally, that created Tull's highest charting albums and most memorable stage shows – Anderson, surrounded by old friends.
4. The fourth Jethro Tull was what resulted once all but Anderson and Barre had departed the third Tull and what would, from this point on, be a band built around that duo plus Dave Pegg, a long time member during the 1980s and 1990s.

Four distinct Tulls – an odd notion, but historically correct. Digest the notion before dismissing it, because at this point I return to the idea of angles and perception. My angle or perception began as a fan. I was introduced to Tull in 1970 by a chance hearing of the group's third album, *Benefit*. It was a landmark day as Frank Zappa's *Hot Rats* was also heard for the first time that afternoon – more about the connection later. In those heady days of album oriented rock, we all knew that every record had an average ten songs, of which two were great, two were good, two were awful, and everything else fell in between – generally. *Benefit* and *Hot Rats* fell into a brand new category – all great. I was hooked, as I have been for over 40 years now.

During the late 1970s, while still in university studying Communications and Theatre, I was overwhelmed by the lashing Tull was receiving by the local press, both for live performances and albums. One review was so off kilter, the song titles listed weren't even correct. I stormed into the editor's office demanding a retraction. Of course, they didn't do that sort of thing, so I said I would write a better review to which he responded, 'You can't do that either, there's no point.' I was a neophyte, plodding the fine line between fanaticism and justice. He relented, was caught off guard for a moment, and asked if the group had released an album recently. Smart fellow! Obviously keeping up with the latest trends.

'Of course,' I bellowed, 'it's called *Stormwatch* and it's brilliant.' It really was; brilliant, that is. 'Why don't you write a review of the album for me and we'll see about getting it printed?', said the editor.

Needless to say, I had no journalistic training and no idea of how to approach this. 'Help,' I cried, and it duly arrived. For the next eighteen hours, my best friend at the time (who was a writer) and I wrote and re-wrote until we were exhausted. The review ran and, from that point on, I became a regular champion for the artistic integrity, not only defending Tull, but other bands I felt were being dealt a skuzzy hand.

The angle has changed, the relationship with the band has metamorphosed and it is now with the keen eye, ears and thought process of the seasoned writer (I hate the term journalist, it conjures up visions of little men with cameras around their necks running after people), that I enter into this project: to capture a snapshot of the 40 year history of all the Jethro Tulls, tempered with the slightly subjective 'feelings' of a fan of 40 years standing.

As for the 40 years part: The first Tull, The Blades, goes way back, much further than 40 years and, for those familiar with the various names attached to the group, it was during a conversation with John Evans – not Evan, as was always printed, for effect – that he mentioned the first time he noticed a new boy in his class named Ian Anderson in 1959: 'A quiet fellow at first, with a thick Scottish accent who had just moved down to my home town of Blackpool from Edinburgh. I remember him desperately trying to get rid of that accent, which he did quite successfully and, at the same time, employing a regionless English accent so that he could not have been recognised as coming from any specific part of England. That was very extraordinary of him, I thought, and I figured our paths were destined to cross, sooner or later.' He was right!

Introduction

Since the average reader of this book will probably be acquainted with Jethro Tull, to at least a small degree, the names mentioned will be familiar in this introduction. If you are a newbie to the band, however, read the full introduction which follows.

Jethro Tull are one of those rare bands that have lasted for over 40 years without breaking up or going on some extended hiatus. At the time of writing however, their future seems uncertain and they haven't appeared as a band since 2011, though Ian Anderson plays their songs live. They have maintained a firm fan base, selling records consistently – about 60 million to date – garnered 40-something industry awards, and performed a couple of thousand sell out concerts from one corner of the globe to another. And they had the great ability to maintain a solid back catalogue of albums without any stinkers in the bunch.

When they began as Jethro Tull in 1968, they thought they had a shelf life of a couple of years. Indeed, Ian Anderson thought the whole thing would be over in a matter of a few short years, as did many bands of the era. After all, with rock'n'roll music being a little over 10 years old, they had no historical perspective from which to judge the possible longevity of the music. Instead, they climbed the ladder of success with none of the trappings and hit making paraphernalia to aid them until, by the early 1970s, they were poised for superstardom. It is a popular misconception that it was *Aqualung* that was their first hit. Truth is, *Thick As A Brick* and *A Passion Play* were back-to-back number one albums in America in the summers of 1972 and 1973, respectively, a feat *Aqualung* didn't achieve.

Aqualung is, however, their most constant and bestselling album over time, but it was never Number 1. The real unsung hero in the breakthrough of Tull – in America, at least – was *Benefit*. The buzz that arose from the completely unusual timbre of that album opened the gates and the minds of the critics and punters to accept the next album with open arms, which was *Aqualung*.

Even more ironically, the album just before *Benefit*, *Stand Up*, has been lauded the breakthrough album for the band in their native UK, where it sailed to the Number 1 position on a seeming cloud of fairy dust – and was also considered their best ever effort by many of their countrymen, if the chart position is anything to go by. It was the young Ian Anderson's most ambitious and personal statement, and the vehicle that made the critical community aware of the fact there was more to this fellow than had been witnessed in the band's earlier years and first album, *This Was*, with all its blues oriented posturing.

Albums like *Stand Up* and *Benefit*, regarded by Anderson as a bright album followed by a darker album (more is devoted to this topic later), showed the world why Ian Anderson was to emerge as the leader of what had begun life as a democracy. However, he is the first, always has been and always will be, to denounce his place as supreme leader and argues that Tull have been a band, not simply one man leading a group of session musicians. I go along with that notion, to a degree, and with the many, many hours of recorded interviews with the past members of Jethro Tull that have gone into preparing this book, that notion has become more and more evident to me.

But Anderson does, and always did, run the show; otherwise, there would not be a Jethro Tull. Look at all the bands that have broken up and drifted off into oblivion after two or three albums over differences, musical or otherwise. With Anderson in the driver's seat, the answer has always been to revamp the lineup or the attitude and that is what separates the one hit wonders and overnight sensations from the institutions. It's also what being a committed musician and artist is all about.

Jethro Tull's ongoing standing as a vibrant and enduring live band is no doubt due to its remarkable ability to navigate complex song arrangements, while maintaining a wildly paganistic, theatrical edge. The band's basketful of classic rock hits, recorded during its high water mark in the 1970s, certainly hasn't hurt either – they are all staples of the live show. Indeed, Tull have taken great pains to only play songs that work in a concert setting, as Ian Anderson explains: 'In most cases, my favourite Jethro Tull songs will be determined by how I feel about them as live performance songs, not by the recorded identity.'

While the band is more often recognised by Anderson's signature flute playing abilities, an underappreciated facet of the Jethro Tull experience is the guitar finesse exhibited by founder Anderson and co-guitarist Martin Barre, the latter of whom was with the band almost since the beginning; a remarkable feat considering over 25 different players have come through the band's ranks. These two exceptional guitarists are unsung heroes of the instrument, song stalwarts whose trademark is to leave the flashy, self-indulgent guitar pyrotechnics out of their repertoire and stick to the composition at hand.

Anderson's creative spark hasn't waned over the years; in fact, rather than fall into stale songwriting patterns, he has never deviated from his own ruggedly individualistic path – and if that means the hit song days are long gone, at least Jethro Tull has stayed true to its vision.

There is one constant that you will find within these pages and that is, as much as is possible, the musicians do their own speaking. It would be an easy task to simply write a story based around what people have said and interject a few quotes here and there. The members of Jethro Tull are now (and probably always have been) a literate group and have the ability to speak rather eloquently, succinctly and say what's on their minds better than any other group of musicians I've encountered in the past 30 years as a writer. Due to the fact there are over 25 musicians who have, at one time or other, been within the Tull fold, I have decided to feature most of them here right down to some of the shortest lasting – probably a distinction Tony Iommi of Black Sabbath is saddled with as his part as lead guitarist lasted two full weeks.

There have been attempts made at putting books together on the band. Ian Anderson intimated that there was even a well known journalist touring with the band at one point in the early 1970s, but that nothing came of it: 'He didn't get along very well with a lot of the people in the organisation, so maybe he just packed it in. I never really found out what happened there.

'Not a month goes by without my receiving some sort of pitch from a hopeful biographer, but usually they haven't got any backing or haven't got any idea how much trouble a biography on a band can be. So these offers come in and I tell the writer to come back to me with a contract or something a bit more solid and I don't hear from them again – I think you're actually the first person who has offered that,' Ian told me. Which is partly why this book is being done today. But it also seemed the right time from a musical and historical perspective.

There has been a resurgence in the popularity of all things progressive. ELP reformed for the High Voltage festival in London in 2010, and Yes continue to record and tour. King Crimson have been turning out group, solo and mini-Crimson recordings for the past few years and Pink Floyd can still command any price for any number of concert nights any day anywhere in the world. The popularity of magazines such as Future Publishing's *Prog* is another good barometer of the renaissance of the genre, as are the many websites devoted to the subject.

Lastly, quality is a constant. You can run through as many fads and fancies as you like, but the truth remains that if you have a piece of art that has quality to it, it will stand the test of time. Jethro Tull stand as one of those institutions that will hold up in the grand scheme of things, whatever the odd critic may say, because the fans and the following continue and are actually replaced as new listeners discover the music.

Part 1

A History Of
Jethro Tull

1

The Birth Of The Blades

Ian Anderson's first introduction to music was big band American jazz. Music by artists like Benny Goodman was perpetually emanating from his father's record player – probably an old Dansette. Anderson recalls:

My father had a few records and an ancient record player. That's the sort of thing we heard, and I suppose my brothers heard it before me. Being the youngest of three brothers, the other two being much older than me, I kind of heard this stuff when it was probably already fairly worn out, but it was the rhythmic nature of it and, I guess, some of that big band stuff also had part of a toe in the world of the ethnic black American music. It was not so far removed from the essence of black American music – I didn't know that then, I was, of course, only 6 or 7 years old, but I think by the time I was 9 or 10, I was aware of what was about to become the beginnings of rock'n'roll.

One of my two brothers had emigrated to Canada and believing, as a 10 or 11 year old would, that this was somehow the home of this new phenomenon, rock'n'roll music, I asked for a pair of jeans and a rock'n'roll record as a Christmas present from him. I'm not sure if I ever wore the jeans. If I did, it was probably the last time I ever wore blue jeans, because that's something I've always stayed away from [laughs]. So I listened to this rock'n'roll record, but instead of being something like Elvis Presley or a cutting-edge style of music, it was by Bill Haley & His Comets. It was not quite what I had in mind; it wasn't the perception I had at that moment in time of rock'n'roll, because what I thought of at that moment was 'Jailhouse Rock', 'Blue Suede Shoes' and 'Heartbreak Hotel'.

Early Elvis Presley was something over the moon. There was just something interesting about the rhythm. The rhythm was something that just naturally appealed to the rebellious whatever. As a pre-pubescent child you just sort of got a whiff of what was going on, which was where it really began. By then, around the age of 12, I got a cheap guitar and began to learn to strum it and play it a bit – something that was popular at the time, called skiffle. Skiffle was fairly popular in the UK, probably closer to what you would call bluegrass in the US.

Shortly after that, Anderson's family moved from Edinburgh, Scotland (although his birth place was actually the ancient town of Dunfermline) to the seaside resort of Blackpool in the north west of England in the very late 1950s. The young Ian was enrolled in Grammar School, what North Americans call High School, where he eventually met John Evans and Jeffrey Hammond. 'Then I picked up playing in a slightly more serious way at age 15, going on 16, when I met John Evans and Jeffrey Hammond who were at school with me and we started the embryonic garage band,' Anderson recalls.

'The things you don't want to talk about tend to be the things that get buried in the back of your mind and, therefore, forgotten. And it's not because somebody has asked the questions, it's perhaps that, if it does come out, it will hurt. Quite honestly, I don't really mull over my previous life's experience all that much, mainly due to lack of time, because I find it difficult enough to make a living,' say John Evans today.

He relates how a group of Blackpool lads got together and through some crazy mixed up scheme decided, despite the fact they all had the intellectual abilities to become lawyers or something equally high-powered, to become musicians. But before recounting the musical beginnings, he insisted on telling the story of how he first met Anderson:

> My father was a school teacher, and he was quite old when I was born. He retired when I was very young and spent the rest of his life teaching me, so I didn't really have too many problems passing the [11 Plus] exam, not through my own abilities. So I went to the Grammar School at the age of 11 in September of 1959. I was 11½ when Ian came into the same class in January 1960. I know it was a few months later, because his family had just moved from Edinburgh to Blackpool and, because he was in the same level in Edinburgh, he was put into the Grammar School in Blackpool. We were considered of equivalent abilities and he was put into my class room.
>
> That was the first time I clapped eyes on him, and I remembered him because of his accent. I think children are very discriminatory, particularly in the north of England in a place like Blackpool back in the 1950s, because you didn't really come into contact with many people who weren't of your particular background, accent, colour. Anybody who was different was picked out; not necessarily in a nasty way. I can remember when the first Chinese restaurant opened in Blackpool,

it must have been in the very early sixties about three miles from my house. In the evening after school, we used to walk there and stand outside hoping to see a Chinese person, because we had never seen one before, just out of interest, something different.

So here was this boy who spoke with a Scottish accent, it just sticks out in my mind. But he only had it for a short time, because it quickly disappeared and was modified into a general British accent rather than a local Blackpool or Northern England accent that the rest of us had. So he developed this classless, regionless accent – I was only about 11 at the time, but that sticks out.

And that showed a definite pitch or quality of pitch. We talk about perfect pitch in music, and you could tell that he knew exactly how he wanted to sound. It must have been determined by his personality, whether consciously or not, he must have thought, 'I don't want to be different, I don't want to be different in the way of being identified as from Scotland, or any particular region and I definitely don't want to take up the local accent.' I believe that demonstrates a facet of Ian's strong personality.

Evans didn't form any close relationship with Anderson at that time, because they belonged to different cliques. As a child, Evans was hit with a bit of a pedagogical double whammy as, in addition to his father being a retired school teacher, his mother taught piano. 'I was pretty well surrounded,' he laughs 'and I had been taught to play the piano from about the age of 4 or 5. Most kids like myself weren't really ready for it at that age. And today, I don't even have a piano, have no inclination to play at all; that's odd isn't it? I used to advertise our piano in the local want ads in the hope someone would take it, but I didn't succeed [laughs]. It was an instrument of torture ... not really, it got better as I became more proficient.'

By 1962, the 14-year-old Evans, like 14 year olds today, had to be up on the current fads in music to gain acceptance amongst his peers:

On Saturday mornings, there was one radio programme dedicated to popular music which was called *Brian Matthew's Saturday Club*. Now this was just before the era of The Beatles, so the pop music that was available, and therefore was featured on this programme, was largely American music which, quite honestly, I found boring, especially at 14; it just didn't seem to relate to me. It all seemed the same arrangements but, because that was what was available, you had to pretend to like it so you could then talk about it with your friends on Monday.

All that changed one evening in late 1962, when I was watching a regional news magazine programme called *Scene At 6:30*, which was from our regional television station, Granada in Manchester. Occasionally they would just feature a local artist, singer or group, most of whom would play rehashed versions of American music, but this particular evening they said they were featuring a new group from Liverpool who had a new record out called 'Love Me Do' and, I don't know, something electric happened. It was something like 'Where were you when Kennedy was assassinated?' or 'Where were you when Princess Di was killed?'

But I didn't immediately think this was going to be the next big sensation. It was just 'There's something interesting and different about this bunch.' I remember the drummer had this very strange face. He didn't look like a rock star, his nose was far too big, but there was something appealing, so appealing that it just stuck in my mind. I didn't really understand them either. 'Love Me Do' was a very strange record. It's not exactly what you might call a rock classic hit from that particular time, it's very different, but I thought 'That's what I want to do.'

The young Evans was daunted by the fact that piano – the instrument he had been taught to play since infancy – was not one of the instruments the new bands were featuring on stage, and decided playing the piano was actually a big drawback. So he decided to overcome that and take lessons in forgetting how to play piano and play something else. 'I didn't want to play guitars. I think guitars are silly [laughs]. You can't really do very much with a guitar, but with drums you can do what you have to. I thought that what I could play was the drums.'

By 1963, The Beatles were becoming firmly established with records like 'Please Please Me' and their first album (in the UK) with the same title. Evans recalls: 'It's still at my mother's house somewhere, I can't find it though. I listened to it with an ear to what the drummer was doing and by this time my father had, unfortunately, passed away, which I think may have removed what could have been a block, a parental veto on it.'

At that point, Evans reached the next big hurdle for the British school kid to cross which was the 'O' [Ordinary] Level school examination, normally taken at 16. Essentially, it was a school leaving certificate in as many subjects as you took, and the passage to the 'A' [Advanced] Level, which paved the way for university and freedom. Evans asked his mother if she would buy him a set of drums if he could pass in at least six subjects. He remembers that:

Fortunately, I got seven and she bought me a drum kit which, at that time cost about £70 and it did the job. I immediately began to drive all the neighbours insane, trying to learn how to play the damn thing, laboriously learning bits of records and trying to reproduce what the drummer was doing.

Before I actually got the drum kit, I had started becoming more and more friendly with Ian, because we had both discovered that we each had ambitions in the music world. Ian had a Spanish acoustic guitar that he had taught himself to play and I think it could well be because of that I decided to get drums. I remember going to his house, which was a sort of a small hotel, boarding house, and he had a military side drum – that's where I first hit a drum – it was Ian's father's drum, probably a World War Two souvenir, a military side drum snare. We tried to do something along the line of reproducing records; Ian playing his Spanish guitar and me hitting this military snare.

The first time that I ever went to Ian's house was the first time that I heard him playing guitar. It was thrilling to hear somebody playing – he had a very strong rhythmical sense. I had never heard a guitar before in real life and all the live music I had been exposed to up until then – classical music mainly on the piano or concert artists – paled. To feel this rhythmical strumming was a totally different thing. It was stirring, the hairs stood up on the back of my neck.

From the humble beginnings of a cheap guitar and snare drum, things progressed, but not enough to cause The Beatles to lose sleep. Once the full drum kit was obtained, the rehearsal venue switched from Anderson's home to Evans' house – it was easier to carry a guitar than a set of drums.

Evans recounts how:

We started investing, on a very limited budget, in amplification equipment, so that the sound of the guitar and voice could be heard above my clattering away on the drums. We bought ex-army surplus amplifiers with those big valves sticking out, not big sexy Marshall boxes, just ex-government with 'Department of Defence' written all over them and loudspeakers that were just sitting in their cardboard boxes. You bought a speaker and just sat it in the cardboard box to hold it, and eventually I decided to build plywood cabinets to put them into.

We realised we needed more people in the band. We needed at least a bass guitar, so we started to look around for people we knew who could play bass. We didn't know anybody ... well we did know one fellow named Smith – more a friend of Ian's, who was a bit better off than we were. I think we had tried him out a couple of times, but we'd decided we didn't like him very much. At this point, I think, we had just taken our 'O' Level examinations. We had opted to stay on at school for further education and I had gone into the Sixth Form specialising in Sciences, and Ian went on into the Sixth Form too, but into Art, Politics, Geography and so on. We weren't actually in the same class anymore, and one of the new people he met in his class was this boy who was a bit older than we were, because I think he had to repeat a year or something, which is why we hadn't met him before. And that was Jeffrey Hammond.

Ian said, oddly, if we had met him a few years later we would have thought him a lunatic [laughs]. He wasn't a lunatic, he was just an individual, just different and somehow he fascinated Ian, and Ian wanted to get him in as the bass player, mainly because of our experience with the other fellow Smith. I think Ian might well have formed the idea that it was more the personality and the image of the person, rather than his ability to play music, because you can teach somebody to play music, but personality and image is something harder to find.

Anderson concurs: 'That's pretty much the way it started; I met John and then Jeffrey at school, and we decided to form a band. I had a very cheap guitar and Jeffrey had a cheap bass and John decided he wanted to play drums, so we started off as a three piece.'

Jeffrey Hammond's parents owned a hotel, so he had a little more money and was able to buy records which influenced what the trio were listening to. He began to bring in blues records. Probably due to the influence of Anderson, they were very conscious of having to look a little bit different to the other groups around Blackpool at that time, who were wearing sharp mod suits.

Anderson remembers that: 'We were the complete opposite. We used to wear black shiny plastic macs, very tight imitation suede trousers and pointed shoes – [then] high heeled boots when they first came out, when I believe they were called Beatle Boots. I remember, I had an earring in my ear. It wasn't a real earring, it was a painted tin curtain ring from Woolworth's which I clipped and sort of managed to hook onto my ear to make it look like my ear was pierced. It took me about ten years to pluck up the courage to finally get a real pierced earring.'

The affable Mr Hammond (who acquired an additional hyphenated Hammond added onto the end of his name for effect during his days with Tull), can be described as the neutral corner in the history of the band. He has nothing negative to say about anybody and was involved with The Blades and subsequent bands as well as the *Aqualung* through to *Minstrel In The Gallery* era Tull. He appears to have been there more from ties of friendship than any questing for fame and fortune. He is the link that seems to keep the ties with the older Tull members unbroken. And, I suspect, a bit of a referee, confidant and all around good friend to one and all. He never gave the impression he liked ruffled feathers and, in the end, was one of the few Tull members who left the band simply because he didn't want to be a rock star anymore.

Hammond muses: 'You could hang labels on each of the original members of The Blades. John was the historian and musical director, Ian the creative and writing force, while Barrie [Barlow] eventually became a driving and antagonistic force.' Put together, these qualities are all complementary and make for an interesting chemistry, which is probably why, once they had all returned to the Jethro Tull fold by the end of the *Aqualung*, beginning of the *Thick As A Brick* writing/recording phase, this was to become the most popular and successful lineup in the band's history.

While conversing with Jeffrey, the unfortunate absence of any input into this story by Barrie Barlow was troubling to him, because, although he and John had been there with Ian at the start, so too had Barrie and he is, supposedly, a colourful character who could have added some interesting slants to the history of the band. Sadly, we will not be hearing from Mr Barlow.

Hammond reminisces;

I think Barrie was extremely happy and thrilled to be part of it on both occasions, but I think he was also a very questioning sort of person and was always forthcoming with his opinions about things and that wouldn't always be agreeable to everybody, particularly in certain circumstances, within certain circles within the band. But I always got along well with him. More so the second time, because he was terribly young when he first came along in Blackpool – he was about 14 – younger than the rest of us anyway. I still have a good relationship with him.

The interesting thing about the characters within the band is that there is such a range that you could almost write a book about each person. It was such an exciting time to be living and growing up, the 1960s, when music was such an important thing and, of course, that was part of what pulled people together. Music was important, but friendship, whether it was in the early days or later on, is the one thing that I missed once I left the band. What I missed was not seeing people and, inevitably, going different ways after you have been in a band encapsulated that. I found it a real wrench [laughs] even though I wanted to get away from it, to do other things.

But I'm very fortunate in that, obviously, certain people drift in and out of touch with people, but the five people that were in the band when I was in it for those five years, I think I'm on good terms with them all.

I think I met Ian when I was in first year sixth and John went off to do Sciences and Ian did Arts and Humanities and that's what I was in. I remember meeting Ian in the Geography room and he just came up to me and said 'You look like you should be a musician or a bass player' the exact phrase escapes me. He found out that I didn't play an instrument, but everybody wanted to in those days, so I told him I was interested. It was due to interest and curiosity that I went around with him to some friend's house who was a Jehovah's Witness. I think his name was Hardman [this person's name will pop up again with a completely different spelling] and he [Anderson] said 'Why don't you learn to play bass?' I always loved music, but I never really put much thought into playing an instrument – it wasn't the furthest thing from my mind, because one does have these sort of romantic ideas. I mean, I loved Brahms' violin concerto and I listened to it endlessly, particularly while I played billiards in this small hotel my parents owned.

Ian was quite persuasive, so I took an interest partly out of curiosity. It was a rather strange beginning to one's career, so we mucked about with this Hardman character, trying to learn tunes and then he seemed to drift right out of it. And there had been other fellows who had been in class with John and Ian in the fifth form who were on the periphery, and eventually we went down to John's house and that's really where, for me, the embryonic business got off the ground. I think John's mum played an extremely important role in those days. She was important in helping us out financially and was always there in the background ... or allowing John to do what he wanted to do [laughs]. These were wonderful, formative days. They were very important to me, not just music, but the beginnings of friendships. I do believe that, at that time, I got on better with Ian than John. Perhaps that was because our tastes in music were more similar, because John may have been a bit more traditional in his likes and dislikes.

Anyway, I was persuaded to buy a bass, I think it was a Hofner, and an ex-army amplifier and I didn't know anything about the technical side, but John did, and he got me a speaker which I didn't know you needed [laughs], and he wired it up for me. There was a piano in his mother's living room and I had this speaker sitting on top of the piano, so when I played, it jumped up and down on the piano [even more laughter].

Eventually John did build a cabinet for it and, as we progressed, they grew larger and larger as technology advanced and he painted them black in order for them to look less homemade. He did a good job, so the three of us spent a lot of time in his living room for months and months – it seemed to go on endlessly – and then one day we went round to this youth club near John's place called Holy Family. I think they took me along there to inspire me to want to make a real go of it. The Atlantics were playing there and they proceeded to point out that this is what a live band did, and that there were lots of girls interested (which was a terribly good feeling), and I wanted to be a part of this. I asked who the bass player was, and they pointed out the guy with the guitar with four strings and I said 'Yes, I would very much like to be one of them' and I think that was instrumental to me becoming part of it.

They were the type of band that did covers of the pop tunes of the moment without much depth. Musically it wasn't at all impressive. So they [Anderson and co.] decided to take the time to teach me to play the bass and, for some reason, it was always, or seemed like it was always, winter outside, I always had a cold. Eventually we got to play a couple of tunes, 'I Can Tell', an instrumental, and 'Roll Over Beethoven', and eventually we moved from the front room and started rehearsing in a room at this youth club. We must have had some better equipment by then and it was just the three of us, until some young ladies began to come in, so there was this first audience with us doing this horrendous version of 'I Can Tell' with these sort of ropey instruments, not terribly well played.

But people came and showed an interest, which helped us, and we began to expand our repertoire. The social thing went quite well too and then we began to be able to play a lot of tunes and then eventually it began to become clear that we needed a rhythm guitarist and that's when a fellow named Mike (or Peter?) Stevens, who I believe had been in The Atlantics, eventually joined, and we started doing one or two gigs as The Blades.

The Blades was Anderson's idea, whereas Hammond's contribution was more to do with the band's image. Anderson had been a great follower of Ian Fleming's James Bond which is where the name The Blades came from; a private card club in the novel *Moonraker*. The music they were playing at the time was essentially chart pop music: Beatles' tunes and Stones' tunes and eventually it was The Rolling Stones' attitude that had most effect on the band, as Evans explains:

We found them more interesting than The Beatles, they were rebels. Of course, The Beatles had to be marketed the way they were, to allow for the rebel types to come along and that's what we really latched on to. That's where we got the beginnings of our 'surly' image at the time.

At that time, the interest of bands like us reverted to the roots of black American blues music and Jeffrey was quite instrumental in that respect. He was very interested in that music and he began to search further and further back before, even beyond Chuck Berry and Bo Diddley. He liked what he heard and he started to become our source for ideas with records that were very difficult to get hold of – the American black blues artists, and he very much liked the music of Sonny Terry and Brownie McGhee.'

The Blades were being persuaded by Jeffrey to start imitating this black music, rather than carry on doing cover versions of what was in the British charts at the time. So they started to do some of the blues numbers; audience reactions were mixed, to say the least. After several months of very painful rehearsal and also trying to acquire more sophisticated equipment, most of which Evans' long suffering mother bought on hire purchase agreement [known in Britain as the 'Never Never', because, with the high interest rate, it was never paid off] they were ready, as Evans recalls:

> We started to look for a place to perform, that was the exciting part – to play in front of a live audience. We started by playing local youth clubs and we were paid £2. I think the first few we did for free, just for the experience, and then we were actually paid to play at dances – it must have been excruciating – £2! I think we started to improve our equipment then too, but one of the big problems was getting the equipment to the gigs, which ended up being a bunch of trips with a collection of hand carts – two or three journeys each way. We would set it all up, play for 20 minutes, and then take it down and bring it all home. After a while, we were able to persuade a friend of my mother's, who was a builder, to drive us to gigs in his van which he continued to do until I got my driver's licence, which was a year or two later. That was very much appreciated and is still appreciated now.
>
> We played once a fortnight, then weekly, and then twice a week in local youth clubs as we started to get a little bit better. We would keep our material to topical hits and slip in the odd original black blues number (obviously much adulterated by our white north of England interpretation of it) which was met with mixed reactions. That takes us to about 1965.

One of the big influences in getting the band going in the first place was going to see The Atlantics and the effect they had on the young female population. This was certainly a great motivator, as young girls were perpetually impressed by musicians and the promise of being able to produce quality music could turn a young man's head.

'It was the first time I had ever seen amplified sound played by a rock band [Johnny Breeze And The Altantics] and, again, that was pretty exciting even though their material was more middle of the road than we eventually tried to do. At this point, myself, Ian, Jeffrey and Barrie, who had joined by then, approached The Atlantics' rhythm guitarist when he left them. We asked him to join us, which he did, so we had Mike Stevens on guitar, explains Evans.

Hammond recollects:

> We got some cards and posters printed up and our first gig was at that Holy Family club and then some other places as well. What was really exciting to me,

was getting this thing off the ground with very good friends and then we started to drift toward more blues oriented music. The Rolling Stones had come along by then and we listened to the standard black blues musicians like Howlin' Wolf and that seemed exciting. In some ways more so than The Beatles – it wasn't my kind of music really, but the Stones appealed to me quite a lot, that rhythm and blues. Then there were other bands of a similar type who played songs like 'Shame, Shame, Shame' and 'Fortune Teller' and so the music moved away from that pop thing into the blues and rhythm and blues. We didn't do any rock'n'roll because none of us were ever really interested in that stuff, but we did do some jazzy stuff like Mose Allison.

By '65, we were very much into the Graham Bond Organisation and, by then, John was playing organ. I remember trying to dissuade him from moving from the drums to organ because I had always felt quite comfortable with him playing the drums, thinking it would be impossible to play with another drummer. But he decided that was what he wanted and there was a problem finding a new drummer, who I think was Paul Jackman. He was sort of a bluesy player, but I think he didn't have the breadth we were looking for, a range of styles. So I think we advertised for a drummer and that's how Barrie came in. He was only 14 and young looking, but very enthusiastic. He settled in rather well, and John started in on the Farfisa organ. The organ just seemed to be the right sound for that particular time.

Evans' take on why he moved from drums to organ is that: 'New kinds of music were starting to develop. The ones that interested me mainly were the bands that used keyboard and organ like The Animals and Manfred Mann and Georgie Fame And The Blue Flames and Mose Allison – his piano playing was so deceptively simple and so impressive.'

However, he agrees with Hammond that it wasn't easy to fill his old drum stool:

So I decided to move to the organ, which meant we had to find another drummer, which is not as easy as it seems. What incentive have you got, nobody's making any money, anybody who's any good wants to join a band that's actually got a future as far as the local clubs are concerned and they've got a steady income. So we put an advert in our local paper and most of the replies – we got only a few – came with questions like 'How much money will I make?' and 'How many gigs have you got lined up?' to which we replied, we didn't have either, really, because the money we did make went into transportation and rentals. So it was difficult to find someone who wanted to join up for the sake of the music and we weren't

13

playing very popular places and there weren't many people playing that stuff or had [even] heard of it.

Most of the drummers would be styling themselves on bands like The Shadows. To get somebody who could play rock and blues was kind of difficult, and one reply we got was from this young kid who was 14. You could leave school at 14, and he had an out of town accent from Birmingham; you could hardly understand what he said and he looked far too young. Since we had no one else, we decided to give him a try – at least have him along to rehearsals, which used to take place in a garage at the back of my mother's house. Before you get any ideas, it was a very small house amongst a lot of other small houses. The frontage would probably be 30 feet, so you can imagine that everybody in the houses on all sides would be complaining about the noise.

So we got Barrie in and we thought 'Maybe he could do it'. He seemed more interested in the music than the money anyway, and we thought he was so young that we could probably mould him, stop him from becoming a drummer after the drummer in The Shadows, or the drummers of the backing groups with singers called Bobby. So he played on a couple of rehearsals, and afterwards he insisted on going into the house to say goodbye to my mother, which seemed a very courteous thing to do – she remembers that to this day – he just went from there.

By the time he had done some rehearsals, he got some of the numbers down and he went on the road with us. I changed to playing the organ, which was a big relief to me. It's less energetic, you don't have to hit the thing so hard and we had a complete new repertoire based on bands and groups that had organ: Manfred Mann, The Animals and so on. Then the next thing you begin looking at bands that have organ and brass and so on, to enable you to do music by bands like Georgie Fame And The Blue Flames.

Hammond expands:

The jazz side of it began to creep into it, with Roland Kirk, and I liked Charlie Parker and Mingus, of course, and I remember a Dave Brubeck tune that was very popular at the time, I think, called 'On Square Dance', which was in an unusual time signature, 7/4, and Ian was very taken by that different time signature.

So Bo Diddley and these various people like The Animals were influencing us and even 'Green Onions'. I think we had begun to develop a definite following around Blackpool, and we played a diverse number of clubs. John was building bigger and bigger speaker cabinets and, eventually, we got the use of this van which belonged to this Polish fellow named Henry who was a friend of John's mother. He would clean his kit out of the back of this van and we would stick our stuff in it and John would drive us to the gigs, because he was the only one with a licence.

John had been building a new cabinet for me, and it ended up so big that we could hardly get it in the van. We were worried about getting it out, so that it only had the one outing and he went back to building smaller cabinets. Around this time we must have become The John Evan Band, because I think there were other groups that had interesting names and because we took the S off the end of his name, it sounded better. I remember buying a green van and painting The John Evan Band in red letters to really stand out.

Around then we were getting bookings from a fellow named Johnny Taylor and suddenly it became more organised and professional. I've always had this anarchic side to me that preferred it the other way round. It was good fun, but I think we began to go further afield by playing in places like Manchester and, around that time, I began to wonder about my future and whether this was going to lead somewhere. It certainly began to seem a bit tiresome when we began to play the same places again, and to act a certain way and appear professional. So it became more and more repetitive in other words, performing for other people rather than ourselves.

I eventually decided to leave and go to art school, but I suppose if Ian had been writing the sort of material he eventually wrote, it would have been more interesting to me. But the material at that time wasn't going to keep my interest. It didn't seem to have much of a direction, so I left and that was the end of it for four or five years. The whole business of going down to London was a very hard grind, and I lost touch for a couple of years.

2

The Blades To
The John Evan(s) Band

Finding a decent brass player who wasn't just a musical mercenary proved to be as difficult as recruiting a drummer had been, as Evans explains:

> We started to look around for brass players, so we put adds in the local papers and it all went the same way and the guys who turned up who could play like Stan Getz always had the same first question: 'How much money am I going to make?', to which we replied with 'Sorry the position's been filled.' The ones we finished up with were the no hopers who couldn't play properly, but we decided we could get them to play the way we wanted to play. I shouldn't say 'no-hopers', because there was one fellow who was a student at the local catering school who wanted to be a chef and thanks to us he changed to being a student at the local music school. He left us and the next guy who came in, his main thing in life was being a Jehovah's Witness, but he didn't get too far with that; well he wasn't allowed to really, poor guy, because as soon as he started talking about Jehovah we just sort of took the piss out of him. We wanted to let him know our views about it, so that didn't get too far. Bloody good sax player though – Neil Valentine – who now sells double glazing.
>
> We had a trumpet player who had one lung, so he wasn't loud on account of that, but he filled the spot for a while. Then Tony [Wilkinson] came in and, by then, we were getting a bit of a reputation because we were the only seven piece in Blackpool: drums, guitar, bass, two saxes, organ, and Chris Riley was on guitar at that time. Up until then, Ian had been guitarist, but that was around the time when the flute began to come in a bit and he had decided he couldn't devote his time to singing and playing guitar.
>
> Tony Wilkinson had been a drummer with another rival Blackpool band and he wanted to be in a band where he could play sax – baritone, which went well

with tenor. I think we were going through a change, because the guy with one lung felt he had a better future looking after animals in the circus, and we agreed. The guy who had been at catering school left, and we thought that was fine, and we got Neil to replace him on the tenor. Tony came in on baritone and we were still a seven piece. At this point, Jeffrey had left about six months earlier – early '66. We looked for a bass player, but we didn't use an ad because we were travelling a lot, so we just put the word out and we got this guy from a town called Grimsby named Derek Ward, who everybody called Beau. He didn't have any place to live so he lived in the van, and then he got a place in Bolton near the guitarist at the time, who's name was Neil Smith.

So at this point, Ian is singing, I was on organ and we had another drummer, because Barrie dropped out for a while; his name was Ritchie Dharma. Beau Ward on bass, Neil Smith on guitar, Neil Valentine and Tony Wilkinson on sax. Chris Riley had left by this point, to be replaced by Neil Valentine in '66. We used to call Neil Smith 'Chick Murray' after a Scottish comedian, because he had a peculiar way of talking and we used to call Neil Valentine 'The Forest Ranger' after the guy who was on the Yogi Bear cartoons, because he had a big chin and a permanent dark shadow.

At this point, we were travelling several hundred miles from Blackpool on a basically drive-from-place-to-place basis and sleep where you could, under the van or in graveyards, just to get money (in the order of £100 pounds a night if we were lucky). To fill in midweek, we would go down to £30, which didn't go very far between seven of you. Then we come to changes again, because this guy Derek Ward more or less lived in the van. The whole thing began to smell rather bad, so we had to get rid of him and he kind of disappeared. He was replaced by Glenn Cornick. Now Glenn, we knew from another band. They were probably the best band in Blackpool at the time – they were called The Hobos [Glenn Cornick was in The Hobos, but later, we will see that he came directly from another band called The Executives, not The Hobos] and Chris Riley was the guitarist and I think Chris had left us to join them, but they were breaking up. Glenn was playing with a dance band, in fact they had a hit with a song called 'March Of The Mods', and Glenn wasn't happy about that because it was bubble gum. But he had to make a living, and our paths crossed on the road at two o'clock in the morning in a motorway service place and I said 'Why don't you come and join us?' He liked our music and he was a shit hot bass player, one of the best bass players I've ever known, so that gets Glenn into the band. I think that was bringing us closer to the time when we moved down to London.

Glenn's parents already lived there, which made it seem as though everything wasn't so far away. So we went and, at this time, I think we realised that this Neil Smith wasn't going to be with us full time. Also, through playing much further south we got to know Mick Abrahams. I don't remember how, probably because we were playing the same place or gig or something and the same sort of thing happened. He liked what we were doing and we liked his style of playing, but he didn't want to live up north and we wanted to be down south.

That was around November 1967. We went to live in the town of Luton about 20 miles north of London [35 to be precise] because Mick lived there. It was very difficult to live on the sort of money we were making. There was no way we were going to be able to support seven on that. Within a week, it was obvious we had to lose the two sax players. This meant completely rethinking our repertoire, which meant we couldn't actually go out and play. Most of our material was based on a seven piece band and the only thing we were left with was twelve bar blues, which you couldn't do a full set of. We were a bit stuck until we got a new repertoire.

And there was no money by then, so Barrie and I decided to leave. I think there was a lot of pressure for me to go to university, and keyboard bands were not as popular as they had been in the mid-sixties. So, it was thought that a new band could get by with a guitar, bass, drums and a singer. Mick's friend Clive Bunker was the ideal choice for a drummer, so you had Mick, Clive and Glenn living with their parents – the financial burden was lessened. I went back to Blackpool to school, back to university and that was the end of that episode.

Because the name The Atlantics seemed to figure so prominently in the formative discussions with the various Tull members, Chris Riley (mentioned above), was contacted. He graciously told his tale of how slightly incestuous Blackpool bands could be and how, even at this early stage, Glenn Cornick was almost in the picture. Riley sent a full account of those heady days in verbatim form so that any impertinent interruptions would upset the flow and possibly the reflective quality of his account. Since the best way to let a musician/historical figure recount events of 45 years ago is to not interrupt, the next few pages come directly from Chris Riley, still a musician in Blackpool:

The basic story of the early years for Tull did come out sounding as if The Atlantics, a group of which I was a founder member, was somehow the forerunner of Jethro Tull. This was not true. The group was one of many spawned in the Blackpool area from school days type groups. However, the group was, and I think many people who were around at the time would agree, one of the better groups of its type and of that time. We were an out-and-out covers band, but

I think we did it better than most. We could actually play our instruments and Frank Blackburn, who was the lead guitarist, was an exceptional player. We just did it right! We rehearsed a lot, and learned some fairly difficult stuff for the time. We came to be respected and we worked consistently for a period of about three or four years under various lineups. The family tree of Jethro Tull was only drawn up from that point because of my connection and that of a friend called Michael Stephens, who went on to form The Blades with, amongst others, John Evans and Ian Anderson. I was never a member of The Blades.

The Atlantics started in 1962 as an instrumental group, playing covers of tunes by The Shadows, The Ventures, Duane Eddy and similar performers. The lineup was Frank Blackburn on lead guitar, myself on rhythm guitar, Michael Stephens on bass guitar and Ronnie Brambles on drums. We played mostly youth clubs and coffee bars, until we found a singer who was called, amazingly enough, Johnny Breeze. After he joined us, our repertoire improved considerably and we started playing Social Clubs, Working Men's Clubs and similar places, eventually graduating to theatres and more concert-like venues having, by this time, acquired 'management'. It was at this time that we worked with a lot of the big names of the era, including The Animals, The Hollies, Manfred Mann, Gene Vincent, Georgie Fame and the Blue Flames, The Walker Brothers and The Yardbirds to name only a few. At this time, Eric Clapton was still with The Yardbirds, but we also supported them when Jimmy Page and Jeff Beck were in the band as I think Eric became disillusioned with the direction they were taking.

In a parallel sort of way, I too became disillusioned with the band's direction or rather the direction that 'management' was taking us. I preferred the more bluesy/soul type acts, (I was, and still am, a big Ray Charles fan) and, in general, the bands in England were moving in that direction. Our management had us playing middle of the road 'all round entertainment' venues and the music that went with that style, so I opted out and joined Ronnie Brambles, who had left by this time, in a band called The Hobos – the bass player being Glenn Cornick.

The Atlantics continued until they all eventually saw the light and moved in a different direction, continuing playing for several years without ever making it big. It was always, in its many different guises, a well respected, solid band. The fact that all of the members of the band are still playing in some form or another, and playing well, speaks for itself.

I first became aware of Ian Anderson through Michael Stephens, who had been my closest friend at school and with whom I had formed The Atlantics. Michael's parents were not too keen on him playing in a band after school, as they had great expectations of him academically. University, at least, was expected of him; he eventually became a policeman. I think his mother saw me as some sort of bad influence on him, although I too did not fare too badly academically. To her credit though, Mrs Stephens did make our first stage outfits, a very stylish black and red bolero jacket, which, along with Cuban heel boots and tight black trousers, had us looking like out of work matadors!

Michael, however, had to leave and a very fine bass player called Brian Hood who was a school friend of Tony Williams (who came to join Jethro Tull much later), joined us. Small world, isn't it? When Michael left, he started hanging around with what was jokingly (I think) called an 'Arty Set' of students, who frequented a Blackpool coffee bar called The Brush And Palette. Here he met up with John Evans and Ian Anderson and they played guitars together. They knew Michael had played with a group and, with him, they came to see The Atlantics at a church-run Youth Club called The Holy Family, which was virtually across the road from John Evans' mum's house. Several years after – I have since found out that it was 1970 – I read an interview that Ian had done in the *New Musical Express*, where Ian recalled coming to see us play and deciding there and then that this was a good way to 'pull the birds' (in the quaint phrase of the day) so that possibly is the point at which the seeds for Jethro Tull were sown. Anyway, sometime soon after, Ian, Michael, John, possibly Jeffrey Hammond and a chap called Hartley [seen before as Hardman] started playing at The Brush And Palette and then moving on to Youth Clubs in a band that they called The Blades.

I have to say that at this time, Ian did not make any great impression on me as he was probably too busy 'pulling the birds' to take much notice. I did, however, go to see them play somewhere, although I cannot remember where it was. It could well have been at the same Youth Club. This would have been somewhere around 1962-63. I remember John Evans was playing the drums, Ian was just singing and possibly strumming the guitar a bit. I think Michael and Jeffrey were alternating playing the bass guitar with Michael sometimes on guitar, and this Hartley fellow blowing the harmonica. At that point, The Blades were nowhere near in the same league as The Atlantics, but what they lacked in musicianship they made up for in enthusiasm, and they were playing more blues orientated stuff. I remember John telling me that Jeffrey helped push them in that direction. Incidentally, I always remember him later being a Charles Mingus fan. There was a band around at the time called The Pretty Things [there still is] and I seem to recall The Blades playing some stuff off their first album. Only covers of R&B things, but in the right direction.

There was a growing awareness of black music, but it only filtered through to Blackpool slowly. We, and bands like The Blades, came to it through bands like The Rolling Stones, Alexis Korner's Blues Band, The Graham Bond Blues Band and John Mayall's Blues Band, only later going to the roots of it. The Beatles, as well, in the early years, covered a lot of black artists and did it well, let's not forget!

I saw The Blades on a few occasions later and they had really improved. John was now on organ (and playing quite advanced stuff as he was a good piano player, taught by his mum, Alice, a lovely lady) and Ian's playing on guitar was much better. He was playing the harmonica, doing Sonny Terry and Brownie McGhee, Big Bill Broonzy, Howlin' Wolf and Muddy Waters type of things: I was quite impressed. Jeff Hammond was now on the bass guitar and they had a pretty good young drummer with them, he must have only been about 14 years old. My first recollection of Barrie Barlow! A guitarist called Ernie Robinson, who was very much a 'blues' man, had also joined them and I think he probably had quite an influence on the direction they were to take, even though he was only with them for a short time.

As an indication of the almost incestuous nature of the way bands developed, Ernie was to take my place in The Atlantics soon after, and took them in the direction that I had been wanting to go. Ernie is still playing and is probably one of the more original types amongst us. He writes his own stuff and, in fact, we went to Nashville together to try and sell some songs. Talk about coals to Newcastle – but that is another story. I think I was now, by this time, in The Hobos and we were playing similar stuff, but possibly more commercially slanted and featuring the organ on the lines of Georgie Fame and Graham Bond.

When I started to become unhappy with the way in which The Atlantics were going, Ronnie Brambles, possibly still one of the best rock drummers in the country, had left to form another band called The Hobos. I had been to see them several times and, as luck would have it, their guitarist, a good player called Peter Holder, was leaving and I was asked if I would like to join. I joined them on guitar, although I had actually been playing the organ with The Atlantics towards the end. At this time, the band consisted of Chris Wooton on organ (a Hammond as was the fashion), Ronnie Brambles (stage name Ronnie Lee) on drums, Glenn Cornick on bass guitar, although at different times he called himself Glen Barnard and Glen Douglas. I think his original name was Glen Douglas Barnard, but his mother remarried and he changed his name. Forgive me Glenn if it was the other way round [you got it right the first time Chris, his mother did remarry when he was very young and he took on his stepfather's name of Cornick]!

We played around the country for about two years with this lineup although, at one stage, we were joined by a saxophone player called Mal. I don't recall his surname, but he came from Barrow-in-Furness, as did Glenn Cornick and Chris Wooton. Again this was a pretty good band, we could all play a bit. At that time, Glenn was a good solid bass player. For my tastes he became a bit too 'busy' a player when he joined Tull, a bit 'airy-fairy' but I think that came from Ian's influence and his requirements of a bass player. [Author's note – You will notice that at every mention of Glenn Cornick's name comes the mention of his advanced ability on his chosen instrument!].

Anyway, we worked solidly for two years or so, again working with most of the big names of the time (1964-65). Like The Atlantics before us, we played club dates, including the Cavern in Liverpool. We worked with a pop package tour, which was promoted by a pretty big impresario at the time. I think he was called Austin Newman and may have been indirectly involved with Bernard Delfont, who was Lew Grade's brother. It was all a sort of forerunner to the Stigwood/Goldsmith/Ellis type organisations, which I think Tull may later have been involved with. Once again, because we were all doing it professionally, or semi-professionally, at this time, we drifted into the better paying sort of jobs and, again, lost touch with what we liked to do musically and inevitably this took its toll.

We just decided one day (we were playing in Morecambe at the time, supporting, I think, Wayne Fontana And The Mindbenders or The Hollies or some group like that) that we had had enough. Chris Wooton went solo, if I remember correctly, for a while. Ronnie joined a band backing a guy called Paul Raven (later to become Gary Glitter) and went to Hamburg, doing all the same clubs that The Beatles had done. I think Glenn went back to Barrow for a while, but I can't be sure.

It was at this point that I was asked to join The John Evans Band, although I can't for the life of me remember exactly how it came about. Anyway, they were, by this time, a six piece band with John Evans on organ, Ian Anderson on guitar and vocals, Barrie Barlow on drums, Jeff Hammond on bass guitar, a saxophone player called Martin Skyrme (later to become a very fine jazz saxophonist and classical flute player, graduating from the Army School of Music at Kneller Hall), and a trumpet player called Jim Doolin who was more of the Salvation Army school of trumpet players but a lovely chap. He could read pretty well, so John used to write the parts down for him and he would play the riffs with Martin. A mini-brass section. We rehearsed in John's mum's garage at the time. It was a bit of a tight squeeze as, at that time, the average sized British garage was built to house something like an Austin! [Author's note – today, the equivalent of an Austin would be the smallest car on the road, whatever that is]

I think the idea of my joining was that, with all due respect, I was a better guitar player than Ian and had a lot of experience in groups. I think also at this time, Ian was becoming more of a front man and dropping the guitar gave him more freedom. We rehearsed a lot: Graham Bond stuff, Georgie Fame, James Brown, Mose Allison, John Mayall, Booker T and The MGs – you name it, we did it. I think I still have a list of songs and instrumentals that we did. In my view, at this point, the driving force musically was John. He was a good piano player and had a very good ear, as did I. Because of this, coupled with my experience in other bands, John and I used to sit and work things out for the others to play.

I remember being in Mrs Evans' front room listening to album tracks with John, deciding what we could or could not get away with musically. Some things that we liked we were obviously not capable of playing, as I remember listening to an album of Oscar Peterson with Sonny Stitt, the great alto player.

I remember seeing Ian sitting in the corner of the room playing a penny whistle; that could have been the start of his flute playing aspirations. He was actually surprisingly quiet and relatively reserved most of the time. I think his stage persona was something quite different from his private one. He went into a sort of act. He was always very well spoken and polite, especially when Mrs Evans was around. I also think that a very relevant point to make, which probably somehow or other affected the way Jethro Tull developed, is that we were all pretty intelligent young lads with reasonable educational standards. I think Ian and John in particular could have been successful in any area that they may have put their minds to.

Anyway, as a result of all this rehearsing we were a tight band. A local agent called Johnny Taylor had become involved with the band prior to my joining. In fact, it may have been through his intervention that I joined the band, as I had done some work for him with The Hobos. When I joined, there were already some publicity photographs that had been done in a studio and already paid for by Johnny Taylor. In order that it would not cost him to have the negatives scrapped and the band re-photographed, I was dispatched to the studio on my own, struck a pose leaning on a Chesterfield recliner and the resulting picture was dubbed on to the original. This became known as the 'seven heads, twelve legs' photograph.

In his wisdom, Johnny Taylor decided that we should enter a local beat group talent contest. It was being held at an ambulance station in a place called Kirkham, near Blackpool. Against our better judgment, we entered and wiped the floor with the opposition (the other groups just could not compete with our well-rehearsed set). We won, hands down, the princely sum of £25! This pleased Mr Taylor no end and we were on our way. He booked us into as many venues as possible in the local area and just branching out a little in the North West of England. I can't remember all of the places I played, or with whom, but some of The John Evans Band's early jobs were memorable. John may remember more, because he did all the driving of the van into the middle of nowhere and all points north, south, east and west!

Working with Eric Clapton? To be quite honest, I don't think it was any big deal to any of us working with any name bands, They were just another band at another gig most of the time. Clapton only really became Clapton some time later and, like a lot of people, joined the Establishment, so to speak. I don't think Jethro Tull can ever be accused of that, although I think Ian has always had aspirations, personally, in that direction. He is now almost one of the landed gentry and why not? Good luck to him! His success has been hard earned and well deserved. 'The Clapton is God' graffiti probably started, though, around 1966. I preferred him in the early days with John Mayall because he [Eric] is without doubt a very good blues player. I was never very keen on The Yardbirds, although they did produce a couple of imaginative singles for the time. I never got into Cream either, I thought they were very overrated. Barrie Barlow was a big fan of Ginger Baker though. In fact I think they may have had a few drinks (or something) together on more than one occasion.

The John Evan Band played with the John Mayall band at least twice, as far as I can remember. The venues were the Aztec Club in Sunderland and the Britannia Rowing Club on the River Trent in Nottingham. We may have played with them at the Cavern in Liverpool and at an all-nighter at the Twisted Wheel in Manchester. I played in a lot of places with a lot of bands and cannot remember all the details, although I have to say I am surprised at what I have remembered so far. It is all true, although the dates, sequence and venues may be a little mixed up.

3

What's In A Name?

Glenn Cornick was not an easy person to pin down for an interview. However, once he was on the phone from his home in California, his memory and diaries – almost day-by-day – depicting the early days of Jethro Tull and its antecedents, led to at least eight hours of conversations. He also kindly supplied some of the photographs that are featured in this book.

Here's his story:

I was living in Blackpool at the time, playing with a band called The Executives who, although at one time had a hit record, didn't seem to be going anywhere. So I was just trying to get to the next step in that town; this was in 1967 I suppose. When I was playing, I was always looking for the next step; that's the way local bands were, there wasn't much loyalty.

I don't remember knowing anybody from The John Evan Band, but they had a reputation around town as a band who were doing something hipper than everybody else. They certainly weren't on the same circuit as all the other bands. All the other bands were playing more or less the same venues. The John Evan Band never played in town, so that gave them an air of mystery. I never sought them out and it's not as if they were considered a great band or anything. I remember people thinking they had an attitude, that they were cocky. The thing about Blackpool for the people who visited, was that it was as low class as you can get; it was *the* working class seaside town.

So I was playing with The Executives and getting tired of doing that and I think I got a call from someone who said The John Evan Band was looking for a bass player 'Why don't you come down and check it out?' I honestly don't remember how they'd got my number, but I remember going down to an audition and I guess I got the job – this was in March 1967. And the first gig I did with the band was 25th March 1967. We were still The John Evan band, the period of the multitude of names came later when we were in London.

At the time, I was still working for the Civil Service and, although we were still only playing weekends, it wasn't around the corner; it was the other side of England. So I'd be getting home from the gig just in time to go to work. Needless to say, my job only lasted a few months. And we spent a lot of time in the van which Tony Wilkinson's father had secured for us. He [Tony], sadly, died just recently; he played the baritone sax in the band. John [Evans] was a real night bird. John and I would be the only two who could stay up all through the night while everyone else used to sleep in the back of the van, and I used to stay up to the end to keep John company, which is how I got to know John so well. [Author's note – as this book was being proofed, Glenn informed me that he and John had reunited at a convention in Europe and that they played on stage together for the first time in over 25 years – 'We Used To Know' was the song he mentioned]. We used to travel a hundred or two hundred miles to get to a gig – those were the days. It really goes to show that it was a young person's thing.

I remember that on the 5th April we recorded at Regent Sound [Denmark Street, London] the three songs we performed on the Granada Talent Show which later turned up as collectors' items. I don't remember the exact date, but soon after I joined we ended up competing there. I seem to remember us coming in second or something. Interestingly, the only photographs in existence of The John Evan Band were pictures taken of us in stage gear for that appearance. I recall, rightly now, that was only about my third week in the band. Basically, we were doing one-off gigs trying to play jazzy, swing material, but also having to play R&B stuff. When I joined the band, Barrie had rejoined to replace Ritchie Dharma. The lineup at that point was Barrie on drums, me on bass, John on organ, the guitarist's name was Neil and the other sax player's name was also Neil and there was Tony on baritone sax and Ian.

It wasn't long before we decided we had to be a blues band. Blues was a new thing that was happening. There wasn't much going on with R&B so we thought, 'O.K., we'll become a blues band and more or less jump on the band wagon.' We thought 'What do we need to be a blues band?' so we thought, to start off with we needed a blues guitarist. We met Mick [Abrahams] in Dunstable where we used to play in a roller rink called the Beach Comber and he seemed to be quite the jovial fellow and quite a decent blues guitar player. So, we decided we wanted to be a red hot blues band and began to move in the direction of London. If you weren't based in London you weren't doing much. Any country is like that, just like in the States – you're based in New York or LA. So we decided we were moving to London, but we didn't make it all the way; we ended up in Dunstable where Mick lived, which was about 50-60 miles north of London [more like 35], but certainly within striking distance.

As I recall, everybody moved there except our guitar player who we were replacing with Mick. I don't remember what happened to Neil at that point, and

Barrie quit. We found ourselves needing a drummer and we knew Clive through Mick. (Clive and Mick had been together in McGregor's Engine). So Clive came in and, within a couple of weeks, we realised we just couldn't afford to have everybody. I remember a conversation with Ian about how many people we could get away with and it was decided we could only make it with me, Ian, Clive and Mick. We could manage as a band with the four of us and we had to send everyone else home. Not that the others weren't already thinking of going home, but there was also the decision from our end that the only way we could survive was to be a small band as we couldn't justify it financially with seven.

I remember talking with Ian about John and it was decided, 'Well, he can come back later' [Author's note: notice the discrepancy here, this angle of the story has many interpretations, but it was either well planned or an incredible coincidence]. That was the idea of it, if we can survive as a four piece and get going, then if we want to bring anybody back we can do it later which is, in a way, what happened, except, of course, the sax players who we never heard from again.

At this point, having been very diligent and obviously quite nostalgic for the period, Cornick produced his diaries and listed a series of dates and recording sessions :

April 5th, 1967: 'Recording session Regent Sound. Three songs – "Mama", "Take The Easy Way" and "You Got Me".'

May 3rd, 1967: 'Recorded the Granada talent show. At that point we were called John Evan Smash. In fact, we changed our name to do this television show. Before that we had been The John Evan Band. I believe the show aired 24th May. On 2nd June, 1967 I quit my job.'

June 19th, 1967: 'Played the Marquee as The John Evan Smash.'

September 14th 1967: 'Began recording with Derek Lawrence. He was the producer who did the single with the name Jethro Toe on it, because he thought Jethro Tull was silly [past interpretations show this as a mistake, but Glenn claims the producer did it on purpose] and we did quite a few recording sessions with him including some really ridiculous stuff. Between 14th September and 24th October, we did five recording sessions with him. Some were done at CBS studios, some were done at Abbey Road. Now, although we were called The John Evan Smash, it was pretty well understood that anything that would be put out, would be put out under another name, in fact, at one time, Derek Lawrence wanted to put us out as Candy Coloured Rain.'

September 14th, 1967: 'He had us record a cover of a song called "The Man". Of course, it was singularly inappropriate for us.'

October 5th, 1967: 'At CBS studios we recorded something I'm not sure of, and we recorded on the 19th at Abbey Road studios. One song was called "The Seventh Stroke Of Nine". These songs have all surfaced since.'

October 22nd, 1967: 'Recording at EMI of "Mama", which was the same one we recorded earlier in Manchester. We also recorded "Aeroplane".'

October 24th, 1967: 'Recording at Abbey Road. We did some unnamed songs along with a cover of a hit song by the Lemon Pipers, "My Green Tambourine" [Author's note: "Green Tambourine" was a big hit in North America that year]. If that ever surfaced it would be really funny to hear because I know our hearts were not in it.'

Enter Mick Abrahams, the man who had a reputation as a blues guitarist and was going to lead this seven piece soul/R&B band into a whole new era and embark on the then 'about to flourish' blues scene in England. And for the time, it was, indeed, the right direction as bands with a blues base like Cream and Led Zeppelin were poised to make it a whole new hybrid movement. Abrahams was never really that interested in going beyond the straight blues, but his influence moved the 'cover band' experience of The John Evan Band into new pastures. He explains how he got the gig:

> When I first joined the band they were called The John Evan Smash and they were a seven piece soul band. They had a guitarist named Chick Murray? He was like a jazzy kind of player, really kind of straight. The band wanted a blues-rock player and I was playing with another band at the time called McGregor's Engine. They asked me if I'd be interested in joining them and, coincidentally, that same night McGregor's Engine broke up because of the bass player at time, Andy Pyle, who later became the bass player of Blodwyn Pig. So we talked and I said 'Sure I'll play' especially since our band just split up. And they all came down to Luton where I lived. Within three days of being there they all went back up to Blackpool leaving just myself, Ian and Glenn Cornick in the band. Of course they asked me if I knew a drummer and I said yes, because I knew Clive was looking for a gig.

So, at that point, Clive Bunker was brought into the fold and the foursome that was to become Jethro Tull had come together. The basic thrust at this point was still very much to be a blues band and the blues band formula was to have a guitarist up front. The flute was not yet a part of the act proper and Anderson was still only singing and playing harmonica, which was the way the Ellis/Wright agency wanted the band to work – Mick Abrahams, the seasoned veteran was to be the front man, a role he didn't relish: 'At that time Chris Wright already had Ten Years After with Alvin Lee on guitar and I think they were kind of looking for more bands in that mould, but I never looked at it that way. I didn't want be the hero or the front man, I never thought that way. I didn't want to be another Alvin Lee. I believed the band was formed as a cooperative and that every person had a share.'

Ian Anderson gives his take on why Abrahams was suitable for the band: 'Back when we first encountered Mick, he had formed a three-piece band after the style of Jimi Hendrix or Cream, called McGregor's Engine. When The John Evan Band was playing in Luton in the south of England, with McGregor's Engine on the bill, we first met Mick and kept in touch with him. When The John Evan Band looked like it was about to fold, it was with a view to Mick joining the band that we all moved down south. It was because of what Mick was doing, that sort of blues stuff, not really what The John Evan Band was doing. Mick was really more into the kind of up, aggressive blues style, whereas The John Evan Band was kind of a bit more eclectic with varying elements within the band. Mick was much more down a specific route, but it was something that I felt I would like to go along with.'

So it was around this point that Anderson and Abrahams began to co-write music and by virtue of the fact they were both singing they were, at least at first, considered co-front men. But as Anderson moved the flute more to the fore, and his stage persona began to develop, he also became more the focal point of the band. 'Probably because of the more unusual nature of my performance on the instrument that I played, I guess I got more of the attention than Mick (as always happens) because if you're the guy that people notice, for whatever reason, you're the guy that they [the media] want to talk to for interviews; and you're the guy who tends to get photographed more often than the other guy; and you're the guy they tend to write about when doing a review,' Anderson reasons.

Cornick takes up the story:

So that puts us living in Luton. Before we came down, we spoke to a lot of the agents we used to have dealings with. We use to play a lot of universities.

Universities were some of the better gigs – you could play better stuff, so we did a lot of gigs like that. The two main fellows who booked us during that time were Terry Ellis and Chris Wright. In England they were referred to as social secretaries, which meant they were the guys at the universities who booked all the events; they were each at one or the other of the bigger universities – maybe Manchester or Birmingham, I don't remember exactly. They finished at university and their idea was to come down to London and become big shot producers, and we basically let them know that we were now in London too – as a seven piece blues band. By this time they had become the Ellis/Wright Agency, not the management company yet, just booking gigs. While we were living in Dunstable, they were our agents, so it was all within the same period that we moved down as they did. The only other band that they had at the time was Ten Years After, so we followed after Ten Years After's coat tails because they opened a path for the Ellis/Wright Agency.

Luton is also where Clive as well as Mick came from, but Ian and I were living in apartments that were just too horrendous. I lived downstairs and he lived upstairs. Luton and Dunstable are twin towns – Luton being the lower class section and Dunstable the upper class section. Ian and I lived in Luton; probably the worst living conditions I ever went through in my life, but we had to live somewhere. I remember we used to share a can of Irish stew every day. The song, 'We Used To Know' is about this period. You know the line: 'Remembering mornings, shillings spent'? In England at that time, your gas supply was on a meter and you used to put coins in it. So you'd be in the middle of heating up your Irish stew, and the gas would go out because your money had run out. Hopefully you would have another coin to get it going again or you'd end up with cold Irish stew.

Although the band had reverted to a four piece from the seven piece band the Ellis/Wright agency were booking, they weren't telling anyone for fear of losing bookings, so the band would show at a venue as a four piece and claim the car with the others had broken down, and that it would just be the four of them this evening. This kind of resourcefulness was essential to survival for the struggling musician.

'We hadn't told Ellis and Wright that we had gotten rid off the other guys, because they brought us down on the strength of us being a seven piece band. I think we were a little scared to let them know, so we ended up making excuses at every gig we went to and in the end Chris Wright told us "We've been getting some good reviews about you at the gigs but how come the sax players never show?". So we pretty much had to come clean that we'd been doing it for a couple months, but fortunately the word that had been getting back to the office was good so from that point things were fine,' laughs Cornick. Eventually it got to the point where the band was doing six or seven gigs a week, so they were driving up hill and down dale all over Britain without a single night off.

Clive Bunker explains how they eventually managed to nail down a name for this band which had many guises:

> The first I heard of the beginnings of Tull was from a neighbour who told me he had been to see this band that he enjoyed, called The John Evan Smash. A few months later they played down here, and Mick called me and said 'You've got to come and see this band.' So we went down and saw them and got to know them. They had quite a few gigs then, but they just sort of dried up or something because members of the band started leaving.
>
> Then it got to the stage where it was either fold the band up and go home or try and carry on, and I think it was Mick who came up with the idea of putting together a four piece blues band, but that still wasn't Tull, because we went through a few names. I think it actually only became Tull when we were in the recording studio and we said 'Look we've got to settle on a name now.' That's actually how the band started. By then everybody had left except Glenn, Ian and Mick. Then I remember John coming back at Morgan Studio when we did the *Benefit* album and it just seemed natural for him to be in the band; it seemed natural to have him as part of the group, it just seemed like he belonged.

The interesting thing about The John Evan Band and Tull, was that they were two totally different kettles of fish, and when the four piece first started they were doing some of the gigs that The John Evan Band still had booked. They were, in effect, doing the same sort of thing that The New Yardbirds did as they were evolving into Led Zeppelin.

It wasn't all plain sailing for Bunker in these early days though: 'I remember I borrowed Barrie's drum kit for about six months after The John Evan Band broke up and Barrie left, because I didn't have one.' He also comes up with an honest assessment of the differences between his drumming style and Barlow's: 'The funny thing, is at that time, Barrie had a better grasp of the material and was probably a better technical drummer than I was, although I was probably better at giving a good bash out for the stage act. Barrie was a bit of a tapper rather than a basher and that didn't work on stage, but he got there eventually. The best way to describe the differences between the two of us was that he had better technique while I had more power, but he did get it all together eventually anyway.'

4

Jethro Tull Christened

Glenn Cornick picks up where he left off with his diaries, and a clear view of what the band was called when and where, and when the name – *the name* – actually took root. 'On 16th January 1968, we played the Marquee Club as Navy Blue, so that was the period where we were changing names a lot, including The Ian Anderson Bag O' Blues. On 2nd February 1968, we played the Marquee Club as Jethro Tull. So that gives you a two week period in which we became Jethro Tull,' he confirms.

He also paints an interesting picture of those early days:

During this period we were opening for other bands. Eventually, we began to headline at the Marquee Club. We gained what was referred to as a residency. Originally, I thought it was playing once a week, but in reality it was every second Friday. But we were still playing other places every other night of the week. What was most important was the Marquee, though.

Just to give you an idea what it was like at the Marquee in those days, here are a couple of bands/artists who played there: April 1968 – The Nice, Ten Years After, The Jeff Beck Group, The Nice (again), Aynsley Dunbar, The Crazy World Of Arthur Brown, Jethro Tull, John Mayall. I spent my 21st birthday at the Marquee watching The Who and we opened for them! On the 24th, Al Stewart and Fairport Convention played.

Of course, in England at that time, we didn't really have any radio, so there were only two ways that you made it: one was the music papers like *New Musical Express* and *Melody Maker* and the other thing was getting out and playing to people. With all of the playing we did we were building an audience, slowly but surely. One thing we couldn't do was get into the papers.

At this point in time, as far as the stage show was concerned, things were just beginning. Anderson was just discovering his stage persona at some point after the group had moved down to London. Cornick recalls the gig, but not exactly when it was. They were playing a big hall with many people and it was cold and Anderson had that famous big grey overcoat that his father had bought him.

'For some reason, I have no idea what, Ian decided to bring this coat on stage with him and, of course, clothes can create a persona. Because he walked on stage with this big grey overcoat and people looked at him as if to say "What's going on with this guy?" I think that's what prompted him to become this strange character on stage,' surmises Cornick. 'It particularly worked at places where we had no expectations of doing well. That was the first famous overcoat, which took us around America the first time. I don't think it was ever cleaned in between either so it became more wonderful with time.'

So where did the standing on one leg routine come from? 'By the time we were playing at the Marquee from the beginning of 1968, the persona where Ian was standing on one leg began to develop during the few occasions that he played flute, because the flute was not a major instrument at that time. He was more likely to play harmonica at that point,' says Cornick.

Anderson himself is best placed to explain his predilection for making like a flamingo: 'I've always maintained that the standing on one leg was more an invention of the popular music press than it was my invention. I recall doing the one legged thing while playing harmonica, not the flute, until my image was manufactured for me. I do it now, but not for the same reason, but as a bit of fun. As long as you can see the side of making music as humorous and self deprecating that's pretty good, and I don't think Jethro Tull has ever lost sight of that.

'We're able to take the Mickey out of ourselves, but we know when it's time to be serious, and I think that when we do get serious we want to be taken seriously, but we have become fairly good at mixing up the moments. We know when to concentrate on playing the right note, giving the note the right quality and interpretation and you can also ham it up a bit and have fun with yourself and the audience. It's important not to get those two things confused. It's important to know the time and place for fun and games and the time to play with some meaning, some authority, with some emotion and you mustn't mix up the funny stuff with the serious stuff.'

Although it is only 45 years ago, Britain was a different world in the late 1960s. Anderson paints quite a bleak picture of life for the band in those days, with poverty never far from their door. He also explains how the famous overcoat was more a necessity than a stage prop:

> Once we got going, I was obliged to take a job part time working in a cinema, vacuum cleaning the floor. I worked in the mornings in an empty cinema, which actually had a charm of its own and offered me a lot of time. In fact, I vacuum cleaned the whole cinema in about two days, then for the rest of the month that I worked there I didn't have anything to do as everything looked so clean. So I was able to sit in the back circle most of the time attempting to write songs, so it was actually a very useful time and it paid the princely sum of $15 a week on which I was able to live.
>
> I didn't live very well. You see it was in the middle of winter, the winter of '67, January '68. In England in those days, gas was used to heat and supply hot water and we had meters which used to supply the utilities. You would put coins in the meters, so when your coins ran out you ran out of utilities and I had about sixpence for the meter, which had to supply heating, light, and hot water. In the middle of winter, sixpence does not go very far, so I ended up being very cold. Interestingly enough, that was where I first put on the prized possession with which my father had furnished me upon my leaving home a few weeks before – a huge grey overcoat which I wore on my first American tour. The reason I started wearing it was because I was very, very cold. I was living in an attic room in an old house and I used to keep a glass of water by my bed at night and in the morning, if I wanted a sip of water, I had to break the ice on the top, it was that cold.

Anderson also reveals why the band was reluctant to settle on a fixed name until it was absolutely necessary to do so:

> Of course you know the story of how we changed our name often and, indeed, the first few times we played the Marquee we used different names, which was due to a theory of mine that if we couldn't get a re-booking under one name, the only way get a re-booking was to change the name of the band and be someone else. Of course, by the time the band arrived it was much too late to say 'Oh no, not you again, go away' they had to let you go on. We didn't actually settle on a name until we had quite firm offer of playing at the Marquee on a regular basis as a support group every second week and, at that time, it became necessary to fix on one name if we were going to try and build up any kind of following.
>
> So, somebody in the office of the Ellis/Wright agency came up with the name Jethro Tull and we really didn't care because it might be another name for another week, so we said 'Fine, fair enough, what does it mean?' Of course, it was the name

+

of the man, an 18th century agriculturist, who invented the seed drill, the first one of which he made from the foot pedals of the local church organ. And so we said, 'O.K.,' and Jethro Tull we became and Jethro Tull we've remained.

He also has a fascinating anecdote as to where the early persona of a vagrant character came from:

I used to carry all my belongings in a paper carrier bag from Woolworth's; in it I kept my harmonicas, my flute and a couple of little wooden flutes and I used to have sandwiches. Believe it or not, I used to have Coca-Cola in a hot water bottle; a rubber hot water bottle and I used to drink it on stage. I used to have a sandwich and drink while Mick was playing 'Cat's Squirrel', which the audience found horrendous because it was supposed to be a purist blues thing. But they were intrigued by this sort of squalid character who sucked coke from a mangy hot water bottle that had been in his mother's bed for about ten years prior to that.

There was an alarm clock that went off in the middle of my solo which, to the audience, was dreadful. They were all shocked by that, and I'd stop playing, beat the hell out of it until it would stop ringing and I would carry on. They thought it was an accident. Of course, it was a planned thing to make the audience snap out of whatever daze they might be in.

That punctuation mark within the music, we still use today – perhaps in more sophisticated forms – but with exactly the same intention to never let people start to be predictable in their reactions and, therefore, provoke us into a predictable situation. We have things happen which jeopardise the continuity of the music because I think that keeps them and us on our toes.

It was around the time of the band's migration to Luton, the emergence of the four piece band, and then a move further south to London itself, that Jeffrey Hammond re-established his connections with his old mates from The Blades. 'They did go through a tough time,' he recalls. 'I think John left and went to college and I think Barrie left and they were stationed in Luton at that time with just Ian, Mick, Glenn and Clive. I can't remember which one of them came to look for a flat in London first, I think it was John. I found him a place in Chelsea and he was dead serious about school and won prizes for his studies. So we got back in touch, got together again and listened to a lot of music together too and re-established our friendship. Around then, Ian had come back down and got in touch with me and I helped him get a bedsit in the same house John was living in.'

After that initial re-introduction of what Jeffrey refers to as 'The Blackpool Mafia,' Anderson began to immortalise his friend in numbers such as 'A Song For Jeffrey', 'Jeffrey Goes To Leicester Square' and 'For Michael Collins, Jeffrey And Me.' 'I think I had started seeing them at the Marquee Club around then when they still had the one roadie, Roy Bailey,' remembers Hammond. 'He seems to be the first roadie as I recall. and I saw the band on numerous occasions, but I don't think they had massive success by then.'

[Author's note: Many attempts were made to hunt down the whereabouts of Mr Bailey, as all the members of the band wanted him to be a part of this chronicle. However, when it was discovered where he was working, the company claimed they couldn't track down one man in an organisation of 18,000 people at the MGM Grand in Las Vegas. So Roy, if you're out there, we tried.]

'I think they had settled on the name by that time, because I had begun to see them at the Marquee as Jethro Tull and Ian had begun to get his stage performance together then: he had the overcoat and so on. I remember the one thing I was always keen about was the brown carrier bag, which I used to use a lot and he ended up using one on stage along with the hot water bottle,' smiles Hammond. 'As far as my name being in the songs, we never spoke about it. I don't know what it meant, but it was certainly nice to be mentioned and I remember hearing "Song For Jeffrey" in the summer back home at my parents house – it was flattering in one way, but I don't think it had a lot of meaning to it.'

The popular view is that it didn't, and I'm sure neither of the two men have a great deal to say about it. Anderson has always conceded having a difficult time making friends and/or being sociable, and if you think about it, the music business and spending the majority of your life within its incestuous – nicest adjective I could come up with – confines for 40 years would tend to make anybody wary in general. My interpretation is, that any genuine loyalties on the part of Anderson have been channelled through music, and that the songs were his way of letting Jeffrey know that they were, without actual words, probably best of friends and that they would remain so for the rest of their lives.

Meanwhile, trouble began within the band's ranks and eventually politics began to get in the way. Terry Ellis began to steer Ian toward being the front man in the group – it was inevitable, given what he was developing into. This led to tensions with Mick Abrahams, who recalls how and why he left the band with brutal honesty:

Terry Ellis wanted Ian to be the main chum. The problem was, I wasn't against that; I think the whole thing made me feel put out. So I reacted and, in some cases, reacted badly and foolishly and so, in the end, I just got so fed up with it that I said 'Fuck this, I'm leaving the band'. I actually gave my notice and told Ellis and Ian I was quitting, because at that point it was decided I wasn't allowed to write with Ian anymore. I dearly would have liked to continue, but it was made clear to me that Ian was going to write all of the songs from then on. As far as I'm concerned, that's the way it fell and that's the way it probably should have been – I don't really have any problem with that at all, except to say that my being pushed out, as I say, made me react kind of foolishly. I went out of my way to mess up a couple of gigs to kind of make my point, but I know that was childish, it was wrong. It was done with a certain amount of attitude and I suppose I regret it because it was mean and wrong of me.

The funny thing is Terry Ellis wouldn't actually let anybody leave Tull unless he wanted it. I told everybody I was leaving and I was going to start my own band. Terry Ellis called me into his office two weeks later and told me 'Things are not working out, we're going to have to let you go.' And the way it was done was so patronising that I said 'What the fuck are you talking about?' And this is where the real irony of the thing comes about; I had a new band up and running in three weeks and Chris Wright decided he wanted to manage us. I believe to this day that he didn't take us over because he wanted to manage me, but that he just wanted to prove to Terry Ellis that he could build a bigger and better band. But I remember that I never really liked Terry Ellis to begin with, he really was the main reason I wanted out of Dodge.

Today, fans always ask about the history of the band and how things are within it. Basically, any of the problems we ever had have long since healed; time does heal things. I actually have a lot of respect for Ian. In a sense I feel a bit sorry for him, because he ended up without a lot of friends. So I feel almost, and he'll probably hate me for saying this, protective toward him, although I'm sure he doesn't need my protection; but I have that sort of feeling. I feel more protective towards him now than I ever did. I guess because we go back a long way.

The thing about Ian is you either take him for what he is or you don't. And to a certain degree, I have a great deal of respect for that, because I'm a lot like that myself: what you see is what you get. Ian has insulated himself for some right reasons and for some painfully wrong reasons. And for that I feel sympathetic towards him.

Because Abrahams was so forthcoming about how he felt about his relationship with Anderson, then and now, I was prompted to continue in a similar direction and ask how he felt about the rest of the group, considering he was actually the very first person to leave Jethro Tull proper:

On Glenn Cornick: Fell out with him a long, long time ago. A good player and fortunately we're friends again, which is nice. We played at the New Day evening in London for the 25th anniversary and I was very concerned, because I was actually only told before the concert that the year before he'd been very poorly and that he had a heart operation. All of a sudden, he just kind of turned up at that New Day thing and walked straight up to me and said, 'How the hell are you man?', shook my hand, we had a big hug and looked at each other and said, 'Well now, haven't we both been silly fuckers? Now that we're grown up, let's go and have a beer.' Glenn has always been a hard hitting, hard drinking, rock and roller sort of intellectual, in a nice kind of way, but maybe he just rubbed up against Ian the wrong way, I don't know. They seem perfectly good friends now.

On Clive Bunker: Solid, reliable, looks like his mother, acts like his mother; lovely guy, genuinely good spirited. A great drummer – one of my best friends.

On Ian Anderson: At the time I thought I was Ian's mate and I thought we were better friends than we were. I think a lot of the reason for me going out of the band was his taking Terry Ellis' side. I was very saddened by that, because I wasn't allowed to express my ideas. It was like losing a friend.

It's probably fairly common knowledge that Jethro Tull's major breakthrough came at the 1968 Sunbury Jazz And Blues Festival, an event sponsored and run by the Marquee Club. Prior to that, Anderson explains how: 'We plodded on, playing the small blues clubs, making $50 a night between all of us, so we were definitely below the poverty level. That brought us through to August of 1968. We remained in residency at the Marquee Club at the same time developing a bigger following, which meant we were pulling in about 1000 people in a place which would normally hold 200. Clubs like that don't exist anymore. They were the sort of place that didn't have a bar and that once you got in you just didn't move, you just watched the band – that's all you could do, you couldn't move. Still no press coverage at this point though.'

Every person involved with the band from Terry Ellis to Clive Bunker recounts the Sunbury story in a way that marks the event as a frozen moment in time, never to be forgotten. Along with his faithful diaries, Glenn Cornick has the most thorough recollection:

Every summer the Marquee would have a festival and that year the festival was held at Sunbury-on-Thames, August 9th, 10th and 11th. It was moved from where it had been held for the last two years, the first festival having taken place in 1961. Here's a quote from the programme: 'The final evening on Sunday has a strong blues tinge with John Mayall, Chicken Shack and Jethro Tull.' We were one of the smallest, least known groups to play. Newspapers didn't know about us and our following was nowhere near as big as the rest of the bands.

One thing I should mention, is that one of the band's other props at the time was a paper carrier bag that Ian kept his flute, his harmonica and that Claghorn in. So the stage was all set, and the audience didn't know which order the acts were playing in. The place was an open air venue and it held several thousand. I couldn't tell you exactly how many people, but from my experience at that point it was huge.

The Marquee, of course, was run by John Gee. John Gee was about to go on stage to announce us and he picked up the little paper bag and walked out onto the stage with it and the entire audience stood up and cheered. Every single person recognised the bag, which was really phenomenal because we had no idea that people knew us that well. The people who had seen us at all those little places all around the country had come to the festival, so everybody out there were our fans. We could tell that they had really come to see us, and it was probably the most exciting thing that ever happened to me in my life. That was the absolute turning point of the band.

We walked on stage and everybody was in our hands. I don't remember how well we played but, judging from our own euphoria, we probably played quite well. I just remember the huge roar and everybody was shocked, even the other bands that were there. Nobody could believe it, because we were considered, by some, a little band of no consequence. We pretty well walked away with all the publicity for the three days, because we were the big surprise of the festival. The picture on the inside cover of *This Was* comes from that show.

Just before that concert, Tull had performed a show with Spooky Tooth who, at that time, didn't have a record out yet, but did have a deal with Island Records. After the concert, Spooky Tooth went to Island and told the A&R department they had played this great concert with a band called Jethro Tull in an attempt to get Island to go after Tull and sign them – things were different in those heady days. At that time, Terry Ellis was talking to Muff Winwood (brother of Steve), one of the heads of Island. As far as the majority of the record industry was concerned, Tull had emerged from nowhere – up until the festival they hadn't existed; it was their point of singularity, prior to the Big Bang. Right after the festival, however, they were approached by nearly every record company in Britain; not quite all of them, of course, but it was enough for the band to feel they could take their pick. Ellis decided that Island would be the right choice after all.

'I think Terry made a good decision then, because Island Records was the only label that was working with hip new bands at the time,' says Cornick. 'They were the only company that had some kind of idea what to do with them. Most of the other labels out there were still living in the Frank Sinatra days.'

5

This Was

***This Was* (1968)**
My Sunday Feeling / Some Day The Sun Won't Shine For You / Beggar's Farm /
Move On Alone / Serenade To A Cuckoo / Dharma For One / It's Breaking Me
Up / Cat's Squirrel / A Song For Jeffrey / Round

It may be an inconvenient truth for many Tull fans but, yes, the real Tull grew
out of their second album, not the first. The foresight to call it *This Was* was
inspired. Before the release of *This Was*, however, Tull's first official single release
was Mick Abrahams' 'Sunshine Day', in February 1968 on the MGM label. The
flip side was 'Aeroplane', a previously recorded John Evan Band track, but with
the saxophones mixed out. Although it has been widely believed that this single
was mistakenly credited to Jethro Toe, we have seen that, in fact, this was what
Derek Lawrence wanted because he disliked the alternative. His idea of Candy
Coloured Rain as a band name seems hardly more suitable. The single sold to
friends and relatives, but failed to make a dent elsewhere. It now fetches a pretty
penny on the collectors' market.

The Sunbury Festival, of course, was on August 11th. The first album, *This
Was*, was released on October 4th – not much gap in between, but recording
time in those days was very short; you did an album in a week. The entire album
was recorded on four-track, with the drums and bass on the same track, so
the whole thing barely took two hands to mix. The album was recorded in a
studio in Chelsea called Sound Techniques, a converted grain warehouse. The
actual recording room was about two or three stories high and was made out of
stone. According to the band, it was a wonderful studio for recording acoustic
instruments, which is why Fairport Convention used it for several years.

However, Cornick has his reservations about it. 'It was one of the most
nightmarish places to record electric instruments,' he claims. 'I honestly have

always had a hard time listening to that album. It was never a satisfying album for me. It was an odd mix between what Ian and Mick wanted to do, and I remember the photo session for the cover was hilarious. There were about 30 dogs running around tearing up this studio – it was quite remarkable that we actually ended up getting any pictures out of it.

'People used to ask what the meaning was of the front cover and the skeleton of the fish on the back. There is a definite idea behind that, and the title of the album was a definite statement – *This Was* what the band sounded like when this recording was done, but not now. Of course at that time, a lot of albums were being released with covers that had meanings in them, so we decided to do an album like that, with all kinds of things on it that people could read things into, but in fact it meant nothing. The real hidden meaning is that there isn't any! To me that album didn't represent the real Jethro Tull: the real Jethro Tull came later.'

This Was was released on the Island label to immediate critical acclaim. A mixture of blues, jazz and rock, the album heralded the arrival of a band that would change the popular music ground floor for several years to come. Tull's music was always organic. Backing tracks were usually written and recorded ahead of time, leaving Anderson's lyrics, which were rarely finished before the backing tracks were, to be added at the end of the sessions – more on this later.

This Was was recorded between June 13th and August 23rd, 1968. It hit a respectable Number 10 in the British charts and they were called upon to play The Rolling Stones' *Rock 'n' Roll Circus* film. Since Abrahams had left and the band were in the middle of auditions at the time of the breakthrough, Earth guitarist Tony Iommi was featured on the show even though he was miming to Abrahams playing on the record. Iommi lasted two weeks and went on to transform Earth into Black Sabbath. Meanwhile, Abrahams had formed Blodwyn Pig.

On *This Was* ...

Anderson: 'Since we had been a blues band, we had material that we could easily put onto record. There were a couple of songs that Mick and I wrote together, a couple we wrote individually and the two instrumentals, 'Cat's Squirrel' and 'Serenade To A Cuckoo.' That summed it up, and it was a statement of what Jethro Tull was at the time we were playing in and around the Marquee. It would not be indicative of what we were going to play in the future, just a starting point for introducing Jethro Tull to the public. It was more of an historical document, because albums like *This Was* and *Stand Up* say a lot about our roots in blues and other forms of music from classical to jazz and folk.'

Cornick: "'A Song For Jeffrey' was our first single, which came out after the album and if I remember rightly 'A Christmas Song' was the B side. It was also the first song recorded without Mick. In fact, Mick was furious because he wasn't at the session. Ian simply thought it was a song that didn't need guitar, which didn't go well with Mick, because he thought himself an equal boss with Ian. But he had alienated himself so much at that point that, if it came to a decision, everyone would have sided with Ian.'

⚬⚬⚬⚬⚬⚬

Glenn Cornick believes that the decision to let Abrahams go was made around December 1968, which means he only had about a month to bask in the glory of being a recording artist with Jethro Tull. Cornick recalls that:

Mick had made himself absolutely impossible to work with and it was not a good experience. Anyway, we let Mick go; we actually dropped him off at his house and, as he got out of the van, we told him. We didn't fire him because we wanted someone specific in, it's not as though we had guitarists lining up at the door. The night we let Mick go, we had been playing somewhere in the Midlands, and the opening band for us was a group called Earth, which, of course, became Black Sabbath. We took Tony's [Iommi] phone number just in case we might give him a shot. A couple of days before, we had played with a band called Gethsemane, which was Martin Barre's band in which he played guitar as well as flute. However, the first person that we decided we would give a shot to was David O'List [who had just left The Nice].

He was a strange guitar player, but we were a strange band. The first rehearsal we had with him was wonderful, but as the week progressed he got crazier, to the point where he never showed up and I don't think we ever saw him again.

Mick Taylor was the next person we thought of, and we approached him and he certainly was an adequate blues player. Ian went and talked with Mick and decided he wouldn't be right for the band, and Mick was happy with John Mayall and didn't think that Jethro Tull was going to do anything anyway. I think we offered him considerably more money than he was getting with John Mayall, but he decided he didn't want to do it.

The band then decided to put an ad in *Melody Maker* and also invited three specific guitarists down to make sure that at least someone would end up being right for the gig. The three gunslingers were Martin Barre, Tony Iommi and Tony Williams. There was basically a cattle call and about one hundred hopefuls turned up over a two day period. And out of the hundred people who showed only three could play guitar – the three guitarists who had been invited. The band's first choice was Tony Iommi.

'He was definitely the best lead guitar player,' remembers Cornick. 'We rehearsed a few days with him and then we did the *Rolling Stones Circus* on 11th December 1968. We were supposed to do two live songs: 'A Song For Jeffrey' and 'Fat Man'. In the end we only did one and we had to lip-sync to it. That was Tony's one performance with Jethro Tull. Later he said 'It's been a lot of fun, but I feel I fit in better with my friends up in Birmingham', so he departed on good terms.

'We were at a loss as to what to do next. We had turned down Martin at the auditions, but meanwhile he had gotten back to Ian and tried for another chance. So, eventually Ian and Martin got together, played some stuff and it worked out. We gave Martin another shot and the key point was that Ian was writing some new music which was not blues oriented, so that may have had something to do with Martin being the choice. One song I remember Ian having at that point was 'Nothing Is Easy' which might have been the first thing he had ready for the *Stand Up* album. I recall we may have tried 'Nothing Is Easy' with Mick.

Terry and Chris paid for the first album, because the band didn't have a record deal, so it was recorded in this cheap studio. Anderson recalls:

We recorded some songs that I had written and some songs that Mick had written, and some that were begged, borrowed or stolen from other people, and we hawked it around the record companies in England at the time and got a deal with Island Records. Unfortunately, at that time, things began to come to a head with Mick who still only wanted to play three nights a week. We wanted to go to the States. We couldn't really afford to fly, but Mick wouldn't fly anyway. So we began looking for a new guitarist and Mick found out about it.

We remembered having played a gig with Martin's band so we asked him to come to an audition along with Tony Iommi, but it didn't work out with Tony, and Martin gave me a call and asked if he could try again. I said 'O.K.' and he said that he was just embarrassed about doing an audition in front of a lot of people and he said 'Perhaps I can come to your place?' So he did, and brought his guitar, but didn't bring an amplifier and didn't realise that I didn't have one. So, Martin came along minus amplifier with the solid electric guitar and proceeded to demonstrate his abilities. But, as you know, the electric guitar without an amplifier makes virtually no sound at all and, due to his extreme state of nerves, he was breathing very heavily. I could see his fingers move due to his profound state of nerves. I couldn't hear anything, but I can see his fingers move and I said 'You've got a job' [laughs].

Clive Bunker remembers that:

> Not long after we were put on the blues circuit, things began to gel rather well
> and then we did the first album. We couldn't get anybody to take it: really! So,
> we recorded it ourselves. It was only when we did the Sunbury Festival here in
> London somewhere (which went down extremely well) that we started getting
> offers from quite a few record companies. We ended up getting a really nice little
> deal with Island Records.
>
> Unfortunately, differences began to arise between Mick and Ian – Mick wanted
> to stay a blues band, which was his main thing. Ian was pushing more toward the
> progressive sound, which was just something that Mick never liked, never wanted
> to do, and still doesn't want to do. So, when Ian started doing all his writing in
> that direction, he was also going further and further away from the blues thing.
> And well, I really didn't know what was going on in Mick's head. I think he was
> probably going through the old 'I'm not too happy with this, but really don't
> want to leave the band' sort of thing, but not telling anybody. The two of them
> were both walking around, obviously keeping something in, but not talking, just
> putting it off and it all just got worse. It's the same as anything; when two people
> think the opposite about anything and not talk it through – it just festers. The
> stuff that Ian was writing was absolutely appealing to both Glenn and myself, it
> was absolutely fabulous.

So Mick Abrahams finally made his decision – or the decision was made. One
way or t'other he left the band. Clive and Mick remain best of friends today
– there was no way Clive was going to be able to change the situation at that
point, whether he wanted to or not. No ill feelings resulted from the parting
of the ways, and there were no regrets, as Clive was totally into the music that
Anderson was coming up with at this point.

Interestingly, Bunker says that his greatest musical regret is: 'Not being good
enough to have played with Frank Zappa.' He expands on the point with great
passion:

> That's the sort of band I would have loved playing in, because I don't like to go on
> doing the same sort of style all the time. The freedom that Zappa's drummers had
> to just go in and experiment was inspiring. I know it wasn't freedom when you're
> in his band, but the way that you could play in so many styles under the control
> of somebody, was something that I always looked forward to doing. Frank Zappa
> was the sort of person who wouldn't let them get away with anything. It would
> have been the best kind of training that any of them could ever have had; it's like

going to the best school in the world. Ian was always under the impression that Frank Zappa never liked us although Ian liked Frank Zappa.'

I wonder if Terry Bozzio's greatest regret is never having played in Tull? Bunker, too, gives us his views on Abrahams' departure and some thoughts on replacing him:

Sometimes when you hear certain stories like the one that describes how Mick didn't want to go to America, they tend to be misconstrued. It gave the impression Mick didn't like what he was doing. I know that Mick did do a tour of America with Blodwyn Pig a couple of years later, but he didn't fly, he took a boat and he took a bus everywhere. I think that taught him that flying was better! His trip through Louisiana taught him that's one thing you don't do and he had long hair – not a good idea at all.

My memory of holding the auditions for a new guitarist was that we spent two days in this audition hall with people coming down with various impressions of what we were looking for. Some of them actually tried to do stage acts which was pretty funny. We had seen Martin in another band that had supported us one time, which was called Gethsemane and Martin played flute, oddly enough, which is why we noticed him. I can remember us saying he would be nice for the band, but we didn't know how to get in touch with him, or whatever, and there wasn't anybody from the auditions that I can remember who was outstanding enough to work for the band. Then we had to do that *Rock 'n' Roll Circus* thing for The Stones and there was Tony. I don't know what went on with Ian and Davy O'List – I didn't even know he was in the frame to be quite honest and, loving what he did with The Nice, I still don't think he would have fitted in properly with Tull. As far as Tony was concerned, I think he was pretty set with his own band anyway. And once Martin arrived, that was it as far as I was concerned. My overall impression of the time was 'Now that Martin's here we're a band again.' It was on Ian's shoulders to teach Martin all of the music as Ian was a pretty good guitarist anyway, so a lot of that was down to Ian.

The story of how Mick Abrahams was replaced by Martin Barre has been told by everyone, except the replacement himself. So, here is Mr Barre's take on it:

I was in a band in London called Gethsemane, which changed from being a soul band into a blues band. One of the places I used to go to watch bands was the

Marquee, where we saw the great bands of the day. One day our drummer came to my flat, and was overwhelmed by this band he had just see that had a wild flute player in it (he figured I'd be interested because I played flute and guitar in our band). He described the band vividly, called them a blues band with a flute player who played in the style of Roland Kirk. I decided to check them out and the opportunity came at the Sunbury Blues Festival; our whole band went. Jethro Tull were on and I just thought they were wonderful. I saw in Jethro Tull everything I wanted to be involved with.

The next time I saw them was when we supported them in Plymouth. I remember we didn't meet them until after they finished playing, because they arrived while we were still on. I remember getting along well with them. They were as interested in us as we were with them and it was a great night, we all enjoyed it. Who would have thought that I would be in the band in a matter of months? At that point, our band had run out of steam. I was thinking of going back to college. I saw an ad in *Melody Maker* looking for a guitarist and it said it was for a blues band. I picked up the phone and called, but when I heard it was for Jethro Tull I hung up the phone thinking that there was no way I would be able to fill the shoes of Mick Abrahams. The next thing that happened was we were doing a gig in London and, during the break, someone came up to me and handed me a business card with a little butterfly on it that said Chrysalis Records. I turned it over and it said 'Terry Ellis, please call!' I knew that Jethro Tull were involved with Chrysalis Records, so I phoned and he said they had been trying to find me for ages, because they had remembered me from the gig in Plymouth and they had wanted me to audition for the job. He told me the audition would be held in London in a few days from that date, and persuaded me to go down and have a go; which I did.

There were at least 100 people at that audition. It was held in a room in a basement and I was unbelievably nervous. The room was literally wallpapered with guitarists. It was a square room with quite a low ceiling and guitar players sat all the way around the room. In the middle of the room there was Clive and Glenn set up to play and Ian was wandering around the room. Each guitar player was plucked from his seat to plug into the amp and told to play and everybody played twelve bar blues; it was dreadful. Ian would sort of wander around and listen, prowl around and then he would go around behind Clive and tap him on the shoulder and that was the sign for Clive to stop playing because Ian had had enough. This would go on over and over just like the gong show – some would last longer, others would last a minute or two, and some would last 30 seconds.

When my turn came, I insisted on having my amp. So, I set up my amp and I had a semi-acoustic electric, which had a terrible tendency to feedback. Because there was a low ceiling, it was screaming and making a terrible sound. Rather than playing another twelve bar blues, I decided to try and play something that I knew from my band, some standard which Clive and Glenn knew anyway. I thought it would be at least a breath of fresh air, so off I go screeching and, of course, my eye was firmly fixed on Ian, waiting for him to go to Clive and tap him on the shoulder. You can imagine, the atmosphere was just dreadful. So I played one song and asked if they would like to hear some flute which went a lot better. When I left I thought 'That's the end of that gig.' Ian called me and told me it was a difficult decision, but they'd given the job to Tony Iommi. He was very nice about it.

About a week to ten days later I thought, 'Well, I wonder if things worked out' because I was just very frustrated at the circumstances of the audition being so bad. I thought 'I'd love to have another go at it', so I called Ian to see how things were working out. It was one of those dreadful conversations where I could hardly hear him, but he said things had not worked out because Tony had had an accident with his fingers and there were certain chord sequences he couldn't work out. In fact, the end of his fingers were plastic that had been surgically put on. So I asked if I could have another audition and Ian said 'Yes'. They hired a back room at this pub and off I went again with my gear and a borrowed guitar. We spent a few hours at this pub and things went a lot better than the last audition.

I can't remember if Ian told me then, but I think I knew it had gone well. This was a week before Christmas and Ian called me up and said 'We're going to start rehearsals and see how things go.' We rehearsed in a room in Soho over Christmas. Because the band had gigs booked right after Christmas in Scandinavia and England, we rehearsed literally Christmas Eve, Christmas Day and right through the holidays.

We were effectively learning the songs that would be the *Stand Up* album, and they were the sort of songs I had never learned to play before. I remember learning 'Back To The Family', 'Nothing Is Easy' and they were all very difficult for me to learn. I think that all of the Tull guys were committed to the fact that I was going to be in the band. When we were rehearsing and had a break, I would sit down and they would sit at another table and have a sandwich and a cup of tea. It was a very strange atmosphere. I don't think they were being unfriendly, it's just I wasn't in the group, but something drove me. I definitely wanted to be in Jethro Tull.

After getting through that week of learning the music that we were going to be playing in the upcoming tour, it was still very much one way or the other as far as everybody was concerned. The first two or three gigs in England were dreadful. The first gig was in Penzance and I remember driving all the way down there with Clive. Because we were late, we had to carry all the gear through the audience and because they expected Jethro Tull with Mick Abrahams they didn't seem to like the change, although we were still doing blues things – a few things left over from the original band. I got the feeling we were getting a mixed reaction because Mick had been such a well known guitar player and I wasn't: particularly those first few gigs in Birmingham and Nottingham. And Mick had always been a focus of attention; it was a very difficult time. You could see that Ian had a lot on his mind.

We were about to leave for Scandinavia and the last gig we did in England was in Manchester in a student union and we played with Manfred Mann. That was the first gig where the audience actually liked the music and everything went down well. Finally, there was cohesion in the performance and we all heaved a sigh of relief and, luckily, it was the last one before we went away. From that point things started going right and I started thinking I might be around for a bit longer.

The first few gigs were supporting Hendrix in Scandinavia. That first year was nerve wracking for me because we were playing with Hendrix, Jeff Beck, Jimmy Page and all the superstar guitar players. When we went to the States, we were the support act and there was me up on the stage playing support to the superstar guitarists – I was in at the deep end.

This was, of course, January 1969 and after the Scandinavian gigs we came back to England and recorded *Stand Up*. We had been playing the songs on stage and I think we ended up recording it in a month at Morgan Studios on eight-track. The sessions were good fun and quite exciting. I can remember them not having any glitches. There was a lot of nervous tension and most of it was done live; very few overdubs. I think the high point for me was the wah wah bit in 'We Used To Know' – that was where I was allowed to let loose.

After that we went over to America and everybody was really excited. It was every English musicians' dream to go to the new land; we were just over the moon about it. We arrived in New York and got unceremoniously dumped into a hotel. We were sharing rooms at the time. I think I was sharing with Clive and Ian with Glenn. We were given a few dollars and Terry went out and about to try and get us a record deal and some extra gigs for us. I think we spent the week discovering New York; walking around streets, but we were literally left to our own devices. I know we didn't have a deal to release the album in America and I believe he spent most of the time negotiating with Warner Brothers to release it.

The first gig was at the Fillmore East backing Blood Sweat And Tears. There were two shows a night – that's the way things were done in those days. Even when we headlined a few years later, it was still two shows a night. That tour lasted three months, but we only played a few nights a week. We played a week in New York, then went to the Boston Tea Party in Boston, then on to Detroit,

Chicago, Minneapolis, St Paul, Seattle. Then we went down to San Francisco, which was wonderful because everywhere else was cold and we arrived in warm glorious California and we all went out and bought new clothes – leather pants and suede jackets.

At that point during the tour, Terry Ellis showed up with the *Stand Up* album and played it for the band in their hotel. For the band members and new recording artist Barre, it was a magical moment – it was the first album he had ever played on. There had already been a bit of a buzz in America over *This Was* because of the bizarre front cover which depicted the band as old men – many members of the public thought they actually looked like that. Interestingly, Anderson recalls that 'We began working on the cover of the *Stand Up* album before we even began recording.'

While in Los Angeles, the band recorded 'Living In The Past' and 'Driving Song'. When the single was released in England, it showed the band in their hippy garb which they had purchased upon arrival in LA. The ad for the single read 'America hasn't changed Jethro Tull at all.' In England at that time, everything was singles oriented so the band increased the fan base from the success of 'Living In The Past'.

Glenn Cornick also has some fond memories of this period in the band's development:

Martin came into the band at the end of '68 and we already had a number of important gigs lined up for January '69; so we're talking fairly major panic. We were booked for the 9th and 10th of January to open for Jimi Hendrix in Stockholm and the 24th of January we had the beginning of the first American tour starting at the Fillmore East. We really had only a couple of weeks to pull it together. I remember it quite vividly, we rehearsed from 9 a.m. to 6 p.m. We took a lunch hour but, other than that, it was solid work and we worked right through Christmas including Christmas Eve, Christmas Day, Boxing Day all in the little studio right next to Leicester Square tube station. It was even hard to find people to open the places for us at the rehearsal spaces. We worked for two solid weeks, not only breaking in a new guitarist but new material as well as the material we did with Mick.

We did a couple of gigs in Cornwall on the 2nd and 4th – those were our first dates with Martin. We did a couple more gigs on the 7th and 8th of January opening for Jimi Hendrix – we were special guests which meant there were two bands. To be quite honest, we stole the shows. We did a lot of gigs with Hendrix, so we got to know him fairly well; he was a nice fellow. He was getting tired of us stealing the show, so on the fourth show he made us look like we weren't even there; so he'd been cruising through the first three. But I found with Hendrix, that's the way he was. Out of the 25 times I saw him, there were three or four great shows. When he wanted to kill an audience he could wipe anyone, but he didn't do it most of the time. We actually did phenomenally well. Jimi Hendrix could be phenomenal, but most of the time he just didn't give a damn. I think it offended him that most people were more impressed by his showmanship than his music. We came back from Stockholm a little overawed.

We did a few gigs around home and after that came the first American tour – 24th January 1969 on support to Blood Sweat And Tears. They were the most arrogant band we ever encountered! When we got to the States, the hotel we stayed at in New York was next to a building site where they were putting up a high rise which meant they were dynamiting. I remember being awakened at 7 a.m. by dynamite blasts. Just being there felt very alien. Here we were ready to do a show at the Fillmore East and our equipment had been shipped to Boston. Luckily the equipment arrived for the next day, and I remember we did fairly well. Certainly well enough that they invited us back. We went on from there to Detroit and opened for Mitch Ryder.

Arriving in Detroit, we were picked up at the airport in a limousine and dropped at a cheap hotel. Of course, we were driving in a limousine right through the area where the riots had just occurred, and on either side of us was nothing but burnt out wreckage, which at that point certainly gave us a rather dim view of America. We finally arrived at the venue, which was the Grande Ballroom in an all black neighbourhood. We got out of the limo and going to the ballroom was surreal. But once we got to the ballroom it was great, we ended up having a good time there. We played three nights and we found out that if you had long hair and were weird you were accepted in the black areas. I guess if you were a white businessman you wouldn't fare too well there.

That was our second place in the States – Detroit. We went on to Chicago, which wasn't much different either. I guess we were considered guest stars at this place which was a converted roller rink. The headline act was Vanilla Fudge, with special guest stars Led Zeppelin, and we were the not-so-special guest stars. So we were third on the bill, but it was funny to see Vanilla Fudge headlining over Zeppelin.

The next stops for the band were Minneapolis and Boston, then a week in New Haven, Connecticut. They played four nights in a really small place to about 30 people a night, from 20th – 23rd February. Although the actual concerts were not noteworthy, it just happened that Ian Anderson wrote a snappy little tune called

'Living In The Past' whilst there; only the biggest hit single in the group's history. The other thing about New Haven was that Terry Ellis had brought a wood cutting artist to meet the band who ended up spending an entire week with them in order to get to know the group. The reason was to produce the cover for the *Stand Up* album.

Cornick gives a fascinating account of how gruelling life on the road could be:

I think we were all very pleased at how well he captured us even though Ian had an extra finger. So we finished that tour and the last gig was on the 11th April. So we are talking a monster tour, because it kept getting extended which meant more exposure for us. We went back to the Fillmore East a couple of times, we went back to Detroit and Chicago again and did better every time. We were starting to build up the name – certainly in the bigger cities.

On Monday the 3rd March, we recorded 'Living In The Past' in West Orange, New Jersey. It was a night time session in this studio owned by one of the Four Seasons. For some reason Martin had great difficulty playing that, he had a terrible time getting the right chords. In fact there is one wrong chord on the song. On Tuesday the 18th March, we recorded 'Driving Song' at Western Recording in Los Angeles. We got back from the States on the 11th April. I thought touring the States was wonderful; everyone else hated it. I was ready to go back again; nobody else wanted to go, everybody else thought it was the most difficult thing they had ever done. I thought it was great fun. That was one of the main differences between me and them is that they hated being on tour, whereas I used to love it.

We arrived home on April 13th, went to Paris on the 15th to do a television show. On the 17th we began recording *Stand Up*. On April the 17th we recorded 'A New Day Yesterday'; April 21st, 'Back To The Family' and 'Fat Man'; April 22nd, 'Jeffrey Goes To Leicester Square'; April 23rd, my birthday, we did 'Nothing Is Easy'; Thursday the 24th, 'Bourée'. All the other stuff was recorded at Morgan Studios, a very nice studio in North London. Morgan was booked on the 24th so we went to Olympic Studios which was a big studio in South London, right around the corner from where I lived. It was famous for being the studio where Hendrix did most of his stuff. Olympic 1 was huge like an airplane hangar and was the same room that Hendrix used, because he could use stacks of amplifiers.

My memory of this session was that it was the most disastrous recording session I ever did. We spent most of the night trying to get the song done, but we ended up with rolls and rolls of useless tape. We were very unhappy about it. We left Olympic and Ian went back there later and edited together what is now the *Stand Up* version of 'Bourée'. He edited the song together from bits and pieces and then added some extra stuff and ended up with the finished version. We honestly never thought we would hear something come out of that horrible session. It's actually the only thing we ever did like that.

Thank God he did do that too, because it was such a pivotal song for us. Certainly, all over Europe it was the biggest thing we ever did. It was the only bad recording session I recall. Our usual plan in recording sessions was going in the morning, laying down the backing track and work our way through the day. We were expected to go to the studio at around 9 a.m. and come out with a finished, mixed song around 4 p.m. or 5 p.m. Not the way things are done today, where people do a whole bunch of backing tracks and then mess around with overdubs later. We did it track by track. We had to keep to a schedule because, as we were leaving, Traffic or Joe Cocker would be coming in.

On 1st May 1969, we recorded 'For A Thousand Mothers' and 'We Used To Know'. It looks like those were the last songs recorded. I don't think all the words were written at that time. I think Ian wrote the lyrics later because all we had to work with was a chord sequence; we didn't have a completed song, which is unfortunate. And that's how we worked after that. We never had complete songs after that. I remember by this time Ian had his purpose built coat; the original great coat was confined to the archives of history, so he then started wearing the orange and grey Dickensian coat.

We did a show in Dublin in an arena where we had to play in the centre, it was a boxing arena. As we came off stage, since we were in the centre, we had to go through the crowd to get to the dressing room and as we did that, someone grabbed on to Ian's coat pocket and pulled it off. That happened to be the pocket where he kept his harmonicas and his flute. Of course this was before we had backup gear and so his flute was stolen. He did get it back a couple of months later.

When we were on our way to that gig the taxi ran out of gas, and the taxi driver said to us 'It's O.K. lads, we've only run out of gas. I will just pop out and get some.' He returned fifteen minutes later. So that was our first experience of being in Ireland. We also played in Belfast and we were the only band that would play there, because that's where all the trouble was – tanks in the street, that sort of stuff and everyone would come to see us. I think we were the most loved band there, because we would be the only band to play there. We were really respected for going there, so we ended up being treated like royalty.

In early June, we played *Top Of The Pops* which was pretty funny for us, because we were about as alien to that crowd as anyone could be. But we did it a few times and we drove them crazy, because we never knew what our camera positions were supposed to be, so we would be out of the camera half of the time.

We went back to the States on the 19th June and played the Newport Pop Festival and the Miami Jazz Festival, along with a bunch of regular gigs and a bunch more festivals; that was the year of Festivals. I remember watching the Jeff Beck Group and Led Zeppelin argue with each other about who got to close the [not specified] show. Those festivals used to overrun so much that we would generally asked to go on around 2 p.m. knowing that by the time we actually got on it would be around 7 or 8 at night. We would be the first band to play under the lights, which was actually the best place to be because it had the best impact.

That tour lasted exactly two months to the day. We came home, did some rehearsal, and the album went straight to Number 1 in England. Terry had said 'Since you've done so well, we're going to treat you,' he said 'I'm going to take you to Las Vegas to see Elvis Presley,' and he wasn't joking. We went to the Hilton in Las Vegas on August 11th and saw Elvis. We had to rent tuxedos to get into the room.

The late 1960s were the last knockings of the Hippie movement of course, but that doesn't mean that peace and love were necessarily the order of the day in the competitive music business. 'We did a ten city tour with Led Zeppelin in 1969 on our second American tour. We did lots of gigs with them that summer as a supporting group,' Anderson recalls. 'At a lot of places we played we were just vaguely known; probably less well known than most bands that have supported us. We went on every night to blow Led Zeppelin off stage. We didn't, but we tried to – that was the name of the game. A couple of times the papers said we did. That meant that people sat up and took enough notice of us as a support group to justify coming back a year later with another album under our belt and playing those same arenas.'

6

Anderson's Birth As A Songwriter – Stand Up

***Stand Up* (1969)**
A New Day Yesterday / Jeffrey Goes To Leicester Square / Bourée / Back To The Family / Look Into The Sun / Nothing Is Easy / Fat Man / We Used To Know / Reasons For Waiting / For A Thousand Mothers

The band's second album, in 1969, was such a departure from the first, it's difficult at times to believe this is the same band; there was so much diversity and quality music in one album. It's a fairly common view in popular music that a band's best album is usually it's first, because the culmination of everything they've ever thought of comes tumbling out in one blast. With Tull having Anderson write all the songs for the second album, *Stand Up* had that same sort of spark. *This Was*, in effect, had been a stumbling out of the blocks but *Stand Up* was the pointer to the future direction of this new band: not to be a blues band, but something very different.

Anderson, with his Scottish/Lancashire middle class background was well aware of the 'Can a white man sing the blues?' dilemma and self-aware enough to realise that his voice didn't exactly lend itself to this style of singing. 'I already knew well in advance that as a singer I was never going to sound like Otis Redding, let alone Howling Wolf or whatever,' he muses. 'It became fairly obvious to me right from the beginning, that no matter how long I stood in front of a mirror and learned Muddy Waters licks and tried to emulate that style, I just wasn't going to wake up in the morning with a black skin. And so, I had already made the decision, long before we started on *This Was*, that it was a great musical foundation for which I still have a great deal of fond admiration, as far as listening to music for fun or pleasure is concerned, but it didn't hold much of a future for me.'

So the transition away from being a blues band had already occurred before Jethro Tull started developing an identity. Getting paid for learning to play a bit better and learning to be a professional musician on the job, meant it was better to go along with the early Jethro Tull twelve bar blues stuff; that was useful as a foundation for learning to play.

Ultimately though, it was very frustrating because Anderson said he used to find it really quite weird to be playing the exact same three chord progression. To have built a repertoire of, say, 26 songs all following the same format didn't seem like there was much of a payoff. It wasn't intellectually challenging and Anderson says he always found that music has got to work on different levels at the same time.

'It had to appeal to my brain as well as my fingers and have a more heartfelt response; something that was ultimately satisfying to write, to record, to perform and more importantly, perform again and again and again,' Anderson states emphatically. 'Which is why I'm very happy to have the catalogue we have and to be able to play from this great list of songs. When it comes to there being a diverse number of ideas on the Stand Up album, it shouldn't be all that different for most musicians when it comes to their first outings as writers. You can probably say the same thing about The Spin Doctors first album or The Crash Test Dummies first album or Pearl Jam, who had great ideas on their first albums, ideas which are a product of teenage angst or first experiences of things beyond the classroom. It's about life out there. In my case, there were elements of Asian music on Stand Up.'

This musical diversity comes, seemingly, from someone well travelled. In fact, it came from the world of Indian and Chinese restaurants, rather than a teenage rites of passage backpacking through Asia. 'Of course you hear their music, you learn something about those people, transplanted as they may be to an urban British culture', stresses Anderson. In fact, to Anderson, our youth is the existential wellspring of our creativity which will inspire us later down the line.

'I think it's the most vital and useful time in anybody's life in the creative sense in that it's there for you to draw upon for the rest of your life,' he believes. 'I think it's probably true to say that the majority of people will be consciously, or for some unconsciously, drawing upon those experiences as writers, actors, directors, musicians, painters or whatever. They will be drawing upon many of those experiences for the rest of their lives; these are exciting moments, dimly understood, yet fearfully entered into. Not to say that it's all you use, but it's the part that doesn't just fade away with time.'

Just prior to the release of *Stand Up*, 'Living In The Past' hit the UK charts in May 1969 and precipitated a spot on the prestigious *Top Of The Pops* programme on BBC TV. The miming Anderson out front, with scruffy sidemen just inches away, was almost too much for the otherwise reserved audience of the middle of the road TV show, but the appearance did the trick. The combination of a Number 3 hit single and nationwide TV coverage put the band under the spotlight; Tull had arrived. *Stand Up* would end up going to Number 1 two days after its release and a subsequent single, 'Sweet Dream' to Number 5.

As Tull continued their touring, both at home and abroad, Ian Anderson's flamboyant live performance became even more outrageous. In the year end *Melody Maker* poll, Tull beat the Rolling Stones as Britain's second favourite band (You can probably guess who was Number 1 – a band from Liverpool that was in the processing of slowly imploding). *Stand Up* has a timeless quality that still yields great listening.

The recording sessions for this album had begun in early 1969 in London with engineer Andy Johns. From this point on Ian Anderson handled the production for the band (Paul Samwell-Smith produced *The Broadsword And The Beast*, however). *Stand Up* was far and away one of the most diverse and innovative recordings Jethro Tull ever made.

On *Stand Up* ...
Anderson: 'With Mick gone and the move away from blues beginning, we started to do some experimenting with somewhat exotic instruments – mandolins, balalaikas, and whistles. 1969 was a definitive year for the so called progressive bands like Yes, The Nice and King Crimson – they had very special identities. All those bands were so different from each other, we were all very separate. The same sort of thing was going on in America with Frank Zappa and Captain Beefheart'
Bunker: 'My first reaction to the music from *Stand Up* was 'What are we going to do with this music?' It didn't seem outrageous to us. Don't forget, we were listening to it in acoustic form in a front room somewhere and I was just tapping

my knees coming up with ideas as to what I was going to do. Once it starts going from that acoustic stage and gets into the electric mould, it's sort of like going from Bob Dylan into Jimi Hendrix. I don't remember it sounding anything spectacular or outrageous at the time; it sounded like a pretty good album. What I was most proud of was actually *Aqualung*. It just seems so much better than anything we had done. Sometimes I tend to forget which album we were working on, and I do remember one time (but not which album), that Ian was actually quite sick and he laid down an acoustic track and then went home. The rest of us added what we thought it needed – it was our own ideas. I was very proud of what we did, proud of the way it turned out. I wish I could remember what song that was!'

On 'We Used To Know' …
Anderson: '"We Used To Know" is one we started to play live again and we hadn't really played since about 1970. I know we played it at Carnegie Hall and the Isle Of Wight, so it was part of the Jethro Tull set back then and it didn't make another appearance, that I can recall, for many years. So it was a long time coming back into the Tull set.

'It never occurred to me that it was going to form the basis of 'Hotel California', which quite a few people pointed out. In fact, Martin pointed it out to me and I didn't really take any notice of it, because it's not anything like 'Hotel California'. But when you actually get to the chord sequence, not the melody, but the way in which the thing harmonically progresses, it is actually the verse of 'Hotel California'.

'The Eagles were opening up for Jethro Tull around that time. I'm sure you can probably look at some of my songs and take some chord progressions and say that's one of The Beatles songs, or a title which has been subconsciously lifted in part from somebody else's title. However, 'Hotel California' is a very, very popular song and 'We Used To Know' remains an obscure album track, and I'm sure 'Hotel California' is a much better song. I actually heard the song recently at some concert and it was musically spot on and I thought it was a very good song, a very good American pop song. So, if it was in any way inspired by 'We Used To Know' I am privileged and I feel proud if that was the case. I joke about it on the stage in a very good natured way and I hope The Eagles did, intentionally or not, take it from something I did.

'As far as what that chord sequence is, I don't remember, because I don't read or write music. For me, it's just a bunch of "You put your hand there and it makes that noise". So in a sense, I'm fooling you and me and that's the enchanting and intriguing thing about music; the naivety with which you do something, on a good night, is quite a wondrous and exciting event, even though you are constantly reinventing the wheel as far as a lot of academics are concerned.'

Barre: 'I think we were going for something that we could use as a climax to the show; an encore or the last number of the show with a big solo. This might contrast to what Ian might say, but that is my memory of it. It sort of built up in the studio and the guitar solo was all done in one take – sort of go for broke. I used a Les Paul Special, which is the guitar I used when I joined the band, with a HiWatt amp and a Hamilton wah wah pedal, which I still have. I remember the recording sessions very clearly. I remember playing solos and the chords weren't usually the twelve chord bar chord in those days. I never really sat down and worked out the implications of chord changes, and I never really played around the chord changes, I just played by ear and sometimes you got lucky and you hit a note that went well and on another take it might be a disaster.

It was all fairly naive musically. But because it was, you went for broke and you came up with something that might be just a bit special, something different from the way that anybody else would play. We always recorded songs with the live performance in mind, and I have a strong memory of that one. 'Bourée' was an obvious song written as a showcase for the flute and bass, so we were always looking ahead. I suppose all that emphasis on solos was a hangover from the jazz era where everybody had their solos and, in some ways, it reflects on how boring the music was – but we got away with it.'

On 'Bourée' ...

Anderson: 'I'm not sure how long it would take me to learn it, if I heard it for the first time and had to remember it. I was fortunate enough to hear it daily coming through the floor under me, where a music student was busy practicing on his classical guitar, so it kind of stuck in my brain when I was busy looking for an instrumental piece to play in 1969.

We had quite a lot of different arrangements of that piece, but you don't necessarily remember exactly where it all fits in. Especially since some of it is, shall we say, improvisation, which over the years becomes almost a set part and, therefore, you do have to relearn some of what were once improvised solos. I'm really not convinced about all that reading and writing stuff, but it is probably something that would be very useful to me now. But I suspect that if I ever had to learn that back in my school days, in my early days as a musician, I would have lost something rather than gained something. I suspect that is the same with a lot of people.

A lot of people have a temperament that is better suited to just getting on with it and playing by ear and trial and error, to find how things work. Other people have a temperament which is, perhaps, more suited to taking an academic approach. Given the option, I think I would rather learn by ear and trial and error than off the page.'

7

Benefit And The Return
Of John Evans

Benefit (1970)
With You There To Help Me / Nothing To Say / Alive And Well And Living In
/ Son / For Michael Collins, Jeffrey and Me / To Cry You A Song / A Time For
Everything? / Inside / Play In Time / Sossity; You're A Woman
(US version features 'Teacher' instead of 'Alive And Well And Living In')

Benefit began the beginning of a series of breaks for Tull in America, that had
already begun with *Stand Up* in the UK. *Benefit* became a cult icon of the early
1970s and *Aqualung*, with 'concept album' pasted all over it, completed the
breakthrough for the band in the US.

Bunker remembers:

We were very close in the group, and I don't think anybody felt they could get
very close to us, just because we were that closely knit. I think that's because
we were together all the time, not that we went out together, but the band
was together all the time. We didn't socialise together but we, as a band, stuck
pretty close to home. We had a pretty close relationship, which gave people the
impression we weren't interested in mingling. That's just my impression of what
people have told me afterwards. We were all looking for the same things, we
were close friends, we got on well with each other. With the amount of work we
were doing, if we spent any more time with each other we would have driven
each other mad. So when we were away from doing work we wouldn't go out for
a meal with each other, only once in a while, because days off were valuable to
get away from each other. It doesn't matter how well you get on, if you put each
other in the same place for long periods of time you're going to have problems.

We were not good friends, we were friends. We had a very good working relationship and that was very healthy. Martin and I were probably the tightest, and Ian was always writing in his room or whatever. The guy was always working and lucky for us he did. When we recorded *Stand Up* and *Benefit*, to me, it was a learning process. I don't really remember a lot of it, and it's not drugs or anything, it's just so long ago. It was like going up a ladder, everything was uphill. It was mayhem and the times spent in the studio working on something like *Benefit* was a lot easier than all that crazy gigging we did in the beginning.

When we did do recordings, to me, it was more than just a piece of vinyl and I thought we better get this right, because it's the sort of thing that comes home to you; you're making a record and it's a timeless thing.

Cornick remembers:

We flew back to Britain on the 19th August [1969] and we did some rehearsal. We did a lot of special guest star appearances at that time, because we weren't quite big enough to headline. Most of the time, we did a lot of guest starring for Led Zeppelin. I got along very well with the guys in Zeppelin, but for some reason Ian didn't. We started recording 'Singing All Day' and 'Sweet Dream', Sunday the 31st August. On September 1st we recorded 'Play In Time'. On the 11th September we recorded '17'. I always liked that song, I'm ashamed it wasn't done with a little more care; it was done as a throw away.

We recorded on the 14th September, but unfortunately at that point, as we got into the *Benefit* material, we didn't know titles of the songs until they appeared on the album and I do really remember recording stuff because I was just playing to chord sequences. In September and October, we toured Britain with occasional dates in Europe. In November, we went back to the States by which time we actually began headlining at places. We played the Fillmore West and actually headlined in November, so there was quite a development from one tour to the next. We also headlined at the Fillmore East.

On the 19th December, we recorded 'Witch's Promise' and 'Teacher'. I remember 'Sweet Dream' coming out and doing *Top Of The Pops*. On the 12th and 13th of January 1970, we recorded more *Benefit* stuff. It's a bit of a shame that I didn't know what songs we were doing when we were doing them, because *Benefit* is my favourite Tull album.

Cornick's version of the inspiration for *Benefit*, and writing credits on *Aqualung*, differs greatly from what is usually offered: 'There are two primary things that were the subjects of *Benefit*, particularly the British version: How much Ian was in love with Jennie, his first wife, and how much he didn't like his family.

'At that time, Ian's mother was not allowed to see the concerts. She was literally banned from the shows. My mother used to sneak her in the back, because Ian was ashamed or was worried about what her impression would be. The thing was, though, that she was very, very proud of him. And so she should have been – this was a band that was about to become an enigma.'

Anderson remembers:

To me, quite often, subsequent Tull albums will have an almost polar effect about them and *Benefit* was a rather dark album, which reflected our first experiences travelling in North America, musical experiences and to do with just the general feel of the music and lyrics in a more or less constructed way. The riff nature of a lot of the *Benefit* stuff was probably influenced by our working with some of the bands that we were with in the US, whether it was Led Zeppelin or some of the other US bands that we played with. But it was a dark album and it's not one of my favourites.

I would have to say though, that it does contain a couple of Martin Barre's favourite tracks; he likes it a lot more than I do because he probably felt more at home with that record than he did with *Stand Up*, because he was the new boy in the band. From one day to the next he had the wolves coming at him, he was barely a competent guitar player in the style he was being called upon to play in during *Stand Up*. Whereas by *Benefit* he felt a lot more competent and probably felt it was a lot more his kind of album.

I understand that a lot of the fans would like to hear more of the *Benefit* material played on stage. But it's rather difficult for me.

I had a talk with Martin about doing an album of some of the music of Jethro Tull with other artists, not with anybody else in Jethro Tull, but a bunch of other folks doing instrumental versions of Jethro Tull material, because a lot of it is stuff that we don't do, because I don't feel good about singing it. I do not like the lyrics, or really feel comfortable with some tunes and that applies to a lot of the stuff on *Benefit*. Martin would love to do 'To Cry You A Song', but I just don't really like it. I remember playing it back in 1969, 1970 but I just, somehow, don't feel the point of identification anymore with those songs. I wish there were some way of doing them to give them a lease of life, where I don't have to feel that I have to approve or disapprove of them. I quite like the idea of taking some of the Jethro Tull material, musically speaking, and doing it in a way that is kind of different. Like the idea of doing some stuff with just me and Martin and a string quartet or something, or maybe working with some Asian musician for one piece, and doing another piece with a famous rock god guitarist and bringing in some other people to broaden the input. I quite enjoy playing around with certain things in various periods. I must say, I rather enjoy the purity of it, to get away from the jarring lyrics with which I've become disenchanted.

After listening to a few opinions about the origins of the ideas behind the *Benefit* album, particularly the diametrically opposed ideas of Cornick and Anderson, there was a need to confront Anderson about the idea the album may have been mostly, or at least partly, devoted to his ex-wife. This was more a case of trying to find out why an album that Cornick refers to as his favourite, an album that Barre would like to play and enjoyed recording, is a dark, unlikeable album for Anderson. Anderson calls it dark – it was primarily responsible for making North America aware the band existed. So was it about Jennie?

'Absolutely not,' he states emphatically. 'I don't think that argument would work at all, it has to do with something that's actually much more intuitive. It has to do with words and the way you choose to sing them and constructions of things, it's not to do with the subject material. It's to do with the mechanics and how they've been put together, technically. I don't have a problem with other people having an idea about something I've done – that's wonderful. It's long ceased to worry me that there has to be any reliable correlation between what I like and what other people, broadly speaking, are not a million miles apart on.

'Quite clearly there's going to be a lot of divergence with music that spans many different moments of Jethro Tull's music, because there's been so many different people who brought some little interesting things into the band, stylistic tendencies toward the music. The job is trying to sort it all out and make something that is eclectic, but it all has to go together as opposed to it just being a mishmash. Sometimes I think I've done quite well. And usually it takes the objectivity that comes with a few months of sitting back and looking at it from a different perspective before you realise, yourself, what you think is good and what is bad. Other people may be drawn to something for a very specific reason; as long as they don't expect me to necessarily share in that enjoyment for the same reasons. A lot of people are coming to Jethro Tull concerts now because of nostalgia; it is something to do with their growing up.'

Anderson remembers how 'John [Evans] returned to the band because of 'Witch's Promise' and 'Teacher'; they both had keyboards on them, so I asked him to come back as a session musician. John was living in the room next to mine and, every now and then, I would ask him if he wanted to come and do a session and he said "Sure I'll give it a try". So, he came along and did the session and we decided to do *Benefit* and asked him to play again on the album, and we asked him to join the group. His mother freaked!'

John Evans recalls in some depth how he joined the band:

I managed to get a place at London University in September 1968, and kept in touch with Jeffrey who was at art school in London, I think, for about a year before that, around September 1967. He had developed contacts for accommodation and Ian had taken advantage of that and was living in a one room studio [apartment]. When I went to university, I managed to get a studio through the same source, you know, the sort of thing that hadn't been redecorated for 40 years with patches that brightened things up a bit with the mould. I paid £4/5 shillings a week – about $10 – and that was near central London. It was at the same place Ian was living in. He would be off with this new band Jethro Tull seven nights a week and, occasionally, he'd come back to his studio flat and I'd see him and we'd talk about what was happening. He kept saying 'Why don't you come and do some playing with us?' and I kept saying 'I've got no time really'. But you know how it is, sooner or later you think, 'I'm getting bored with studying, I think I'll take him up on the offer to come and put some keyboard tracks down'. Especially as a student who is a bit short on money.

I think I was paid around a $1,000 for doing the *Benefit* sessions and that was a lot of money for me back then. One evening, I was studying in my studio and the communal phone rang (just a single phone in the entire boarding house), and someone shouted up to me that I had a call from Germany. It was Ian, who said it was absolutely vital that Jethro Tull get a keyboard player to continue playing the sort of music they want to play and to continue to perform *Benefit*. They would have to do that and, naturally, they wanted me. I didn't want to do it, because I had been studying pretty bloody hard for two years. I had exams coming up and didn't want to throw it all away but, of course, I wanted to be in a band that was making money and going abroad, and what young man didn't want to be in a band? So I went to see my tutor at university and he said 'You can't miss a chance like this. It doesn't come along every day, and, because you've been here for two years and you've got pretty good results, there won't be any problem for you to come back in two or three years.' I thought 'All right,' so I did it.

It was a culture shock. I had taken my exams in March 1970, and at the same time rehearsing with Jethro Tull, and by April we were performing in California. The first place we played at was called Mammoth Gardens in Denver, Colorado, where somebody committed suicide with a kitchen knife. The next gig somebody jumped, or was pushed, off a balcony and killed himself, which was very different from playing in clubs in the north of England where, as a seven piece band, we often outnumbered the audience. At the third gig, we played Anaheim Stadium or Coliseum which holds about 18,000 people. For some reason, Jethro Tull were really, really big in LA from very, very early on and this was April 1970. But it was still very localised, because I remember playing at the Fillmore West for several tours and we struggled to fill it. In [some] areas of the States we wouldn't be a big attraction, but in other areas we could fill a large auditorium, so it was still pretty patchy. I can remember being in a very downmarket hotel in New York on 48th and 8th, for what seemed like weeks at a time, just watching TV, waiting for an old English movie to come on at 3 in the morning, because we were just waiting for a place to play.

At the age of 21, 22, it's a case of out of sight, out of mind, isn't it? In quite a lot of different areas, when you're young, it's a case of go with the flow, as they say. At that time, I was very much in the flow. As I said, it was a very strange experience to be a penniless student in a one room apartment and then, a couple of weeks later, you're headline attraction at Anaheim Stadium; the difference in life styles is mind blowing. Just as the reverse of coming out of that situation and back to normal, or seemingly normal, life as it happened in 1980 was just as mind blowing. What do you do without all that? That took quite a bit longer to get used to – three or four years. Once you're in it, you embrace it at that age and you don't think about anything else. The furthest thing from your mind is going back to a one room apartment and studying.

After two or three tours through 1970, I remember playing at a place called Rambles Island in New York, a sort of stadium. One of the acts was Jimi Hendrix. I distinctly remember meeting Hendrix walking along the underground tunnel from the dressing room into the middle of sports field where the stage was, and the look in his eyes was just like a hunted animal. He was somewhere else. It was frightening, very frightening, because, believe it or not, I had very little to do with drugs, hard or soft, certainly not hard. The number of times I smoked grass I could count on my two hands. I used to drink quite a lot of beer, but that was it.

With Evans back in the fold to add keyboards to a session or two, prior to his full, formal re-introduction into the band that he and schoolmate Anderson had created over five years before, the line up from *Stand Up* remained, plus one.

'Witch's Promise', another single from the band, saw them miming again on *Top Of The Pops*. Then the album was released. Martin Barre has always been very positive about the album, but Anderson has always leaned toward it being a dark album: 'It didn't have the warmth, the humour, the lightness of *Stand Up*'. Mostly recorded in December 1969 and January 1970, Anderson did some experimenting with his production techniques on this album.

The band toured again, headlining some of the biggest concert halls across America, selling out the Los Angeles Forum in just a few hours. Yes opened for Tull while on this tour and Tull, in turn, opened for Jimi Hendrix at the Atlanta Pop Festival. The legendary Carnegie Hall Concert of November 4, 1970 also featured in this tour [and part of that gig turned up on the *Living In The Past* compilation]. Reaching Number 3 in Britain and Number 11 in the US, *Benefit* became Tull's first million seller. After the tour finished in December 1970, original bassist Glen Cornick was 'invited to leave'.

On 'Sossity; You're A Woman' and 'Nothing To Say' ...
Barre: 'Those were the first times Ian and I played guitar together because "Sossity..." had two guitar parts. I remember it very well and which guitar I played – an old Echo acoustic. We played together on that and on 'Nothing To Say'. We sat in the studio, I played finger style guitar and Ian played plectrum.'

On 'Play In Time' ...
Anderson: 'That was done very unusually. That was done, I'm pretty sure, in a studio in Los Angeles on our very first visit to the US as a B side to something: maybe 'Living In The Past' or something very early on. Again, for me, it's one of those riffy period songs.'

On 'To Cry You A Song' ...
Barre: 'The influence for that song was the Blind Faith song 'Had To Cry Today' which was a really nice track, although you couldn't compare the two. Nothing was stolen, it was just a nice idea, a nice riff, a bit back to front, starting on the nose, beat one of the bar, unusual riff crossed over the bar in a couple of places. Ian and I both played guitars on the backing tracks, it was more or less live. Ian played my Gibson SG and I played a Les Paul both through Hi Watts. I've always liked that track. In fact, I was playing it on this tour at a sound check and everybody sort of turned round and joined in and said "What's that?", because the guys in the band don't know the music from that era and they were saying "That's really good" and Ian had a go singing it. It's really nice.

'I remember all those songs and I can play them without relearning them again. It was also Lesley West's favourite song. We did a lot of gigs with Mountain in the 1970s and he loved that one. He comes to our gigs in New York, he was at the last one. We have a longstanding relationship. We got along well and are friends and he's a fabulous player. I suppose if anybody ever influenced me at all, he was the only one that did. He was one guy I felt if I could play like he did then I'd be very happy.

'It was recorded at Morgan Studios in Willesden, London. It's a favourite album of mine because *Stand Up* was a bit nerve-wracking for me having just joined the band and sort of feeling my way, but *Benefit* was more fun because I was more confident. We had just done an album which had been successful. Certain albums have different pressures and some albums are more laid back, but it doesn't mean they end up being better albums. Sometimes, the ones that are done under the direst of pressure end up being the big albums, like *Aqualung*.'

Anderson: 'Not one of my favourite pieces. I know Martin always seems to like playing that, but Martin likes a lot of the pieces from the *Benefit* album. That was one that I suppose I'm not sure whether I also played guitar on. I think actually Martin and I did play harmony on that. I might be wrong, but I think we did. Basically it was just a riff that I came up with, a repeating riff and said "Here Martin, this is the riff" and left it to him. That was at a point where John Evans had just joined part time to play the piano on a few tracks. He may, or may not, have been part of the original record. I haven't heard that one for quite some time actually; it's not one of my favourite songs. I couldn't sing that song.

'Most of our songs fit into categories lyrically. There are those that I'm happy to get up and sing and feel honest about, and there are those that instantly I know I just cannot sing. I know I'm not gonna be able to get up and do certain songs because they don't feel right. Some of those songs are among Jethro Tull's most popular songs and I've tried – it just doesn't work. I would much rather go on and sing a song that means something to me, even if the audience didn't like it. Luckily, the audience will usually like it. And then, there are songs that I can do sometimes – if I'm in the mood.'

8

Bunker Does A Bunk

Clive Bunker was the first member of Tull to leave without animosity or stress; the first member of Jethro Tull to depart the band for reasons that didn't include anything beyond wanting a different type of life; without any ill feelings, odd stories or weird circumstances. He just walked away from what was about to become one of the world's biggest bands and he did it for love. You've got to admire that.

Here's his story:

I don't think there was a band in those days that thought they would last longer than five years. I think it was one of those periods from which the bands that did very well, looked at the Rolling Stones and said, 'Let's do that.' We were in at the tail end, if you like, of the first lot of bands that came out of the late 1960s and we've been around long enough that we're still annoying people into our sixties which is great, really, because before that what did you have? Your Bobby Vees and that sort of clean cut stuff.

But to jump to the inevitable question of why did I leave the band? To get married. At the time we had been working really non-stop and I remembered thinking that if I found the one (woman) I wanted, then this isn't the life I would want with a marriage. When I did meet this lady I did decide to leave. If we had not been working so much I might have stayed on a little longer, but the way it was going, if I had finished the next tour we were going to do, I think I wouldn't have gotten married. We were going off for the first world tour and then back to work. Then we were going to move to Switzerland to live for a year. So I would have come back to a complete stranger. She couldn't go to Switzerland to live, because she had been previously married and had a child who was about to start school. So it just really didn't work out. I stuck around right up until the first full world tour where they went to Australia and everywhere else.

It's interesting that you brought up my marriage because that's the reason I'm actually back playing seriously again – my marriage broke up. You just expect a good marriage to go on forever, so music is about the only thing I really know how to do now. I figure I've only got about five more years to go before I start to seize up, so I might as well drum right now.

It's an interesting coincidence, or I've always thought it was interesting, that drummer Doane Perry was a fan of ours back when I was in the band. His mother sent me a letter when it was his birthday one year, he may have been 11 or 12, and she brought him to a Jethro Tull show and then brought him backstage and he met us. I let him play my drum kit for a while. Now that he is actually in the band, he still can't believe it's actually happened; perhaps even the longest lasting drummer they've ever had. I wonder if he now knows that nobody's going to beat his record [laughter]. [Perry has since left along with Barre ... for the time being. One can never be sure in the world of Tull]

As far as any tensions or problems within the band are concerned, I was never aware of, nor was I ever really interested. If there were things like that, they usually begin with just one small bit of information and that gets blown out of proportion. So you know, you might start off with something really small and suddenly you've got the band that started World War III. In all honesty, I don't remember any real problems and I don't think it really mattered, not to me, personally. The only thing that I can remember going on, was the Mick leaving thing and that was really because nobody said anything and it was just going on and getting worse.

As far as Glenn's leaving was concerned, I don't remember there being any problems. I never had any problems with Glenn; never had, never will. I don't really remember the circumstances of Glenn's leaving. I mean, it was out of my hands anyway and I'm not the sort of person who likes to change things, but we did lose an awful lot when Glenn left and, on the other hand, we gained something when Jeffrey came in. Glenn gave us a lot with his stage movement stuff and playing, whereas Jeffrey gave us stage presence, but without moving. He always looked so outrageous the way he was. Glenn used to play the bass all over the place, á la Jack Bruce, whereas Jeffrey had it down pat like a normal bass part. I liked them both.

Tull had this policy of never jamming with anybody. That went on for years and years and that was a Terry Ellis thing way back in the beginning, when people were looking at us as being something very different and weird, so he discouraged us from going down to clubs and jamming. It was his thing for us to stay separate from other groups, but I do remember Glenn getting up and jamming at a festival and got his face all over the newspapers.

Although the North American tours were fantastic, absolutely fantastic, I thought all the tours were great in any country, anywhere. I mean, I couldn't get over the fact that we would go to different countries and people would actually know us. A year earlier, at home in England, if we played in another town they might not know us.

He should be unbelievably proud, our Ian, because he's been responsible for the writing and it's his writing that's been able to make it possible for everyone else in the group to do their bit. Over the years, I've told him many, many times that he should record an acoustic album, because so much of his acoustic material was so wonderful; I don't know why he hasn't done it, because some of the nicest songs have been the acoustic ones. I get the impression that the big thing in his head that has been stopping him, is that 'Nobody wants to come and see me unless I'm standing on one leg and leaping about'. I think he always has been worried about the fact that he couldn't get away with not leaping about for the sake of the show, and I don't think he needs to. I think those songs alone would carry any show.

I remember doing three dates with Led Zeppelin in Chicago in the same place we did some festivals, and I remember Philadelphia quite vividly. I was surprised to learn there had been any friction between Tull and Zeppelin. On the contrary, we got on really well; at least I got on really well, I wonder who might not have? Bonzo [John Bonham] was a great guy, there was something very special about guys like that, guys who are on the limit and it didn't have to have anything to do with drink or drugs. If you were to take Keith Moon without a drink, he still would have been out on the limit, it's just something there was about these guys that made them come up with material that was one of a kind. People like Ian and Frank Zappa have got that looneyness inside them, but they keep it there and project it through their creative abilities when it comes to music.

I remember there being problems with money when Mick was in the band, and I had said all I wanted was 50 quid a week (which was a lot of money then) and Mick said he wanted £75, but that's the only time I remember money being a problem. As a matter of fact, money's not a problem with me in any case. There was, of course, a point at which we went from the one room flats, which were freezing cold – and that was never an exaggeration – to a point where we could buy houses. Those things did change, but I didn't want them to change that much, which is why I regulated my wages on purpose, because I didn't want to get out of control. If I wanted anything expensive, I would go to the tour manager and ask for the money, and then I would think about it very carefully. There are times when I regret not spending the money. I remember when some of the guys from Zeppelin would say 'Come on, let's go have a good time' and I would say it will cost too much. I regret that now, because I didn't save anything anyway. When the divorce went through my ex-wife got it all.

The funny thing about the amount of time that has passed since I was in Tull, is that I've heard all kinds of things from all kinds of people you wouldn't believe. People have come up to me and told me what we did when we were getting popular, and it's amazed me because I remember being there and those things did not happen. There is an old saying which goes 'Send reinforcements we're going to advance', and it eventually turns into 'Send three and fourpence we're going to a dance'. So most of the stuff I have no firsthand knowledge of. It's pretty amazing, particularly since people tell you things that I don't remember doing myself, and I would say 'No, we didn't do that.' And even more amazingly they would say, 'Yes you did'.

Bunker on …

Martin Barre: 'Wonderful man and I don't mean that because he's a good guitarist – he is a good guitarist – but he's also an all round good bloke with his head screwed on right. The sort of person I'd like to see as often is possible.'

Glenn Cornick: 'I get on with him very well, but I get on well with everyone, that's my problem, really. As far as getting together is concerned we get on fine, it's just I'm quieter when I go out. As a player, Glenn was exactly what the band wanted at that time; in the studio he was precise and good. And on stage he would let fly a bit.'

Mick Abrahams: 'Personality wise, a little overpowering for me but on his own, when we weren't out, he was great. Great as a player. He is his own worst enemy, because he should be way up there with all the other greats, but he had this thing where he just had to stick with the blues, you know. You don't hit the top playing just blues, so that can keep you down.'

Ian Anderson: 'Ian was into what he was doing, whatever that was, which much of the time was writing in his hotel room. I admire everything like that about Ian. Having been there during the time that these things were going on, I would have to say that he was, and is, a genius. I see myself as a bit of a punter, and if I hadn't been playing with him I would still have been a fan. After I left the band, of course, is when they reached their biggest success. I really didn't know much about it at the time, because I was busy getting married'

9

The Return Of
The Prodigal Bass Player

'When Glenn left the group, Jeffrey, who had finished art school, was desperately afraid of moving out into the big world, so I bought him a bass for his birthday and I said "Maybe you should think about playing again,"' Anderson says. 'The thing was with Jeffrey, in the original Blades back in Blackpool, he never had been able to play anyway. He didn't know what he was playing!'

Apparently, John and Ian used to teach him the notes. He didn't understand what he was doing, but he could play it parrot fashion. There was a great deal of anxiety in his mind about his musical abilities, so it was difficult to persuade him to do it, but in the end he agreed to give it a go on a trial basis.

'Ian has always been a very persuasive person, so after Glenn Cornick left he bought me a bass guitar for my birthday and tried to persuade me to rejoin the band,' Hammond recollects. 'I was very fortunate, because I was in a position where I had left art school and wanted to attend the Royal Academy, but didn't get in. I wasn't sure what I was going to do and the only other thing open to me at the time was to be a teacher, which I really didn't want to do. I was stuck and my grant had run out. I couldn't afford to carry on living in London, as there were no prospects of work, and he very kindly offered me the opportunity to redecorate his house while he was away on tour.'

So Jeffrey got a free billet and did the place up for Ian. The band came back from the States *sans* Cornick, and Hammond officially rejoined the group on 22nd November. Almost immediately, the band began rehearsing songs for *Aqualung*. They had commitments for a European tour coming up in January, so once again Jeffrey was thrown in at the deep end, as he explains:

We rehearsed *Aqualung* for this tour, I don't think that went particularly well. The recording didn't go well either. There was one tune that did go well, a sort of one-taker, but the rest didn't. We went away on tour and Ian wrote some more, scrapped some of the tunes and recorded the newer ones and that became *Aqualung*. One thing I do remember were power failures, because it was the middle of the winter, and always being in two overcoats, coming home at 2 a.m. and climbing into bed freezing cold. We could also hear Led Zeppelin in the other studio.

On my first tour of America in 1971, we seemed to still be playing in smaller venues. Later on that year, places and shows began to get bigger, going from 5,000 and 6,000 to 15,000 seaters. I remember that aroma of marijuana [none of the group did any of that stuff] and the smell was so powerful that my head began to spin. I am allergic to alcohol and I remember being naive enough not to know why I found my head swirling around, but as the audiences grew it became quite thrilling.

Jethro Tull was always a band that reflected the people who were in it at the time, and many people thought of Ian as being Jethro Tull. But if you look at the various groupings, you will hear definite differences as with any band. In the early days in Blackpool, John certainly played a very big part in the band because of his education, and being able to write down all of the music and the parts in notation form. People say that the time that I was in Tull was their most successful and magical, but I have nothing to compare it with. I came as they were almost at the top of the ladder, and left of my own accord while they were still there. In that entire time when we played on stage, I can't remember a time when the whole experience wasn't absolutely wonderful.

John Evans recalls:

At the end of 1970, it was a question of Glenn out and Jeffrey back in again, and we set to work on *Aqualung* which was very, very hard work. Musically, it was very taxing. We struggled on with it. We recorded the whole album after many, many takes and overdubs and late night sessions.

I think the best thing to have done would have been to pack it all up and go on holiday, but we just forced it and forced it and forced it, mixed it, cut it. Then Ian listened to it, and it sounded so turgid that he scrapped the whole thing. We went back into the studio and did the whole thing again – redid it in one week at Island Studio – and that was how that it was done. It was like hammering something out of a piece of iron on an anvil, but eventually, when we redid the whole thing it flowed a lot more easily [1]

So I think you got the best of both worlds with that one: you get all the sweat and blood and toil and hard work, but then you lose the turgid side to it and it becomes fresh again. It's unbelievable. You're sitting there in front of speakers and, after awhile, it's like you're looking at a Picasso from two inches away. You just can't see the thing, all you can see is a blob of paint where he accidentally blobbed the canvas a bit and that's all you can see. It's only when you come back years later and walk into a room and go 'Wow, that's incredible!' that you can appreciate what you've done. It's very unfortunate, it becomes very rewarding much later on; that distance in time.

I must say I was very impressed, quite recently. One of our drivers, who had been a Jethro Tull fan, had got a couple of live recordings he had made from radio broadcasts in the 1970s; he brought me copies. They were just home recordings, straight from the radio show, and I was quite impressed by the band and quite impressed by the keyboard player who was me [laughs]. I was bloody good actually, because it was mixed stuff, it was really driving the band along, but you don't realise it at the time and back then I was just thinking 'It's just me playing here, what's everybody going on about? I'm not whoever your hero is.' And you just can't take it in that, to the people in the audience, you are their heroes. Just as much as someone who might be your hero.

[1] Author's note – I brought this up with Ian Anderson and he denies that *Aqualung* was re-done. He believes Evans has somehow confused *Aqualung* with the aborted *Château d'Isaster* sessions that eventually were re-done as *A Passion Play*. The fact that Evans has the studio correct is a bit odd, but when it comes to definitive versions of stories like this there's usually three separate accounts – his, his and the correct one. I wasn't there, they were!

10

Aqualung

Aqualung (1971)
Aqualung / Cross-Eyed Mary / Cheap Day Return / Mother Goose / Wond'ring
Aloud / Up To Me / My God / Hymn 43 / Slipstream / Locomotive Breath /
Wind-Up

The Jeffrey from 'A Song For Jeffrey', 'Jeffrey Goes To Leicester Square' and 'For
Michael Collins, Jeffrey And Me' was now a re-born Tullite, but with an extra
Hammond added on to his last name for effect. His parrot-fashion learning of
the bass back with The Blades was to begin anew, but this time he had been flung
headlong into a band that was about to record the biggest selling album of its
career. It was called a 'concept album' by the press, a pronouncement Anderson
vehemently disagreed with.

'It's an album with songs that have some sympathy for each other,' he
agrees, but the press went on at length with the famous statement: "My God,
now Ian Anderson wants us to think."' Whoever that journalist was has long
since bitten his tongue. *Aqualung* became a multi-platinum album and the title
track and 'Locomotive Breath' have been live fixtures ever since. The meat of
the matter is organised religion's role in society. A few songs on Tull's previous
Benefit album had touched on that idea, but no rock band ever dealt with the
subject so thoroughly as Jethro Tull did on this album. Recorded during the first
three months of 1971, *Aqualung* maintained the same lineup as the previous
album, except for the switch between Cornick and Hammond on bass. As usual,
virtually all of the material had been written in motel/hotel rooms whilst on
the road. The backing tracks were recorded before the lyrics were finished and
Anderson handled the production. John Burns engineered.

The first side of the album, when it was originally released on vinyl, was
subtitled 'Aqualung' and dealt with the downtrodden and helped along the

notion of the album being conceptual. The second side was subtitled 'My God' and clung to the organised religion vein a little more cohesively than the subject matter of the first side – little wonder it was taken for a concept album.

On *Aqualung* ...

Barre: 'Island Studios was new and they had a lot of problems there, hence we had problems and, musically, it was a struggle. We weren't as tight a band as we wanted to be and things either fall into place, or they are a struggle, and, in the case of that album, things were very difficult and very tense. But, at the end of the day, it was an important album and I think the songs were so good that it really carried the album through. I love all the acoustic songs, so I couldn't pick any one song as a favourite and the album itself is tremendous.

Anderson: 'When *Aqualung* came along, it combined the best of both of those two previous albums, because it had the amusing, surreal moments on some of the more acoustic material, things like 'Mother Goose' and 'Up To Me'. They had a slightly more surreal element to them and they were upbeat too, and fun. They were seemingly inconsequential, but still musically substantial. They sounded quite different compared to what most other people were doing. And there were also the bigger sounding songs which were more dramatic, like 'My God', 'Aqualung' and 'Locomotive Breath'. There was a good balance of material and *Aqualung*, I think, really does hold up fairly well today in as much as it's probably given us, over the years, more material which works on stage than most of the others.

'When it comes to *Aqualung*, I can't think of a single outtake. There is, perhaps, once song that was recorded for the *Aqualung* album but not used at the time, which subsequently appeared on the 20th anniversary box set, called "Lick Your Fingers Clean" in its original form, and in a different form on the *War Child* album. *Aqualung* was recorded very much in an unbroken time period.

'I noticed, talking to Jeffrey Hammond about something, that he had a completely different recollection to mine. We talked it through, and I think we realised that there was a definitive version of the story and his wasn't right. Martin Barre is probably the best guy at remembering things; he actually has the best recollection of all of us – places, names and dates. I think John Evans is pretty unreliable in that respect, bearing in mind that at the time [much laughter] these things were going on, poor old John was a pharmacy student at university and the next thing he was in a rock'n'roll band and travelling the world making lots of money [even more laughter].

'The rest of us at that point were a little more down-to-earth. Martin and myself, particularly, because we didn't drink or party – in fact neither did Jeffrey – so I think Jeffrey, Martin and myself probably have a slightly less controversial set of memories [laughter] of that time than John did. Knowing John as he was then, you literally sort of had to pick him up by the scruff of the neck and put him in front of his keyboard and say "This is what we're going to do". He was a lot of fun. He was a confused boy sometimes. I look back at it with a lot of fondness.

'*Aqualung* was pretty well done in one straight period through the end of the year, and in an unbroken set of sessions at Island Studios. It was a pretty miserable time. We didn't have an easy run of it; for technical reasons we came out of it with the feeling we had intrinsically quite a good record, but from an audio quality it just didn't sound good at all. We really struggled with the mastering of that to make it sound good and yet, the irony was, listening to the multi-tracks as I have done in recent months, it sounds pretty good. It sounded so awful in the room at Island Studios, but what was on tape was actually pretty good and sounds really not too bad at all.

'Literally, I took three of those tracks from the original multi-track master as the bed tracks for some live TV show we did in Europe. I mimed the vocal and flute parts, because we had to lip-sync to a recording and it was easier for me to do my bit again, because the camera would be on me most of the time. But it just amazed me, listening back to those tracks, how good they sounded and remembering how bad they sounded at Island Studios. Led Zeppelin, who were in the room below us, were having an equally difficult time as we were recording simultaneously. Technically, those records were really hard to make. But in both cases they did ... O.K. [chuckles]'

On 'Aqualung' The Song ...

Barre: 'Ian really wrote all of it, in as much as he wrote the riff and the verses and the form was just verse/riff. We sort of came to a point where we needed a guitar solo, so I said, "Why don't we just base it on the chords of the verse, but break it down into half time and then take some of the chords of the verse to do a sort of round sequence to do a solo over." So we tried that and it worked well, so that became the solo.

'Led Zeppelin were recording downstairs at Island Studios and while I was doing the solo (it might have been the second take and it was going really well) Jimmy [Page] walked into the control room and started waving wildly and I thought "Should I wave back and mess the solo up and have to do another one, or should I just grin and carry on?" So, being a professional to the end, I grinned and that was the solo that is on the album – it's true!

'And there never really was a rivalry, we got on really well most of the time – because Zeppelin were an out and out rock band and we were always a bit left field. In those days, you only had half an hour with an eye to blowing off the headlining group, but it was all rubbish because the audiences were just great; they really liked us and loved Led Zeppelin. We actually owe them for helping us get to the point where the next time around we headlined.'

Anderson: 'Since I feel a responsibility to the people who buy our records, and who come to the concerts, I'm interested to know what it is they like. *Aqualung*, at the time it was released, arrived as Tull was becoming popular in America. So although it wasn't terribly successful that year, it has continued to sell consistently since. I will usually hear from the younger fans who may have discovered Jethro Tull because they heard *Aqualung*. These people who are becoming Jethro Tull fans are half of my age, or less than half of my age, in most cases they weren't even born when we released the first albums. So it's more difficult for me to understand what it is they see in the group. Believe it or not, I like to know who it is I'm singing to. Every night I play I have to keep in mind that, for some people, this is the first time they've seen Jethro Tull, so it's the most important Jethro Tull concert they have ever been to. It's an important part of the act of entertaining people. When we first played the music from *Aqualung* in America, the audiences were just about able to cope with the acoustic sections of some of the songs, probably because they knew they were going to get the big bang for their buck any minute.

'The title track has always been jointly credited to Jennie Anderson, my first wife, and myself. We were only married for about a year. We got divorced a couple of years later – not unhappily, it was just that we were both kind of young; she was Jewish and I wasn't.

'In fact, she had been taking photographs because she was at some sort of college and, at that time, was very much into tramps, very much into dirty old men. Which explains why we came to meet because, that's the sort of image I had. Well, her mother certainly made her aware of that fact if I didn't before. She had taken some photographs of this particular guy, who was a very striking figure. He had a defiance and nobility about him, and indeed, it would have been so much better to have used her photograph with the guy's permission instead of that, I think, really not very attractive or well executed painting on the front cover of *Aqualung*. I've never liked the *Aqualung* album cover; although a lot of people think it's terrific.

'I didn't like the fact that it was made to look like me, or loosely look a little bit like me. Terry Ellis was wanting this to be a character: it could be like me, or it could be somebody else. Anyway, Jennie had scribbled down some lines about this guy. I said, "Hey, let's make this into a song." We talked about the guy and she came up with a few lines, and I tried to show her how that could become a song. We wrote the lyrics to the first couple of verses and so she contributed to the lyrics of "Aqualung." It's a good song, and it's probably the only time that I have ever written anything with anybody else lyrically.'

On 'Cheap Day Return' …
Anderson: 'That was based on a trip to visit my father. In fact, "Cheap Day Return" and the song "Nursie" were both drawn from that. At that time, I was away from home and he was in hospital. I had not enjoyed a happy relationship with my father for some years and, around that time, we were starting to get along again. I was very aware that I might not see him again. I'm sure that, for a lot of people of my age, it's one of the things that you fear, because when you're thousands of miles away and somebody very close to you dies at that moment, you feel very guilty: very much cut up at being denied an opportunity to make your final farewell with somebody. The possibility of all this occurred to me on a Preston platform, waiting for a train back down south. So all that was a sad and slightly nervous moment. I think I wrote that on my way back on the train, but I do that a lot on trains.'

At the end of a brief swing through the US to promote *Aqualung* in early May, Clive Bunker left to get married – a marriage that lasted about 25 years. Back onto the drum stool came former Blades/John Evan Band drummer, Barrie Barlow, completing the original foursome from the Blackpool days when the band played 'I Can Tell' to a lukewarm audience. Meanwhile, *Aqualung* went to Number 7 in the US and Number 4 in the UK. Barlow's first recording with the group, was the five song EP 'Life Is A Long Song' which featured prominently on the *Living In The Past* album.

The 40th anniversary box set for *Aqualung* was extensive, with a hard outer shell box, a full book about the making of the album, a reproduction of the gatefold album cover with a 180 gram vinyl album and two CDs with various extras and remixes in standard CD format, a DVD of the album and extras in 5.1 surround sound and a Blu-ray with the whole package of remixes in multiple formats. A far cry from the 12" vinyl on which the original album was pressed on. More about this later.

For those who hail from a gentler age of stereo, or even mono, or who thought Mike Oldfield's *Hergest Ridge* in quad was as good as it gets, here is a word about 5.1. This is 5 separate tracks and a subwoofer track, meaning the sound has to be split into 6 separate channels instead of what we've had since vinyl appeared, mono or stereo. So the mix will be, by virtue of there being more channels to fill, different from the straight stereo or mono track from the original. When an album is recorded, as Ian does, with 24 tracks on an Otari 2" recorder there are 24 separate tracks to direct to the left or right in stereo or centre. With 5.1, the new mix will have 5 separate places for that music to go with the sub woofer track taking the low frequencies which is the .1 part. So stereo goes by the way and 5.1 moves in.

11

Superstardom – Thick As A Brick

Thick As A Brick (1972)
Thick As A Brick Part I / Thick As A Brick Part II

In the summer of 1972, Jethro Tull hit the dizzy heights of Number 1 in the *Billboard* album charts, toppling the mighty Rolling Stones' *Exile On Main Street*, and thus could justifiably lay claim to being the world's biggest band at the time with *Thick As A Brick*.

Thick As A Brick, a 45 minute continuous piece of music, whose lyrics were a sociological examination of a child's experience in the modern world, pretends to be based on a poem written by child prodigy Gerald Bostock. These purposely obscure lyrics were supposedly based on Anderson's childhood. The album sleeve, which Anderson claims took as long to complete as the album, carried the joke to its absurdist conclusion. The humour translated to the live show as well, and saw the group becoming more and more flamboyant in terms of stage clothes and on-stage personas; Jethro Tull concerts now featured comedy sketches, weather reports, white rabbit suits, walking tents and 30 yard dashes across the stage.

Almost six weeks were spent in rehearsals, recording and mixing. Anderson handled the production, and Robin Black was recruited for the engineering. *Thick As A Brick* quickly became Tull's first American Number 1 charting album and reached Number 5 in Britain. An outstanding tour followed, and Jethro Tull were hailed as the Kings of the Castle. The aforementioned five song EP, 'Life Is A Long Song', was released a month after *Thick As A Brick,* and also included 'Up The 'Pool' [Anderson's homage to his old hometown of Blackpool], 'Dr Bogenbroom', 'From Later' and 'Nursie'

On *Thick As A Brick* ...
Evans: 'That was good. That really seemed to flow. Everybody in the band put a lot of original musical ideas into that one. It's funny, I look at that as an album

of two sides: the first side is almost one side of coherent music in its own right and then, on the other side, it becomes more fragmented into different musical statements. That's the way it seemed to me, anyway, but it seemed to have a lot of energy especially on that first side, which carried right through to the end of the side. That was a good one to make.'

Anderson: '*Thick As A Brick* seemed an important album – to try and come up with a worthy successor to *Aqualung*, which hadn't been hugely successful yet. At that point, the words "Concept Album" were being used way out of context. The whole thing was really over the top. It was done with a sense of fun that we wanted our audience to share with us. And the whole album cover and everything about it was all done to make it pretty obvious that it was a joke. Many got it; surprisingly, many didn't. And, of course, some people still thought that there was a Gerald Bostock who really did write all this!

'It ended up being a very successful album. When we first started playing *Thick As A Brick* in America, because the opening was acoustic and quiet and the audiences were whooping it, it first occurred to me that I didn't want to do this anymore. That was the only time I ever felt like I didn't want to do any more concerts. Today, as soon as I start playing *Thick As A Brick* there's a great wave of recognition, but then immediately people go quiet.

'Barrie came into the picture when Clive decided to leave and get married – he had had enough and wanted to settle down. So Barrie came in when we did another single called "Life Is A Long Song", and he came in to play the drums on that. We asked him to stay on a trial basis, but he turned out to be all right and we did the album *Thick As A Brick* with him, which was his first real taste of working with the group.

'In all sincerity, I started with an idea, started writing a song and didn't stop. That's really the end of it in terms of a simple answer. I started to write with an acoustic guitar in a hotel room somewhere in America and I didn't stop. Usually you stop after four minutes, well it just kept going and kept going from one thing to another, and some places were repetition and original themes sort of came up again in different keys or in different time signatures, or whatever to change the sound and effect of it. All in all, it was a very mobile kind of music. It was a great sort of monster that was taking shape.

'We found as we were shaping it up for recording, that part of the second side wasn't working, so we re-wrote that very quickly and it went in another direction toward the end of the second side, which was different. Then we returned to the first theme again. It was a very exciting album to do, one which I think all the group found rewarding because we really had to work hard to play together on that record, and it was the first album that we played together in the sense of the complete group.

'As a piece of music, it was a response to the critical assumption that *Aqualung* had been a concept album, which to me it was not. Although, clearly, there were a few songs that did hang together, but *Thick As A Brick* was a deliberate attempt to come up with what Saddam Hussein might have referred to as "The mother of all concept albums". It was, of course, a preposterous idea that it had been written by a 8-year-old boy and it was all delivered with a certain tongue in cheek, almost Monty Pythonesque sort of delivery, particularly in terms of its live performance on stage.

'So it was a bit of a light hearted put on, but in a way that, perhaps, puts you in mind of some of the more British forms of humour. We delivered it in a way in which people were clearly not quite sure whether it was a very serious exercise or whether it was a bit of light comedy. It was, in truth, both of those things and some people take it incredibly seriously and others just find it a frivolous waffling. Whatever it was, it was a lot of fun.'

Barre: 'We toured fairly hard on the heels of *Aqualung* and I think Ian, in many ways, wanted to take the Mickey out of the concept album thing, the sort of grand and overblown thing people were doing, overtures with orchestras and double albums. So in many ways it wasn't a concept album in as much as there were a lot of songs in there and we just tied them all together. We would rehearse a song and then do a link which would go to the next song. It was fun doing it.

'We rehearsed about 90% of the album at the Stones' studio in London. I remember working very hard on that album and staying up working until four or five in the morning, have four or five hours sleep and then get up and start again. We literally started exactly where we left off the night before, and very often Ian would come in not knowing what the next piece of music was going to be and we'd just sit down and do it. He'd just say "Got an idea for the next bit?" It was good fun. Other people added ideas, and lots of things that John Evans came up with on Hammond organ became classic Tull bits. A lot of *Thick As A Brick* was very much of his making. It was an album where everybody had their little bit and I had my guitar solo in "The Poet And The Painter"; Barrie had his drum solo on the second side; Jeffrey had his talking bit – it was nicely formed because everybody had their say and it was very difficult to record. It was the hardest music we had played up to that point, there were lots of odd bars and time signatures. It was intensely hard work, lots of pressure and many times we thought we'd never get to the end, but we did.

'We never took ourselves seriously, but obviously other people did and it was labelled a concept album, maybe that's what made it work, it had humour. With everybody else, they didn't have the humour, except for Frank Zappa. Everybody was so full of themselves, but we were always having a dig at ourselves and when we played it live we added to the humour and made fools of ourselves.'

12

Living In The Past

Living In The Past (1972)

Song For Jeffrey / Love Story[1] / Christmas Song[2] / Living In The Past[3] / Driving Song[4] / Bourée[5] / Sweet Dream[6] / Singing All Day[7] / Teacher[8] / Witch's Promise[9] / Alive And Well And Living In[10] / Just Trying To Be[11] / By Kind Permission Of[12] / Dharma for One[13] / Wond'ring Again[14] / Hymn 43[15] / Life Is A Long Song / Up The 'Pool / Dr Bogenbroom / From Later / Nursie

(This is the US track listing, the UK version has 'Inside' instead of 'Alive And Well And Living In')

[1] The last song they recorded with original guitarist Mick Abrahams, 'Love Story' was finished in November 1968, just after the band's *This Was* album was completed. Previously unreleased in America, 'Love Story' was the third British single, reaching Number 29 in January 1969.

[2] 'Christmas Song' was recorded in late November 1968 without Mick (who was on the verge of leaving the band). The strings were conducted and arranged by David Palmer.

[3] 'Living In The Past' was one of the first songs Tull recorded with guitarist Martin Barre. Recorded in New Jersey in February 1969 before work had begun on *Stand Up*, 'Living In The Past' reached Number 3 in the British charts when it was released in May 1969. Reaching Number 11, it became Tull's highest ever US charting song.

[4] 'Driving Song' was recorded in Los Angeles in March 1969, just before the band started *Stand Up*.

[5] 'Bourée' had been recorded in April 1969 for *Stand Up* (Not included on the compact disc).

[6] 'Sweet Dream' was recorded in London in September 1969 during the *Stand Up* tour. A British Top 10 hit in November 1969, this was previously unreleased in America. The flip side, '17' was eventually released in 1988.

[7] 'Singing All Day' was another outtake from the same September 1969 sessions.

[8] This version of 'Teacher' was recorded in December 1969 for *Benefit* (Not included on the compact disc).

[9] 'Witch's Promise' recorded in December 1969. With the original version of 'Teacher' as the flip side, this reached Number 4 in the UK charts.

[10] Recorded in January 1970, 'Alive And Well And Living In' was deleted from the American version of *Benefit* to make room for 'Teacher' but appeared here (Only on the US version of this album). Recorded in January 1970 for *Benefit*, 'Inside' replaced 'Alive And Well And Living In' (Only on the UK version of this album).

[11] The previously unreleased 'Just Trying To Be' was recorded in June 1970 by keyboardist John Evans (who had yet to officially join the band) and Ian Anderson.

[12] 'By Kind Permission' and [13] 'Dharma For One' were both recorded live at an anti-drug benefit at Carnegie Hall on November 4, 1970 during the *Benefit* tour.

[14] 'Wond'ring Again' was recorded during the *Benefit* tour in June 1970, several months before being re-written and re-recorded as 'Wond'ring Aloud' for the *Aqualung* album.

[15] Hymn 43 is from *Aqualung*.

'Life Is A Long Song', 'Up The 'Pool', 'Dr Bogenbroom', 'From Later' and 'Nursie' all featured on the British EP 'Life Is A Long Song'.

Released just six months after *Thick As A Brick*, the first two sides of this compilation were filled with near hits and flip sides previously unreleased on albums, while the third side of this was devoted to a live recording made at Carnegie Hall during the *Benefit* tour on November 4, 1970. The fourth side was mainly filled with songs recorded just before *Aqualung* was released. The American release peaked at Number 3. A slightly different song lineup was used for the two-sided British version of this album that charted at Number 8.

When Tull began the rise to superstardom, both the band and their label oriented themselves towards scoring hit singles and albums. When *Living In The Past* was released, in the summer of 1972, it created excitement in North America because it contained both tracks previously unheard on the continent and material which had never appeared on any previous LP. In addition, an entire side featured a portion of a concert at Carnegie Hall; the first offering of a live Tull recording to that point and the only one until *Bursting Out* appeared in 1978.

The odd thing about *Living In The Past* is that it was released in three different versions (each with slightly different selections). For the first time, the three different versions have been gathered (including the collectable 36 page booklet) into one set by Mobile Fidelity. As usual, the company used 24 carat gold and re-mastered the album with the GAIN system for the best sound quality. The album is a testament to the high quality of music Tull had created. Every track, from the hard driving 'Sweet Dream' and 'Driving Song' to the melodious ballads 'A Christmas Song', 'Wond'ring Again' and 'Witch's Promise' stand out as revolutionary.

13

A Passion Play

***A Passion Play* (1973)**
A Passion Play, Part I: Act 1- Ronnie Pilgrim's funeral - A Winter's Morning In The Cemetery: i. Lifebeats ii. Prelude iii. The Silver Cord iv. Re-Assuring Tune. Act 2 – The Memory Bank – a small but comfortable theatre with a cinema-screen (the next morning): v. Memory Bank vi. Best Friends vii. Critique Oblique viii. Forest Dance #1
A Passion Play, Part II: Interlude – ix. The Story Of The Hare Who Lost His Spectacles. Act 3 - The business office of G. Oddie & Son (two days later) x. Forest Dance #2 xi. The Foot Of Our Stairs xii. Overseer Overture. Act 4 - Magus Perdé's drawing room at midnight xiii. Flight From Lucifer xiv. 10:08 To Paddington xv. Magus Perdé xvi. Epilogue

Like *Thick As A Brick*, *A Passion Play* was a continuous piece of music with lyrics which were possibly an exploration of life after death and the even more absurd possibility that if it wasn't your time, you could come back to the living. The music had Anderson playing soprano, sopranino and alto saxes along with the flute – the two former instruments have long since been sold. However, in a later interview Anderson said they were still around somewhere. Whatever, they didn't make much of an appearance from that point on, apart from being a part of *War Child*. David Palmer was probably the last to blow a sax in anger on a Tull record for 'Too Old To Rock'n'Roll'.

Whether on purpose, or due to a lag in record company efficiency, the world tour that promoted the album commenced before the album was released. It featured the album in its entirety including the short film 'The Hare Who Lost His Spectacles' and the 45 minute build up to the band's actual stage entrance, complete with film of a dead ballerina coming back to life was, to say the least, memorable. It finally made its appearance on film as part of the re-mastered version of the album when the catalogue was redone ... the first time ... or was it the second? The record industry, along with musicians themselves, have taken masters in hand and continually redone their recordings as technology has permitted. So, just because an album says re-mastered version, it is a good idea to check which. Be aware that now we have the 5.1 re-releases and, at last notice, we had just come to the release of the special editions of *Thick As A Brick* as well as a double box set of *Thick As A Brick 1 and 2* on 180 gram vinyl with a hard covered book accompanying the two albums.

A Passion Play sold for a series of reasons, including its first spins on radio, showing off a series of very hot, rocking songs that were destined to become classics, as well as a series of ballads and oddities with even a song about Mother Goose. And, of course, the concept album debate.

There were no fence sitters; like Marmite, you either love or hate *A Passion Play* – take your pick. The critics, of course, hated it; the fans loved it. Enough that the album went to Number 1 in the US and remained in the charts for the duration of the summer it was premiered. The poster for that concert still hangs in the office of Canada's largest promotion company. It was a memorable show and the album is more than likely the finest piece of overall production Tull have ever managed.

A Passion Play began as a collection of individual songs recorded in Paris at the famous Château d'Hérouville, where notable rock musicians had recorded, amongst them Elton John, who even named his album *Honky Château* in tribute to the place. Enough material had been recorded for a double album when the sessions broke down, and all but two missing tracks were shelved and later believed to have been lost. 'Only Solitaire' and 'Skating Away' showed up two years later on *War Child*. Three unnamed tracks were performed live and later included on 1988's *20 Years Of Jethro Tull*.

After this fiasco, the band returned home to England where Anderson quickly re-wrote the album which became *A Passion Play*. The band recorded the album soon after, but the music evolved during additional rehearsals, so the entire album was recorded a second time. Due to the lambasting the album took in the press, the record company issued a silly press release stating the band were so upset by the backlash that they would stop touring for good. 'For good', in reality, lasted two weeks. *A Passion Play* was Tull's high watermark in the sense that it was the last to reach Number 1 on the American charts, but, equally, was their first not to crack the Top 10 in the UK.

A track called 'A Passion Play, Edit #8' peaked at Number 80 on the American singles charts in June 1973, a month before the album was released. 'The Story Of The Hare Who Lost His Spectacles' was credited to Jeffrey Hammond-

Hammond. With the appearance of a man in a large rabbit costume, this very brief song became a focal point of the band's live show.

The supposedly lost sessions were eventually unearthed and three were included on the band's 20th anniversary collection of music, which ran the gamut of types of songs from radio recordings to remixed singles. The music in general, was a smorgasbord of brilliant songs that made the fan wonder why had they been kept off of albums, not used or just passed by? It was one of the best collections of the then new concept of unreleased and remastered box sets ever recorded. It had a smaller single disc release and both disappeared never to be seen again – very rare and sought after.

In addition, the double CD of the material that made up the early versions of songs that were recorded at the château, called *Nightcap*, was the third part of the boxes released for the 25th anniversary five years later and contained all of the then thought lost recordings that had been shelved and led to a re-recording of the *Passion Play* material.

It was a stellar set of songs and took up one whole disc and showed the early themes which emerged as *A Passion Play* afterword. It is one of the band's best efforts, even though shelved for decades. The second disc was a series of also thought missing, plus outtakes, all of excellent quality, posing the question again: why was this material not used on the albums from the sessions they were recorded for? In fact, to take the *20th Anniversary Album* and *Nightcap* and place them side by side, if released at the time they were recorded, they could have charted in the time periods they originated. But the question today is moot. The four disc 25th anniversary box, although well done, did not reach the same heights as the previously mentioned albums and seemed more made for the event.

On *A Passion Play*:

Barre: '*Passion Play* was probably a mistake in as much as it was presented in the same way as *Thick As A Brick*. People compared it to *Thick As A Brick* because it was continuous. So we went to the same formula, because it had worked once, which we probably shouldn't have, because a lot of people pointed at it as a lesser album, which I don't think it was. We should have gone in a different direction. We also started by recording an entire double album in France and, because we had so many problems with the studio there, we ditched the album and came back to England and completely started again from the songs upward. Those French sessions did get released on the *Nightcap* album. At that point in time, I think we reached a high – it was a difficult point in our career and, really, it isn't easy for people to review a new album and give it equal billing; the obvious way is to go down and that's how people saw it – as a lesser product.'

Evans: 'A Passion Play was a downer. That's funny, they seemed to run in opposites – one up, one down. I still think the music bears the marks of those hammer blows. It was forged on an anvil more than coming out easily, which may not be a bad thing. If you take Mozart and Beethoven for example, with Mozart, the music wrote itself. Mozart was just a medium between divine inspiration. With Beethoven, quite often, you get this feeling that it was forged out of solid rock and forged like a piece of iron with a lot of effort. As far as albums getting their just desserts, I think that War Child was underrated; I thought that was a bloody good album. Minstrel In The Gallery was a painful album to make, similar sort of thing. It seemed very forced. I don't know, sometimes you just don't get something right in the ambience. I suppose a lot of it is subjective. It's the times you might be going through, personally, it can be very hard to make an album when there may be something you're not too happy about.'

Anderson: 'A year later we started another album and we reverted back to a number of songs again. Then we started recording in France at the château, which is a sort of ancient place where people can actually live at the same time. It was going to be a double album. Suddenly, I thought "I'm really missing the excitement of the album before", and we just stopped and went back to England. And in two weeks I wrote A Passion Play with a view to trying to get this thing going again, this great sort of exciting way of working. And we did it again, and we did it on stage again as we had done with Thick As A Brick the year before. On stage we did A Passion Play in that way and it was terribly exciting to work that way.

'When it came to the next album, I guess we all felt we should try to be more serious and I think that was a problem with A Passion Play. It didn't have the humour or the warmth that Thick As A Brick did. It doesn't mean that one or the other is a good or bad album, maybe just that the mood was wrong or that it was the right mood for the wrong time.'

Jeffrey Hammond was totally unaware of the release of Nightcap and the Château d'Isaster tapes and exclaimed, 'I guess I must have been on that'. He also admitted he wasn't aware that much had been recorded at that studio. 'I do remember some good things happening at the time at that studio,' he mused, 'so it's not surprising that it did get released. My impression at the time was that what was being done was not essentially what Ian wanted the music to be, not quintessential Tull; perhaps a bit experimental. It's too bad that it didn't get released until recently, because I enjoyed it as well as did other people. I know Barrie enjoyed it a lot. I also felt that, perhaps some of it was irresponsible, because we mucked about quite a bit, because it was a unique situation where we were working and living at the same place. You stayed there on the grounds. Usually we would live at home and then go to the studio, where we basically went to work.

'There was that opportunity to do things in a haphazard or less constructed way, so some of the music may have reflected that instead of the hard-edged, very focused way of working which was the normal way. In the end, I liked *Passion Play*. I know not everybody did, but I quite liked it and, again, I don't think it was what the group was all about. I don't think it was a good follow up to *Thick As A Brick*. I think, in itself, it was all right. I think it was unfortunate to have to be compared with *Thick As A Brick* ... it suffered from that and the publicity angle where the management said something to the effect that the group weren't going to do any more gigs, which was a silly thing to say, and people in the group were not pleased to hear that. I thought the album was a strong piece of music on its own. It stood the test of being able to stand up next to other records, except maybe *Thick As A Brick*.'

Jeffrey was astonished to learn that *Passion Play* had hit Number 1 in the US back in its first month on the shelves: 'You would think that by being in the band you would be aware of that. There seemed to be little time for reflection, we just got the news that it had been panned. I don't think people were as upset as management made out, we just got a certain amount of feedback and that was that. It wasn't that well liked.

'I remember going on tour with that and, as I recall, the rehearsals for that were in Tennessee. At the beginning of the tour we had two or three days of rehearsal, and I remember Ian having some technical difficulties with saxophones and various instruments and sounds, that was proving difficult for him. There were also other people having some problems, but I personally found it thoroughly enjoyable and I was feeling very ready and comfortable about the whole thing, which was very unlike me. I was all for it, but I know other people did have technical problems and it's very difficult to fit that into a set with other lengthy tunes like *Thick As A Brick*. It's also quite a strange thing to go through; recording an entire album and then scrapping it and starting over.'

The irony about the popularity of *A Passion Play* is that, in many quarters, it was considered the group's finest hour, their *magnum opus*. It will inevitably be compared to *Thick As A Brick*, unfairly or not, as the two albums shared something in common – their length. Other than that, they were chalk and cheese and the fact that both reached Number 1 was not a coincidence, they were both brilliant, but different reasons. The fact that *A Passion Play* was never played in concert again, due to the critical bashing it received, is very sad. The album was better than most albums recorded in the rock idiom, and represented more than the basic boy meets girl, boy loses girl, girl finds love, love goes away *ad infinitum*. It reached places lyrically that other records could only echo, but never hope to better. It was a piece of music/lyrics Tull would never equal again and the reasons for keeping it off the concert song list for the next 40 years were just plain wrong. End of story.

14

A Gradual Fall From Grace – War Child

War Child (1974)
War Child / Queen And Country / Ladies / Back-Door Angels / Sea Lion /
Skating Away (On The Thin Ice Of A New Day) / Bungle In The Jungle / Only
Solitaire / The Third Hoorah / Two Fingers[1]

[1] 'Two Fingers' was a slightly rearranged 'Lick Your Fingers Clean', an outtake from the
Aqualung sessions originally scheduled for release as a single in early 1971.

Although the fans loved the group's albums, the critics were less enchanted. So,
Tull returned to a style more familiar to the average punter – shorter songs – and
released another big seller, 1974's *War Child*, which gave them a Number 1 single.
But that was to be the last time Tull had a hit – *War Child* only broke the Top 5
hitting Number 2 in the US and a disappointing Number 14 in the British charts.
From there, their popularity began to slide. *Minstrel In The Gallery* and *Too Old To
Rock'n'Roll … were* not big sellers. It was obvious the band's tastes were headed in
a more eclectic direction than mainstream.

'When it came to doing the next album, it was obvious we had to record
material oriented toward an onstage situation,' Anderson says. 'So, we had to
revert back to short songs that we wouldn't have to cut up like *Thick As A Brick*
or *A Passion Play* because with *Thick As A Brick*, for example, we had to take stuff
and play them as "sort of songs" and they don't really work that way.'

War Child had actually started life as a film project, which was shelved due to
a lack of funds. Much of the music, which had been written for the script, and
two songs from the sessions prior to the recording of *A Passion Play* – 'Skating

Away' and 'Only Solitaire', ended up on what became *War Child*. Some tracks even featured members of the band playing with a full orchestra. Reverting to the format of a collection of separate songs results in a solid, accessible album. The live shows continued to be extravaganzas, incorporating a female string quartet in platinum wigs, plus the usual outlandish stage gear worn by the rest of the band, of which the most memorable was Jeffrey Hammond's matching black and white striped suit and bass. A five night stint at the Los Angeles Forum prompted headlines such as 'Jethro Tull – now the world's biggest band'. In the studio, Robin Black once again engineered while Anderson produced.

On 'Skating Away ...' ...
Anderson: '"Skating Away ...", which had been recorded as one of the disastrous *Château* tapes from a couple of years before, along with 'Just Solitaire', ended up on this album. It was back to just a bunch of songs – a nice, good, accessible album. I came back to England to live after having gone, for tax reasons, to spend a period of time in Switzerland. When I came back, I found myself living alone in a rented mews cottage off Baker Street. I think I was writing the *War Child* album when I first moved there, but I continued to live there at least into the period of writing the music for the next album. So the Baker Street references are really to do with my post-first-marriage life, living alone again, as I then had got very used to doing. I didn't have too much in the way of things in my life. I didn't have a car, everything was simple.'

On 'Sea Lion' ...
Anderson: 'Slightly ecological in content, probably influenced by being brought up in Blackpool, where the sea was dirty because of the dumping of the town's sewage a very short distance off the shore. As an adolescent, I used to go there when there was a storm and watch the waves and great clouds of spray. We used to dodge them. Little did we know then, that what we were dodging was every kind of variation of *E coli* bacteria known to man. As the tide came in, you could see sewage floating in the water. And children, little kids, would be playing in that water.'

The tongue in cheek song 'Bungle In The Jungle' was a surprise hit, and actually charted, although a throwaway song. It was the group's last hit single. Tull's whole career was a mixture of songs recorded with thoughts of 'This is a great song, we're going to have a hit here' and 'What a silly ditty, why are we bothering with this?' Ironically, the throwaway songs hit the charts, while the serious attempts went ...well, not very far'

15

Minstrel In The Gallery

***Minstrel In The Gallery* (1975)**
Minstrel In The Gallery[1] / Cold Wind To Valhalla / Black Satin Dancer / Requiem /
One White Duck / 0[10] =Nothing At All / Baker St Muse: i. Pig-Me And The Whore ii.
Nice Little Tune iii. Crash-barrier Waltzer iv. Mother England Reverie / Grace

[1]The title track featured a very rare co-writing credit for guitarist Martin Barre. The
heavy guitar riffing had been a staple of the tour before and was a solo Barre had come
up with as he had for almost every tour the band ever undertook – this time, however, it
was incorporated into a song. This track peaked at Number 79 on the American singles
charts in October 1975. Its flip side, 'Summerday Sands' was eventually included on
1988's compilation *20 Years Of Jethro Tull*.

Group leader Ian Anderson, guitarist Martin Barre, keyboardist John Evans,
bassist Jeffrey Hammond and drummer Barrie Barlow had spent four years on
the road – with occasional breaks for recording sessions, before making this
album. The band's lineup had been stable for the course of five albums and the
threads were beginning to show – this would be Hammond's swansong.

The album was recorded in Monte Carlo in a mobile studio. Anderson again
handled the production, and Robin Black engineered. But Anderson was not
happy with the atmosphere of the recording or the finished product. Although, in
retrospect, much of the music stands up well compared to the group's catalogue
in general, it suffered in sales quite probably due to a lack of radio exposure and
the fact the band did not tour to promote it. The album reached Number 20
in Britain and Number 7 in the US. Hammond left Tull to concentrate on his
painting, three months later in December of 1975.

Although a tour was not mounted for this album specifically, by the time the
War Child tour reached Canada the album had been released and many thought
it was a tour to back up *Minstrel* ...

A large format video was recorded and played on television featuring many of the songs and although Anderson – his own hardest taskmaster – hadn't liked the end product, the recording went over well and Martin Barre, to this day, states it is one of his favourite albums, citing 'Black Satin Dancer' as a stand out. The album as a whole stands up well after all these years and features a mini-suite in the guise of 'Baker Street Muse'. The album is solid and should be viewed as a very artistic and solid statement to the abilities of a very well-versed group about to begin to fracture, but not a dud in any way.

On *Minstrel In The Gallery* ...

Barre: 'I'd write a guitar solo for each year and it would be an instrumental. I redo one each year, so I wrote one for the *Passion Play* tour which ended up being tacked on at the beginning of *Minstrel...* The thing about those solos is that they got better as we went along. We used to call them "Martin's Tune" [laughs] and it was "Martin's Tune" 1, 2, 3, 4, and so on [laughs] and we finally got tired of doing that. I actually have a song called 'Martin's Tune' from before my joining the band, which I used as my audition. I have a recording of that from 1969. They've improved over the years, but just riffs and ideas glued together. Jumping ahead to the present, I think I've gotten to the point where I can say I can write music to a reasonable standard, whereas in those days I was still learning. But I don't regret anything, it was all right for the time but I'm glad I moved on.'

16

Jeffrey Takes A Bow – M.U.

'Musically, there is some pretty good stuff on *Minstrel In The Gallery*, but I think the band was suffering by then,' Anderson reflects. 'Jeffrey Hammond left soon after and John (Evans) was endlessly playing classical music, seemingly removed from the world of rock and what Jethro Tull was about. He was also drinking far too much, probably due to a marriage breakdown. A lot of things in the band were beginning to crumble. Barrie was another story altogether. Jeffrey put down his guitar in 1975 and that was the end of his musical career.

'Jeffrey would be looking back upon his life, being the same age as me, or a year or two older than I. And I think you become reflective on the subject of people you've known, on what you've done and all the rest of it. I think Jeffrey does look upon it being part of a period of his life where the camaraderie of it all was the main force behind his interest.'

Hammond used to go and see the early Jethro Tull at the Marquee Club when he was at art college and living up the road from Anderson. They were friends and had played together briefly in school in The Blades, but at that time, Hammond was the group's fan – the only one. 'He was the guy who came to see us all the time,' Anderson mentions. When the band became popular and had lots of fans Hammond melted into the background because he wasn't the sole supporter anymore and, not being a very social sort, he wasn't going to hook up with the other fans.

'Jeffrey sort of faded away until he returned to Jethro Tull in 1970,' Anderson recalls. 'At that point, of course, it was a commitment for a limited amount of time and he did what he did for five years. He had a clear cut idea in his head that it was going to last only so long. When Jeffrey began to realise it wasn't as much fun anymore, and he also had a pretty keen idea of how much money he had made and how much he needed to live on, then I think there came a point where he thought it was better to switch and go back to what he really wanted to do, which was paint,' Anderson reckons. 'And he decided to do it then rather than let something go downhill. Around the time that Jeffrey left, we had all been hit with enormous amounts of tax and most of the guys had gotten married, had families, and suddenly a lot of things became very demanding in terms of not only having to worry about each other and playing music.'

Hammond's leaving left some pretty big shoes to fill and, as intimated by members of the group, there was a certain sadness concerning his departure. 'We all tried to persuade him to stay, but he probably made the right decision at the right time, because Jeffrey was never a natural musician. I think he always felt that he was a bit of an imposter – he really had to learn things the hard way, it didn't come naturally to him. But I think Jeffrey was much more of a musician, in the best sense of the word, than he ever realised. I always thought that he had a much better sense of musicality than he himself appreciated at that time,' Anderson recalls fondly.

The old saying goes, 'Join a party when it's in full swing and leave before it dies down.' Whether intentional or not, for Jeffrey Hammond, he was a part of this great band as it hit big and before it stopped charting high. He entered the band in time to be included in the most successful string of albums in the band's canon – *Aqualung, Thick As A Brick, A Passion Play, War Child, Minstrel In The Gallery* and *Living In The Past.* It was the pinnacle of Tull's success; and the most theatrical period.

The last words on this subject are, of course, best left to Jeffrey himself: 'After I left, I went to see them when they played near where I lived. Apart from that, I didn't really stay in touch with what they were doing. I really have these massive voids of ten years in which I have no idea what was going on in Jethro Tull [laughing] which can be pretty embarrassing at times, you know, not even knowing who was in the group through various times in the eighties.

'I really loved going to see them before I joined when I was an art student and they were playing at the Marquee Club in London. I also used to go around with them in the van when they were just getting going before the first album. I did quite enjoy the album *Roots To Branches*. In fact, now that Ian lives a lot closer to me we've been seeing more of each other. He's only about an hour away and he gave me a copy of that album and I loved it instantly.'

M.U. – *The Best Of Jethro Tull* (1976)
Teacher / Aqualung[1] / Thick As A Brick, Edit #1[2] / Bungle In The Jungle / Locomotive Breath[3] / Fat Man / Living In The Past / A Passion Play, Edit #8 / Skating Away ... / Rainbow Blues[4] / Nothing Is Easy

[1]The compact disc version of this compilation featured a remix because the original master tape was supposedly lost.

[2]This was the single edit from *Thick As A Brick*.

[3]This was released as an American single, peaking at Number 62 in March 1976.

[4] Previously unreleased.

This album featured one previously unreleased track and covered material from Tull's second to ninth albums. Initially selling over half a million copies, it peaked at Number 13 in the US, but only Number 44 in the UK. In England, where the band had become a hit so fast, the strain of releasing albums too often was beginning to show. By the way, M.U. was short for Musician's Union.

17

Too Old To Rock'n'Roll

Too Old To Rock'n'Roll: Too Young To Die! (1976)
Quiz Kid / Crazed Institution / Salamander / Taxi Grab / From A Dead Beat To An Old Greaser / Bad-Eyed And Loveless / Big Dipper / Too Old To Rock'n'Roll: Too Young To Die / Pied Piper / The Chequered Flag (Dead Or Alive)

When Hammond left the band, a suitable replacement was found in John Glascock, formerly of the band Carmen, who was dubbed Brittle Dick. Anderson and David Palmer, the band's orchestral arranger since *This Was*, had been writing a stage musical about an old fashioned rocker who comes back into fashion. They had Adam Faith in mind for the lead role. This was another project that didn't get off the ground, like the *War Child* album, which was to have been a movie soundtrack. It was not written on the road as all other albums had been. It charted at Number 25 in the UK and Number 14 in the US, where it was the first of the 1970s albums not to go gold. Anderson fervently denies that the main character, Ray Lomas, is in any way autobiographical.

On *Too Old To Rock'n'Roll* ...
Anderson: 'I was in Switzerland over Christmas. I had some ideas for songs and David Palmer came along and we did some work together. We rehearsed with the band and worked out some ideas with an eye to doing something different, something musical, theatrical and sort of performance oriented. I can't remember if we had anybody in mind. It had the light humour and the warmth that wasn't on the preceding album. Unfortunately, it's not a very satisfying album. It doesn't have enough blues or R & B for me.'

On 'Salamander' ...
Anderson: 'I was just thinking about that song in bed the other night when I couldn't sleep, when I got back and was a little bit jet lagged. I was just thinking

"What is there I've never played live on stage that would really be a kind of a buzzy thing to play?" and that song came to me. It employs one of those hybrid tunings; it's not really an open tuning, but it has a number of open strings which allows you to play things that you can't play on a regular concert E tuning.

'As an acoustic guitar piece, it was one of the rare occasions when Martin and I actually sat down in a studio and played live together during that piece, and it just occurred to me that that might be one we might resurrect as a live piece. The only problem is that you don't have a lot of time in concert to fiddle about tuning up, because it isn't just the question of dropping the pitch of a couple of strings. If you do that on any guitar you have to re-tune everything; you change the tension of the untouched strings by virtue of reducing the tension of the strings you are detuning. So it's not just a ten second operation, you're looking at 30-40 seconds to re-tune two guitars and our band is not very well known for being able to cover for each other while tuning. However, we will figure this one out.'

Barre: 'We recorded that in Monte Carlo, and it's a very difficult piece of music. Ian suggested we do that on a tour and, I swear, I spent two whole days learning it, because it's an open tuning and I didn't know which open tuning it was – it's not a normal one. It took me hours to work it out. I tried one tuning and then figured I'd got it wrong. I re-tuned the guitar again three or four times before getting it right and then I could learn it. I do remember it was a very good piece of music. It was the best thing we did together, but at the time it was just another song. It was difficult to play and sounded great.'

18

Tull Renascent

Songs From The Wood in 1977 and *Heavy Horses* a year later, along with the live album *Bursting Out* in the same year, saw a resurgence of popularity in the band's fortunes. They also entered the history books by being the first band to transmit a live show via satellite to the world. Things were very Tull once again, though mega-stardom was a thing of the past. Tull had become a big band with a large, faithful following – their cult status was born. 1979's *Stormwatch* was also a successful album, but by the end of that decade, Tull was changing rapidly, and the punks were like barbarians at the gates of Rome trying to kick out the old order.

Songs From The Wood (1977)
Songs From The Wood / Jack-In-The-Green / Cup Of Wonder / Hunting Girl / Ring Out, Solstice Bells[1] / Velvet Green / The Whistler[2] / Pibroch (Cap In Hand) / Fire At Midnight

[1] Released as a 1976 Christmas single charting at Number 28 in Britain.
[2] Released as a US single in May 1976 charting at Number 59.

The bucolic frolic that is *Songs From The Wood* benefited from Anderson's move from the city to the country – he began to embrace all things woodsy and reflected his new-found surroundings in song. Needless to say, it was one of those brighter albums. But Anderson didn't just retire into a wooded area, he took on the responsibility for an actual working farm. All of this showed through on the album – a combination of English and Celtic folk roots, but with some 'heavy metal mandolin' influences to boot. The portative pipe organ made its debut into the Jethro Tull live show, which saw Anderson with his hair shorter and sporting riding breeches and crop like some English country squire – which, you could argue, he was.

David Palmer finally debuted as a full band member, as opposed to just providing arrangements as he had done since the first album: he would remain until 1980. In late 1976, the band released a three song EP that foretold the change of direction this album was about to take. Included on that EP were 'Ring Out, Solstice Bells' (a minor hit which gets an annual airing on TV and radio every festive season and has probably been a nice little earner down the years, and was the last song Tull played in the flesh on *Top Of The Pops*), 'Pan Dance' and 'March The Mad Scientist', supposedly a Christmas present to the European fans. The public's acceptance of this collection of excellent songs was seen as a comeback for the band. The album charted at Number 8 in America and Number 13 in the UK.

On *Songs From The Wood* ...
Anderson: 'After only ever living in hotels in the middle of London, or in other cities, I was the last member of the group to move out of town and go to live in the country. Suddenly, what had been part of my childhood, being outdoors and being in more remote and rural places, was now a reality of day to day life. So that part of my life – owning a house and being in one place, had a stabilising influence on me. It gave me a place to put down some roots, and I think that was reflected in the music. It also brought the guys in the group together, musically, in terms of their involvement. I would deliberately leave the studio and let them come up with some arrangements and ideas. It was an attempt to try and get the band working as a unit and add a social as well as musical identity.'

On 'Pibroch (Cap In Hand)' ...
Barre: 'I remember doing the introduction to that – turned the amps up full and went for it. Just sat and played. Of course, the idea comes from bagpipes, a certain style of music, and I remember Ian lending me an album of bagpipe music and saying "I think you should have a listen to this and get an idea of the notes they play." And, of course, if you analyse what bagpipes do and try to do that on the guitar you're really on a sticky wicket. I can't remember how the actual notes came about, but probably between me and Ian we figured out what to play and we used to do that as an instrumental; lovely melody.'

Repeat: The Best Of Jethro Tull, Volume II (1977)

Minstrel In The Gallery / Cross-Eyed Mary / A New Day Yesterday / Bourée / Thick As A Brick, Edit #4 / War Child / A Passion Play, Edit # 9 / To Cry You A Song / Too Old To Rock'n'Roll: Too Young To Die / Glory Row

Also in 1977, another 'Best Of' was released, which charted at Number 94 in America making this something of a damp squib for the band. Odd really, when you consider that the first Best Of , *M.U.*, went to Number 13 in the US. Like *M.U.*, *Repeat* had a previously unreleased track in the shape of 'Glory Row' to tempt the faithful who already had the other songs on the original albums. Maybe two 'Best Of' albums in as many years was too much? Maybe two albums in the same year was overkill? Maybe the whole world had turned punk? Maybe not!

Heavy Horses (1978)

... And The Mouse Police Never Sleeps / Acres Wild / No Lullaby/ Moths / Journeyman / Rover / One Brown Mouse / Heavy Horses / Weathercock

1978's *Heavy Horses* followed in a similar vein to its predecessor. It could easily have been called *Songs From The Wood Volume II*, but true to Anderson's nature, he preferred the former to the latter claiming, once again, that *Heavy Horses* was a darker album. He cited the possibility of increased friction within the group as a possible reason for this. It's entirely plausible, as the band was only two years from being completely overhauled. The album was recorded in London in January 1978. It reached Number 19 on the US charts and just scraped the UK Top 20. As this album was released, the band started another world tour.

On 'No Lullaby' ...

Barre: 'That was one of those really loud songs – amps up loud and I was playing Hamer guitars at Number 10 in the studio with Marshall amps. I used to use a Gibson Les Paul Sunburst until it got so valuable that I had to buy tickets on airplanes for it and it went everywhere with me: breakfast, lunch, you couldn't trust it out of your sight. And I thought, "This is wrong and they're irreplaceable" so I started playing Hamer guitars at that point. And technology caught up and you could get just as good a sound from guitars that weren't antiques – the Gibson is worth $30,000-$40,000. Since then, I've gone through Ibanez and Anderson guitars and the only strings I use are GHS.'

Bursting Out (1978)

No Lullaby / Sweet Dream[1] / Skating Away (On The Thin Ice Of The New Day) / Jack-In-The-Green / One Brown Mouse / A New Day Yesterday / Flute Solo Improvisation – God Rest Ye Merry Gentlemen – Bourée (Medley) / Songs From The Wood / Thick As A Brick / Hunting Girl / Too Old To Rock'n'Roll: Too Young To Die / Conundrum[2] / Minstrel In The Gallery / Cross-Eyed Mary / Quatrain[3] / Aqualung / Locomotive Breath / The Dambusters March

[1] Missing from the single CD
[2] Missing from the single CD
[3] Missing from the single CD

1978 also saw *Bursting Out*, the first full length live album the band had ever undertaken. With the exception of the two songs on *Living In The Past*, it had taken the group ten years to put out live material, odd for a band that is so accomplished on stage. For the occasion, Anderson utilised an eight-track recorder and then sold it after the album had been completed. However, part of the reasoning may have been that Anderson maintained that this album marked the end of an era for Tull and that the group was about to embark on new territory.

Tull played to their biggest audience ever in October 1978, thanks to the technological miracles of satellite television as their Madison Square Garden show was beamed live all over the world – they called it Tullevision. Standing in on bass was an old Blackpool mate, Tony Williams, who played on the entire US tour in place of John Glascock who was seriously ill (he sadly passed away due to complications during surgery in 1979 aged only 28). The album was recorded in the early summer of 1978 at several concert sites throughout Europe. The album charted at Number 21 in the US and Number 17 in the UK. Unfortunately three songs and a great deal of the stage banter was deleted from the single CD release, including the two pieces by Martin Barre. A double CD with the entire album is available in Europe.

Stormwatch (1979)

North Sea Oil / Orion / Home[1] / Dark Ages / Warm Sporran / Something's On The Move / Old Ghosts / Dun Ringill / Flying Dutchman / Elegy

[1] 'Home' was released on a British EP with 'King Henry's Madrigal'.

It's difficult for the surviving members of Tull who recorded *Stormwatch* to talk about the album due to the passing of John Glascock. He sadly died at the end of the tour to promote that album. He had played some bass on the tracks, but the majority had been done by Anderson.

Stormwatch has a foreboding tone to it and is very much to do with environmental issues. Overall it's a well written and recorded collection of songs that very often gets passed over in favour of more popular or well-known recordings. 'North Sea Oil', 'Orion and 'Home' begin the album with a lot of flare. 'Dark Ages' is a mini-epic with enough imagination and guile to stir emotions. The trilogy of 'Dun Ringill', 'Old Ghosts' and 'The Flying Dutchman' are wistful masterpieces perfect for a rainy autumn day.

But punk had come to power and the album was less than successful. In early 1980, Tull set off for another American tour with Fairport Convention's Dave Pegg on bass. Shortly after, Barrie Barlow announced his plan to depart the band. Unknown to the rest of the band, it would also be the last recording John Evans and David Palmer would be a part of. As the decade came to an end, so did the involvement of the Blackpool Mafia from the 1960s. *Stormwatch* sold a respectable half a million copies, peaking at only Number 22 in the US and Number 27 in the UK.

Stormwatch, like several earlier Tull releases, is an album written around a concept rather than a random collection of commercial ditties. *Stormwatch* considers the anxious challenges of the omnipresent energy shortage, paying special attention to our rapidly dwindling oil supplies and the risk of annihilation from nuclear disaster. The first cut on side one 'North Sea Oil' expresses the central theme:

> '*Ten more years to lay the fears, erase the frown before we are all nuclear ... The better way! Oh, let us pray; we want to stay in North Sea oil*'

The tempo is speedy and Anderson's treatment of the word 'Oil' is a drawn out jeer. All tracks on the album were written by Anderson except for 'Elegy', a David Palmer composition. Typically, all members of the group – John Evans and Palmer on keyboards, John Glascock on bass, Barriemore Barlow on drums, Barre on lead guitar and Anderson as flautist and musician-in-chief – perform superbly. *Stormwatch* was their best album in quite some time, and is clearly and favourably comparable with *Thick As A Brick* and *Aqualung*. It's a certain antidote to more complacent lyrical creations and less musical constructions.

Because this was a pivotal point in the history of the band – on the brink of the departure of three long time members and the death of another, Jethro Tull were about to, in effect, become a duo of Anderson and Barre. Dave Pegg augmented that duo bringing it to a trio. And thus it remained until future members became ensconced in the organisation.

19

A New Decade, A New Tull, '*A*' New Record

In 1980, Anderson embarked on what was to be a solo album by enlisting new players. Dave Pegg had just joined Tull and was, therefore, still considered a new kid on the block, so he, along with Martin Barre, was invited to play on the Anderson album. Eddie Jobson was asked to come on board because of his keyboard prowess. Jobson had been with UK as a support act to Tull on tour in 1979, and his impeccable C.V. included work with Curved Air, Roxy Music and Frank Zappa. He brought along Mark Craney to play drums.

Unfortunately, a local English paper was about to print a story about the group splitting up. Anderson headed off the arrival of the news in print by sending a note to the other members of the 'working' Jethro Tull to warn of the impending falsehood. But ill feelings ensued and Barrie Barlow, who had already left the band, never returned, and John Evans and David Palmer left in a huff and formed the ill-fated Tallis. The band continued to get the wrong idea when the album was released as Tull, at the suggestion of the record company who felt the album sounded like a Jethro Tull album. All this only served to exacerbate any problems within the ranks.

A (1980)
Crossfire / Fylingdale Flyer / Working John, Working Joe / Black Sunday / Protect And Survive / Batteries Not Included / Uniform / 4.W.D. (Low Ratio) / The Pine Marten's Jig / And Further On.

The album had the working title of *A*, simply because the initial was on the tape boxes. Chrysalis persuaded Anderson to release it under the Jethro Tull name. That meant explaining the lineup change with a record company press release that has to go down in history as one of the biggest clangers in the music business. It quoted Anderson as saying he had fired John Evans, David Palmer and Barrie Barlow. Not one to take things lying down, Anderson immediately countered with his own press release putting the record straight about his solo project. It didn't mend anything. It is quite probable that the ill feelings from that mess have never been fully mended.

Dave Pegg's first recording under the Jethro Tull banner was a long way from the folk direction of recent Tull albums which, as an ex-Fairport Convention stalwart, he would have appreciated. Electronics had taken centre stage in the music business and synthesisers, computers and sequencers began to rule the day. This was meat and drink to Jobson, and Anderson followed the trend, so that *A* was a light year away from the previous *Stormwatch*, but a powerful album nonetheless.

On joining Tull, Dave Pegg was summoned to Ian Anderson's home to discuss business. Pegg remembers: 'We met at a huge table in Ian's home to discuss my upcoming involvement in the band. For some reason, Ian proceeded to tell me exactly what each member of the band thought of him, which I found an odd thing to do. I can't remember what he said about each of the guys, but within a short time I discovered that he had been 100% correct in his assumptions.'

The live show had each band member attired in matching silk parachute suits. 'Black Sunday' rivals anything Tull have ever recorded and a few other pieces were almost equally memorable. *A* charted at Number 25 in the UK and Number 30 in the US.

On *A* …

Anderson: 'We worked very quickly together. It was the first time I had worked with an almost completely different lineup of people altogether. We ended up recording about seven or eight songs in only a couple of weeks, and then enough to finish an album.

'Several of the songs dealt with things to do with current scenarios, happenings within the world – relationships took a back seat. "Black Sunday", one of the strongest tracks on the album, suffered from some technical difficulties, unfortunately, and much effort was spent working on that in the mixing process. It's probably my favourite on the album. It was a boy / girl song – the breaking up of a relationship.'

A was not a huge success, but it did offer the remainder of the band an opportunity to work from a different mindset for a change and the album still has its high points.

Eddie Jobson was only available to answer questions from me via e-mail:

Jobson: 'Let me try to give you a quick overview of what my position was in the band at the time: First of all, I was never a member of Tull. Ian called me in 1980 and asked if I would like to collaborate with him on a solo album. I was just beginning my own solo album, *The Green Album*, at the time, but agreed to participate in the project. There was never any intention of this being a Jethro Tull project. In fact, I asked Ian if I should bring along Mark Craney – the drummer I was then rehearsing with for my project. Ian agreed and the *A* album was born. The synthesiser/drums/bass backing tracks were so fresh sounding (remember – it was the beginning of a new decade) that Chrysalis Records requested the album become a new Jethro Tull album. Ian asked me if I was O.K. with that and I said I was – as long as I received "Special Guest" billing.' Jobson's first impressions of the organisation was: 'frugal', 'but very organised'.

As this was the first and only time Jobson worked with the Tull musicians, it was interesting to learn of his take on their characters. 'The members of Tull are some of the nicest people in the business, and remain, sincerely, friendly to this day,' he replied. Anderson and Barre being the nucleus of the band, I asked how he described their relationship, he replied: 'Symbiotic.' Succinct, to say the least, but interesting and the first time such a description has been given, I believe.

So would Jobson work the same way with the band if the album were done again? 'Yes' Again, succinct! And who contributed what to the album and in Jobson's opinion, who, besides Ian contributed essential aspects of the group's material, sound and music? Jobson: 'Overall, of course, Martin provides a key element of the Tull sound. I think, however, that on the *A* album my keyboard approach added a new element to Ian's usual sound (that being the intention of my participation). I also contributed compositionally to some small degree.'

Where, then, did he see himself as a part of the history of the band? Jobson: 'A small footnote. A "Special Guest" performer brought in to offer a different character for a brief period.'

Was he aware ahead of time how long he would be with the band when joining? Jobson: 'After the album was finished I returned to the US, but, it was difficult for them to tour with that material without my participation. So I agreed to do the one tour with them – provided, again, I received "Special Guest" billing throughout. It turned out to be the most enjoyable tour I've ever done. Afterwards, as planned, I returned to my solo projects.'

With regard to the technical aspects of instruments and outboard gear – what did he use on the album? After all it was the beginning of the synth-heavy years of the 1980s and a decade easily identifiable for the almost over-used gear known as synths, synths and ... synths.

Jobson: 'With Tull, I used primarily a Yamaha CS80 Synth, a Mini-Moog, and a Yamaha CP70 Piano, as well as my custom electric violins.' And, not surprisingly, Jobson found the tour to be a particularly strong one. 'Although, I understand why the "futuristic" approach didn't sit too well with everyone. Even I prefer the Olde-England folksy style that typifies the Tull we all know and love. However, the *A* album and tour were meant to be different – and serve as a colourful departure in the long view.' And as quickly as the busy soundtrack composer came into the conversation, he was off to continue his busy schedule, but not before adding: 'I hope this gives you enough ... my participation in the Jethro Tull chronology, as important to me as it was, doesn't warrant too much space.' He is being too modest.

20

The Broadsword And The Beast

The Broadsword And The Beast *(1982)*
Beastie / Clasp / Fallen On Hard Times / Flying Colours / Slow Marching Band / Broadsword / Pussy Willow / Watching Me, Watching You / Seal Driver / Cheerio

A was an experiment with new technology, but *The Broadsword And The Beast* was a storming album that combined modern with more traditional sounds, while *Under Wraps* furthered the electronic experiment. Unfortunately, the Broadsword tour was the last time Tull averaged 16,000 seaters in North America. From here on in, nothing would bring the band back into the public eye at the level to which they had been accustomed.

With Jobson and Craney returning to their other lives, the drummer's seat and keyboard position had to be filled. Gerry Conway played drums on the album, but was replaced for the ensuing tour by ex-10cc drummer, Paul Burgess. Peter-John Vettese's cherubic face peered out from behind the mountain of keyboards for both the album and tour – his talents far exceeded his obvious youthfulness. From a strictly quality driven standpoint, *Broadsword* ... was vintage Tull in all its glory. Enough material had been recorded to release a double album and was one of the only albums where Anderson did not produce. Several producers were invited for the position, with Paul Samwell-Smith (ex-Yardbirds founding member and producer for Cat Stevens) edging out the competition in the end.

The electronics of *A* had obviously been maintained to some degree via Vettese's nimble and youthful approach, so the mixture of old and new was perfect for what is one of the best later albums in the Tull catalogue. The remainder of the material, which did not make it onto the single LP (in hindsight it may have been worth releasing as a double at the time), surfaced on various anniversary packages and EPs. These songs included: 'Jack-A-Lynn', 'Overhang', 'Too Many

Too', 'Down At The End Of Your Road', 'I'm Your Gun', 'Mayhem, Maybe', 'Motor Eyes', 'Rhythm In Gold', and 'Jack Frost And The Hooded Crow'.

Had you been paying attention to the rumours floating around prior to the Jethro Tull concert promoting *The Broadsword And The Beast*, you would have half expected a group of old men to limp onto the stage and stumble through some ancient ritual. Instead, Anderson, Barre and the other minstrels in the gallery were in top form despite Anderson's battle with a lingering sore throat. The newest incarnation of the live show was slick and intense.

Gone were the lengthy drum, guitar and flute solos. Instead, the musicians offered up unrecorded instrumental passages which blended well with the vast Tull repertoire. It's no secret Tull had been regarded as dinosaurs for years; indeed, at the time of the Broadsword tour, they celebrated their fifteenth anniversary. At a time when many groups had to settle for performing in 4,000 seat halls, Tull constantly filled 15,000 seaters, hardly the death throes of a dying dinosaur even if they weren't playing the vast stadia of yesteryear.

The album reached Number 19 on the US charts and Number 27 in the UK. When Tull was invited to do the 1983 Prince's Trust Benefit Concert, drummer Phil Collins sat in with the band. After the tour was finished, Anderson sold his Maison Rouge studio and began recording at home. The result was his first solo album, *Walk Into Light*, in collaboration with keyboardist Peter-John Vettese.

On *The Broadsword And The Beast* ...

Anderson: 'For some reason that album, although not popular in the US, was very popular in Germany. We didn't have a keyboard player at the beginning, so I did the first tracks. Peter Vettese came in later and finished things up. But that album was done in a slightly different way in that I joined in on the backing tracks. That made for a band feeling, a live situation and I think it is reflected in the quality of the material.'

The music of Jethro Tull had evolved over those years and, in doing so, left certain sections of their audience behind. Even back in 1982, rumours that this was the group's last foray across the continent were abundant. Martin Barre put those rumours to rest quickly: 'We received bad press all through that particular tour, you know, about our age and so on, but we can keep going just as long as people still want to see us perform; I don't see there being any limit.' Barre is not your average guitarist. Contrary to the stereotypical rock star, he is quiet, soft spoken, polite, and claims to like Bach and the music of Elgar; quite the opposite of what you'd expect. But what of the man who has lasted so many years with a group where members have come and gone like clockwork, where Ian Anderson appears to be in complete control?

In conversation, Barre reacted surprisingly to the question of whether there was acquiescence between himself and Anderson. 'I've never really thought about it,' he explained 'I've never even considered the subject really, but yeah, I'm sure there is. I'm sure that if we weren't going to get on and work well together it wouldn't have lasted two months. I would have thought, "This isn't for me, I'd better go," or he would have thought, "He's not the one, he'd better go", or "I'd better go and work with somebody else". Obviously that's apparent in all of us, that we are all capable of working together, but I just accept that rather than trying to figure out whys and wherefores.'

Barre has said that this was the first Tull album he truly enjoyed recording, his increasing familiarity with his own home studio enabled him to approach the project in a different light. Unfortunately, *Broadsword...* was not considered a hit. Barre was not happy about this and spoke rather sombrely about it: 'We haven't had a hit for a while. The reviews we receive tend to be less than kind. We want to have a hit. It costs so much to tour and if you don't sell enough records it can become too costly to tour.' The emphasis on touring is paramount in the scheme of things for Tull. Most rock artists tour to promote record sales. Tull, on the other hand, seem to sell records in order to tour. 'The nature of the band's performance,' he offered 'is such that the live show is the core of what makes Jethro Tull work, it's the most important aspect of the group.'

21

Anderson Flies Solo – Walk Into Light And Under Wraps

Walk Into Light **(1983)**

Fly By Night / Made In England / Walk Into Light / Trains / End Game / Black And White Television / Toad In The Hole / Looking For Eden / User-Friendly / Different Germany

More a collaboration with Peter-John Vettese than a solo album, in 1983 the duo recorded one of the most electronic-sounding albums any member of Tull was ever a part of. Many of the songs were brilliant and overlooked by both the record company and the public. Given the opportunity to re-record some of the highlights today, they would be amongst the strongest Tull material on record: 'Different Germany'. 'Looking For Eden' and 'Fly By Night' come to mind immediately.

Under Wraps **(1984)**

Lap Of Luxury[1] / Under Wraps #1 / European Legacy / Later, That Same Evening / Saboteur / Radio Free Moscow / Astronomy / Tundra / Nobody's Car / Heat / Under Wraps #2 / Paparazzi / Apogee / Automotive Engineering / General Crossing

('Astronomy', 'Tundra', Automotive Engineering' and 'General Crossing' appeared on the cassette, and on later CD versions, but not the vinyl LP)

[1] Released as a single, which charted at Number 70 in the UK and received extensive air play in the States.

Electronics had begun to creep into the Tull mainframe during *A* and had been on the rise over the course of the next two albums. The *zeitgeist* favoured synthesisers, with the New Romantic movement (not that Anderson or Tull could be accused of being part of that scene, but they must have known which way the wind was blowing). In 1984's *Under Wraps*, they prevailed to the point that a drum machine was employed rather than a human drummer. Not the best thing they ever recorded, but it was proof they had the mettle to meet technology head on no matter what the consequences and, in retrospect, the foundation of the material holds up. It's just that the instruments themselves sound dated, as did anything else recorded during that era – it was inescapable.

Both Anderson and Barre find it a rewarding and totally palatable album. More than notable was the quality of the production. Anderson was at the helm once again and this was recorded at his home studio. Lyrically, it was obvious Anderson had delved into the writings of Craig Thomas and probably other spy novelists – fun stuff all around, but most Tull fans were probably happy the distraction lasted for only one album. Disappointingly, the album only reached Number 76 in the US and 18 in the UK.

Ditching the drum machine, thankfully, they brought a human being in the shape of Doane Perry for the tour to promote *Under Wraps*. However, during that tour Anderson developed throat problems that were to keep Tull off the road for two years. This allowed him time to develop his fish farming business in Scotland. The band performed at Bach's 300th Anniversary concert in Berlin in February 1985, and played Tel Aviv and Budapest for the first time during a 1986 tour.

Original Masters (1985)
Living In The Past / Aqualung[1] / Too Old To Rock'n'Roll ... / Locomotive Breath / Skating Away (On The Thin Ice Of The New Day) / Bungle In The Jungle / Sweet Dream / Songs From the Wood / Witch's Promise / Thick As A Brick / Minstrel In The Gallery / Life Is A Long Song.

[1] A remix, as the original tape was supposedly lost.

This third greatest hits package from the band, released in 1985, served as a good introduction to the band's earlier material for anyone who had joined the party via later albums, or for those who had recently bought a CD player and wanted the best known songs on the relatively new format. The unheard remix of the 'Aqualung' track offered something new to the hardened fan.

22

Crest Of A Knave And The Anniversaries

Crest Of A Knave (1987)

Steel Monkey / Farm On The Freeway / Jump Start / Said She Was A Dancer / Dogs In The Midwinter / Budapest[1] / Mountain Men / The Waking Edge / Raising Steam

(Original vinyl version didn't feature 'Dogs In The Midwinter' or 'The Waking Edge')
[1] The first version ran over 22 minutes.

After a three year break from recording, Tull returned with a vengeance with 1987's *Crest Of A Knave*. This album saw Peter-John Vettese pack up his synthesisers and decamp, though the band couldn't resist the lure of drum machines on all but two tracks, on which Doane Perry made his recording debut for Tull. It also saw Martin Barre's heaviest guitar input in living memory. The result was an album that brought back the faithful and landed numerous new fans. It also found Tull high in the charts and even won them the first ever presentation of the Heavy Metal/Hard Rock album of the year Grammy award. This didn't endear them to Metallica fans whose heroes were hot favourites to scoop the prize

On the subject of the Grammy win, Anderson is magnanimous in victory: 'I'm very pleased to have won, because it is something of an accolade, coming from one's peer group of a large number of people who have been creatively involved in the music business for a number of years. It's recognition from them, and to them I say a very warm "Thank you".'

For the live concerts Don Airey, who had played with just about every heavy metal outfit, stood in for Vettese. However, there was more than a rock feel to the album – some could almost detect a Dire Straits and ZZ Top sound being filtered in on some songs. The album began life at Dave Pegg's studio with just the trio of Pegg, Barre and Anderson purposefully writing songs in a lower key to protect Anderson's voice from strain once the music was brought out on the road and put to the test – the last thing the band needed was to cancel a tour.

Anderson remembers that: 'During that period we had not done a complete tour, but we had not been inactive as a group. We did concerts here and there. I wanted to take a year – which turned into two – away from doing music partly because of the vocal strain I experienced on tour in '84.' That vocal strain resulted in the cancellation of many concerts on their North American tour following the release of their last album. The change in pitch was intentional: to avoid strain which could result in another cancelled tour.

'I remember writing the song "Budapest" in a hotel the morning after a show, about the vision of some slender and tall athletic creature who was serving sandwiches backstage. It was an easy lyric to write, ten minutes to scribble down half the lyrics for that one. I was having a cup of coffee, overlooking the not-so-blue Danube,' Anderson recalls.

At the suggestion of branching out into video with these sort of visions in mind, he responded, 'It's not the sort of area in which an artist would have tangible direct control of what is going on. I can go into the studio with my equipment and I don't need an engineer, producer or tape operator. Just me, the tape recorder and the equipment in between. I can operate that while sitting in front of a microphone playing an instrument – it only takes one hand. What I can't do is be in front of and behind a camera at the same time; the old arms are not that long and the equipment is not yet designed to be programmable and operable so that the operator is also the performer. It's possible that in a few years we might see some programmable cameras, which will pan and focus to a programmed plan, so that one can actually be in front of the camera and let the camera do all the work that you programmed into it earlier. That may come about, but I think by the time it does I'll be far too ugly to want to appear on video.'

With drummer Doane Perry, the group moved briefly to engineer Robin Black's studio, then finished the project at Anderson's home studio. Near the conclusion of the sessions, Perry had to return briefly to the US, and drummer Gerry Conway was brought in to finish some tracks. The album charted at Number 19 in Britain and Number 32 in America. Anderson previewed the music to a few focus groups of Tull fans, then used their response to solicit support from the record company.

The tour that followed featured Pegg's other band, Fairport Convention, as opening act so he was doing double duty. The tour was a success: Tull were back in the big time.

On *Crest of a Knave* ...

Barre: 'That's the album where a lot of things were of my invention. There are still chunks of the music where Ian very much knew what he wanted, but I think my input was far greater on that album than any other album. On "Budapest" there are bits of acoustic guitar that I wrote. I think that I've dabbled here and there and come up with some significant ideas for what they were.

'On *Under Wraps* I co-wrote a couple of songs with Peter [Vettese] and put the lyrics on, so that's the nearest I've come to writing a song for Jethro Tull. I think the formula works where Ian writes the music and the band arranges the music and adds ideas and then Ian writes the lyrics and performs the vocals. I don't offer songs to the band, but if Ian says "I'm stuck here, have you got any ideas?" I'll go away and come up with something. So I let Ian play the ball within the band and let him take the lead and if he needs help, which is rare, well he never needs help, but sometimes he asks for input and obviously it's very willingly given by whomever he asks.'

Tull released an extensive amount of material commemorating their 20th and 25th anniversaries. Much of it was unreleased material featuring some of their best recordings from across the years.

20 Years Of Jethro Tull: 1988

The differences between LP and CD versions of the package are noted in the following description of the package:

Compilation: Radio Archives

The songs on this side were recorded live in 1968 and early 1969 for the *Top Gear* and *Saturday Club* programmes on BBC Radio.

Side 1

Song For Jeffrey[1] / Love Story[2] / Fat Man[3] / Bourée[4] / Stormy Monday Blues[5] / New Day Yesterday[6]

[1] Performed by Tull's first lineup in late 1968.
[2] Performed by Tull's first lineup.
[3] Performed by Ian Anderson and drummer Clive Bunker in early 1969.
[4] Performed by Tull's second lineup.
[5] Performed by Tull's first lineup.
[6] Performed by Tull's second lineup.

Side 2

Cold Wind To Valhalla / Minstrel In The Gallery[1] / Velvet Green[2] / Grace[3] / The Clasp[4] / Pibroch (Pee Break) / Black Satin Dancer[5] / Fallen On Hard Times

[1] Performed by Ian Anderson and drummer Barriemore Barlow, recorded in April 1975 for a BBC Radio broadcast.
[2] From the then just released *Songs From The Wood*, recorded in February 1977 for the BBC's *Sight And Sound* programme.
[3] Recorded for the BBC in April 1975.
[4] Recorded live in Hamburg, 8th April, 1982
[5] Recorded live in Hamburg, 8th April, 1982

Side 3: The Rare Tracks

Jack Frost And The Hooded Crow[1] / I'm Your Gun[2] / Down At The End Of Your Road[3] / Coronach[4] / Summerday Sands[5] / Too Many Too[6] / March The Mad Scientist[7]

[1] An outtake from *The Broadsword And The Beast*, used as the flip side of the 1986 release of 'Coronach'.
[2] Previously unreleased outtake from *The Broadsword And The Beast*.
[3] Previously unreleased outtake from *The Broadsword And The Beast*.
[4] Written by keyboardist David Palmer. Theme for a UK TV show.
[5] Flip side of 'Minstrel In The Gallery'. An outtake from the Monte Carlo sessions, spring 1975.
[6] Previously unreleased outtake from *The Broadsword And The Beast*.
[7] Released on the 'Solstice Bells' EP in November 1976, the *War Child* outtake was recorded by Anderson, Evans and Hammond in 1974.

Side 4: Compilation: The Rare Tracks (Released But Only Just)

Pan Dance[1] / Strip Cartoon[2] / King Henry's Madrigal[3] / A Stitch In Time[4] / 17[5] / One For John Gee[6] / Aeroplane[7] / Sunshine Day[8]

[1] Released on the 'Solstice Bells' EP in November 1976. Originally recorded for the Pan's People dance troupe who opened the 1974 Rainbow Theatre concerts. Racing driver Stirling Moss did the introductions that night.

[2] *Songs From The Wood* outtake, used as the B-side of 'The Whistler'.

[3] *Stormwatch* outtake released on a 1979 UK EP with 'Home'.

[4] Previously unreleased outtake from the *Heavy Horses* sessions.

[5] Recorded by Tull's second lineup in 1969. Flip side of 'Sweet Dream'

[6] Mick Abraham's composition for the manager of London's Marquee Club. Recorded by the group's first lineup, this was the flip side of 'A Song For Jeffrey'.

[7] Recorded by the John Evan Band in early 1967. Tull's first single, credited to Jethro Toe.

[8] Written and sung by Mick Abrahams, this was the B-side of 'Aeroplane'.

Side 5: Compilation: Flawed Gems (Dusted Down)

All of these tracks were completed, several were mixed and ready for release, but then held back at the last minute.

Lick Your Fingers Clean[1] / Scenario – Audition – No Rehearsal[2] / Beltane[3] / Crossword[4]

[1] *Aqualung* outtake slated for release as a single. Instead, it was slightly reworked and released as the song 'Two Fingers' on *War Child*.

[2] Three songs that comprised *The Chateau d'Isaster Tapes*, plus the previously released 'Only Solitaire' and 'Skating Away (On The Thin Ice Of The New Day)', were all that survived from the ill-fated 1972 French recording sessions .These three previously unreleased songs were finally mixed in April 1988.

[3] Previously unreleased outtake from *Heavy Horses*.

[4] Outtake from *Stormwatch*.

Side 6: Compilation: Flawed Gems (Dusted Down)

All of these tracks were completed, several were mixed and ready for release, but then held back at the last minute

Saturation[1] / Jack-A-Lynn[2] / Motoreyes[3] / Blues Instrumental (Untitled)[4] / Rhythm In Gold[5]

[1] Recorded around the time of *War Child*.

[2] Previously unreleased outtake *The Broadsword And The Beast*.

[3] Previously unreleased outtake from *The Broadsword And The Beast*.

[4] *Stormwatch* outtake.

[5] Previously unreleased *The Broadsword And The Beast* outtake.

Side 7: Compilation: The Other Sides Of Tull

Anderson has said that the following two sides contained his favourite Tull music.

Part Of The Machine[1] / Mayhem, Maybe[2] / Overhang[3] / Kelpie[4] / Living In These Hard Times[5] / Under Wraps 2[6]

[1] Written and recorded for this compilation in March 1988.
[2] Previously unreleased outtake from *The Broadsword And The Beast*.
[3] Previously unreleased outtake from *The Broadsword And The Beast*.
[4] *Stormwatch* outtake.
[5] Outtake from the *Heavy Horses* sessions.
[6] Recorded by Ian Anderson and Dave Pegg in 1984.

Side 8: Compilation: The Other Sides Of Tull

Only Solitaire / Cheap Day Return / Wond'ring Aloud[1] / Dun Ringill[2] / Salamander / Moths / Nursie / Life Is A Long Song / One White Duck / 0^{10}=Nothing At All

[1] Recorded live at the Hammersmith Odeon for Capital Radio, London
[2] Recorded at the same Hammersmith Odeon concert.

Side 9: Compilation: The Essential Tull

Except where noted, all of these were previously unreleased live versions of Tull songs.

Songs From The Wood[1] / Living In The Past[2] / Teacher[3] / Aqualung[4] / Locomotive Breath[5]

[1] Recorded live at the Hammersmith Odeon for Capital Radio London on 29th October, 1987.
[2] Recorded live at the Philadelphia Tower Theater in November 1987.
[3] Rare, early version, released as the flip side of the 1970 UK single 'Witch's Promise'.
[4] Recorded live in Hamburg, 8th April, 1982.
[5] Recorded live in Hamburg, 8th April, 1982.

Side 10: Compilation: The Essential Tull

Except where noted, all of these were previously unreleased live versions. These tracks also began the third compact disc of the compilation.

Witch's Promise / Bungle In The Jungle / Farm On The Freeway[1] / Thick As A Brick[2] / Sweet Dream[3]

[1] Recorded live at the Philadelphia Tower Theater in November 1987.
[2] Recorded live at the Hammersmith Odeon for Capital Radio London.
[3] Recorded live in Hamburg, West Germany

When this five LP/3CD box set was released in 1988 it set the standard by which all other box sets would, and should, ever be judged. It was unprecedented in its scope and quality. Yes, there was a comprehensive booklet that went along with it, but the music and the selections and the lengths that the many, many people involved in the project went to, made this a little bit of history. It is, sadly, no longer available, but was truly one of the most collectable items ever assembled. No one ever celebrated an anniversary like this in the music business and will probably never do so to this extent again. There were 65 tracks, comprising live and radio sessions, versions of old favourites, hard-to-find B sides and other rarities, plus sixteen previously unreleased studio songs.

At first the nostalgic overtones of an anniversary package caused Anderson to refuse to become involved in working on a project like this. However, when he recognised the degree to which someone else could re-write the group's history (badly), he began to work on a definitive compilation. Two hard core Tull fans, David Rees and Martin Webb, were recruited to assist with the project, and long-time Tull engineer Robin Black was brought in to ensure that the digital copying and remastering was done properly.

For fans that could not afford, or didn't want, the five album box set, a 27 track double LP and a single CD were also issued. A lengthy world tour saw Fairport Convention's multi-instrumentalist Maartin Allcock added to the lineup on keyboards and guitars.

23

Rock Island

Rock Island (1989)
Kissing Willie / The Rattlesnake Trail / Ears Of Tin (The Mainland Blues) / Undressed To Kill / Rock Island / Heavy Water / Another Christmas Song / The Whaler's Dues / Big Riff And Mando[1] / Strange Avenues

[1]Anderson wrote the lyrics about the true story of guitarist Martin Barre's electric mandolin being stolen and returned.

1989's *Rock Island* followed *Crest Of A Knave* and, whether by design or not, it was a heavier album than the former – heavy metal Grammy winner or not. The band began work on this album in the autumn of 1988. Recorded at both Anderson and Pegg's home studios, the idea for the album was to incorporate re-occurring themes. This idea wasn't maintained. The band did a European tour in the early fall of 1989 and the US near the end of the year.

On *Rock Island* ...
Anderson: 'I think *Rock Island* missed out on having some humour elements there. It was there on things like "Kissing Willie", not a great song, but it's good fun, and another one or two fun songs like that would have been good. *Rock Island* had two or three songs that were just a little too serious.'

Unlike tours by their contemporaries such as The Rolling Stones, The Who, and Paul McCartney, Jethro Tull do not take the 'comeback trail' when they tour because they've never gone away. They've toured consistently over the years, maintaining more of a cult following than pop star status, but have never actually hung up their instruments or announced their retirement.

However, there was a notable renewal of the band's popularity, due to *Crest Of A Knave*. Further, *Rock Island* promised to trump the popularity of *Knave*, climbing the charts with the first single, "Kissing Willie' at Number 6 on the radio airplay chart.

Eight of the ten songs off the album were written in a ten day period, then recorded rather quickly. The reason for this, according to Anderson, is scheduling: 'I just stick to a schedule, which I can tell you this far in advance, already has me back in the studio to write the next album. That will facilitate a focused release. Putting yourself in a position where you have to produce is an excellent way to get the creative juices flowing again. If I know I have ten days before the guys are due to arrive to record, it puts the pressure on me to produce. I like it that way.'

The production on *Rock Island* is the sum of over 20 years experience in the studio for Anderson, and it shows – the album sparkles from stem to stern. The mix has the electric guitar and flute very much up front, while the acoustic, folksy side of Jethro Tull is conspicuously absent.

Although it has been generally understood that Anderson writes all the band's material, and the other members offer limited input during the recording process, he explained that, 'Jethro Tull is, from time to time, an extraordinarily democratic band in the sense that there is a lot of cooperative musical involvement. Albums like *Thick As A Brick, Passion Play, Songs From the Wood* and *Under Wraps* are very much collaborative band efforts as far as arrangements are concerned. I may have written most of the songs as original sketches, but the way they come out can change dramatically.'

24

From Fairport To Tull – The Strange Tale Of Maartin Allcock

Maartin Allcock tells the bizarre story of how he joined Jethro Tull:

Fairport Convention opened up for Jethro Tull in 1987 on the '20th Anniversary' tour of Europe and the USA. I had been in Fairport a couple of years by this stage and there was a good feeling in the Fairport camp, which didn't go unnoticed by Ian. Then I was in the local pub at lunchtime on New Year's Day 1988 with Dave Pegg (who lives about 300 yards away), and he said to give Ian a call, which I did later that day. He asked me if I'd like to play with Jethro Tull on keys. I said that I didn't have any and that it wasn't one of my instruments. He said something to the effect of 'You'd better get one and get practicing then' [Author's note: This says a lot about Ian Anderson's 'salesmanship' for want of a better word. In the 1960s, he persuaded a novice Jeffrey Hammond that he should play bass in his band. By the 1980s, he has gone one better and convinced an already established stringed instrument aficionado, in Allcock, that he could swap to keyboards].

I asked 'Why me?' He said, 'I'm tired of flash keyboard players who overplay everything and you play guitar and mandolin etc.' So, I suppose I had the advantage of the lack of technique! So I bought a Roland D50 and borrowed a whole bunch of other stuff off Ian and practiced about 18 hours a day for three months. I recorded 'Part Of The Machine' on 21st March 1988, using Kieran Halpin's ten string bouzouki. I overdubbed the second guitar on the 25th. My first gig was at Shoreline Amphitheater near San Francisco on 1st June 1988 and my last was in San Francisco Civic Center on 17th December 1991: 231 gigs later.

I had been a fan of the band when I was at school and was very pleased for Peggy when he got the job. I didn't actually get to see them again though until about '86 when they played on the Marillion show at Milton Keynes Bowl with Peter Vettese on keys (Mozart reborn). They were very, very good. I saw the Tull organisation at work when we supported them in 1987. It was quite impressive, but as you'd expect for a band of that calibre. It was clear that Don Airey was not happy in the band, but I never realised that it would be me getting that job next. I hadn't imagined Martin Barre to be such a thoroughly nice chap, one of life's few real gentlemen.

Kenny Wylie was at the helm of the crew and always seemed to be working too hard. Gerd Burkhardt was the tour manager and very unpopular he was too. Peggy, I'd known for about twelve years or so by this time and Doane was very nice. We were dressing room mates for most of my time. The crew were great chaps in the main, with only a couple of exceptions. When I joined, so did Fairport's sound men, Rob Braviner (still with Fairport) and Gareth Williams, my mate from Manchester, who now works with Oasis and was Monitor Engineer of the Year in 1995. Also poached from Fairport, was the lighting engineer Mike Cooper. I thought at the time that it was as if Ian was trying to get some of the Fairport Convention camaraderie into Jethro Tull.

Here's a Q & A that I did with Maartin via e-mail:

I asked Jobson about Barre and Anderson's methods together, so I asked Allcock the same:

Allcock: 'Ian and Martin are indeed the hub of the band, although it's Ian's band and no one else's. They've both tried solo careers without much success. I think they kind of need each other. Ian winds Martin up quite a bit, but as Martin's such a sweetheart he never takes it too much to heart.'

Rabey: 'What is your favourite album from the band'

Allcock: 'My favourites are *Aqualung*, because it says what I was thinking at the time, and *Thick As A Brick*, as it has some really great music in it. I know most people's fave is *Stormwatch*, but I never had to listen to it much, so I'm not that familiar with it.'

Rabey: 'Interesting statement. So which was/is the best Tull lineup?'

Allcock: 'I enjoyed the *Thick As A Brick* tour in '74 or whenever it was [1972] and I liked the first lineup with Mick Abrahams. I think possibly the golden days are gone for good now. I did enjoy my time with Jethro Tull, but the last year or so I was unhappy and wanted to leave. I kept getting asked back for one more tour, but I was glad to leave at the end. But I got to see the world a bit, made some great friends all over and have some fond memories. Do it again? Maybe ...'

Rabey: 'While you were in Tull, album by album, how did the dynamic within the band change? Who contributed what to which albums and in your opinion who, besides Ian, contributed essential aspects of the group's material, sound and music?'

Allcock: 'Ian is the music of Jethro Tull. You play his notes. Nothing else. Most of the time he played my parts anyway. I didn't actually get on too many tracks.'

Rabey: 'In that case, having involvement with both, what were the differences between Fairport and Tull? Why do both?'

Allcock: 'Fairport Convention is more of a good time kind of band on the outside. They're all very pally with the audience and very accessible to their fans, due mostly, I would say, to Dave Pegg's own personality. Peggy had been doing both for years and it was great to tour with him in two bands. I've done more gigs with him than anyone else in my life. So Fairport Convention always worked around Jethro Tull. After I left Tull, it was great to be spending some time at home, but then when Dave left Tull, Fairport started working a lot more until, at the end, I was away from home too much. I have three small children and when I came home from the US in November '96 I asked my 3-year-old what my name was, and she said "Gig". I thought "That's enough then" and left soon after. Also I was getting stale and I was becoming unhappy with what I heard coming off the stage, so it was time.'

Rabey: Was being in Tull fun?

Allcock: 'Mostly, Jethro Tull was fun, although tour manager Gerd Burkhardt's absence would have made it more so. I remember one time in the US, we checked out of the hotel at some ridiculously early hour to go to the small airport, only to get there before the caretaker came to open up. I was not involved a lot with the recording. Performing was different. I used to love Peggy's playing on "Locomotive Breath", he really used to rip it up. I don't know if I could have stayed long without Peggy. He made everything all right.'

Rabey: 'How much of a tight-lip did people within the band maintain? I ask this because Tull was, and has always been, a bit of a mystery type organisation which is part and parcel, I suppose, of why people still call Ian, Jethro?'

Allcock: '"Tight-lip" is a good phrase here. There was a lot of it about in my day, kind of "I'm telling you, but don't tell him" stuff. It might make for an effective organisation, but it doesn't make for a happy one, really, but as it's one man's band you have to do it his way.'

Rabey: 'So did that kind of mythic quality help the band?'

Allcock: 'I think it helped to attract quite a few nutters, who were always gutted when they found out that Ian wasn't the hippy he appeared to be. He's a very astute businessman and rules with a firm hand. He doesn't like to give too much of himself away.'

Rabey: 'Do you think the band has gone beyond what it should have?'

Allcock: 'I think maybe Jethro Tull have over-saturated their own market. Even *A New Day* magazine [the fanzine] think so! They seem to be playing smaller and smaller venues. Like Spinal Tap's manager says, the audience is becoming more selective.'

Rabey: 'So can musicians carry on almost indefinitely?'

Allcock: 'Musicians never retire – they can't think of anything else to do. But we did one gig in Phoenix, Arizona, which Ian added himself instead of a night off. It was very hot during the day, but as soon as the sun went down, so did the temperature and it was very dry. Ian's voice packed up after about 15 minutes and I think it was one of the shortest Tull shows ever. *Aqualung* lasted about 30 seconds before Ian threw the towel in. We got caught in the traffic jam coming out and Ian was muttering darkly to himself "Stupid. Never again. That will teach me" etc. We got back to the hotel and Peggy, Martin and myself found a nice bar with a jazz guitarist playing who was very good, so we had some drinks and an early night.'

Rabey: 'So where do you see yourself in terms of the band's history?'

Allcock: 'Guest multi-instrumentalist – stayed for four years. Youngest member before Jonathan Noyce; with insomnia and Manchester attitude. 20th person to join. I figured I'd be in for a couple of tours, then they'd get a real keyboard player. I would have preferred being in bands more like Led Zeppelin, Lindisfarne, Peter Gabriel, Rolling Stones and Planxty. I really liked my first US tour, both trips to Brazil, and every German tour, although later US tours were weaker. The last one especially, when it was obvious that the voice was a problem.'

Rabey: 'Anecdotes?'

Allcock: 'It would take forever and some of them you couldn't print. I'll try and think of some for you.'

Rabey: 'Disappointments?'

Allcock: 'The realisation that I would not be contributing anything to the music myself apart from playing Ian's notes. Not getting to go to Japan or Australia.'

Rabey: 'High points?'

Allcock: 'Working so much with Dave Pegg, having a laugh with Doane and the crew, playing the intro to "Locomotive Breath" at Hockenheimring in Germany to 130,000 people all by myself. Standing on the centre spot at Wembley Stadium two days earlier, the day before we supported Fleetwood Mac. I've seen my heroes standing there from being very young.'

25

Tull In The 1990s

Live At Hammersmith '84 (1990)
Locomotive Breath (Instrumental) / Hunting Girl / Under Wraps #1 / Later
That Same Evening / Pussy Willow / Living In The Past / Locomotive Breath /
Too Old To Rock'n'Roll ...

Funny that Tull's first offering for the new decade was recorded six years earlier
in the depths of the 1980s on the *Under Wraps* tour. However, this was on the
Raw Fruit label, which specialised in putting out live albums well after the event,
from acts as diverse as Welsh rockers Man, Gillan and Ten Years After. Not a
momentous album, but of note to fans as this was one of the first times that
Doane Perry appeared with the band.

    Soon after this recording is when Anderson began to experience the well-
documented throat problems and took time off, delving into the world of fish
farming. Interesting that it took six years to get this album out and that it is not
on the Chrysalis label. It comes from a BBC broadcast.

Catfish Rising (1991)
This Is Not Love / Occasional Demons / Roll Yer Own / Rocks On The Road
/ Sparrow On The Schoolyard Wall / Thinking 'Round Corners / Still Loving
You Tonight / Doctor To My Disease / Like A Tall Thin Girl / White Innocence
/ Sleeping With The Dog / Gold-Tipped Boots, Black Jacket And Tie / When
Jesus Came To Play

Anderson's favourite quote about this 1991 album revolved around the music
being played on instruments that originated from trees. It was an attempt, in
fact, to return to the blues roots of *This Was* over 20 years after Anderson had

moved on and 'progressed'. The result was that fans didn't quite know what to make of the album – they either loved it or hated it.

A Little Light Music (1992)

Someday The Sun Won't Shine For You / Living In The Past / Life Is A Long Song / Under Wraps / Rocks On The Road / Nursie / Too Old To Rock'n'Roll: Too Young To Die / One White Duck / A New Day Yesterday / John Barleycorn / Look Into The Sun / A Christmas Song / From A Dead Beat To An Old Greaser / This Is Not Love / Bourée / Pussy Willow / Locomotive Breath.

1992 saw Tull tour almost unceasingly promoting *Catfish Rising*, and giving in to the whims of the fans by re-arranging a number of their lesser performed catalogue items and recording them while on tour in Europe and Middle Eastern countries. Andy Giddings, who had just joined for the recording of *Catfish Rising*, did not take part in that particular venture, but Dave Mattacks (another Fairport member) sat behind the drum kit for Doane Perry who took some time off. Inevitably, the nicknames Jethro Convention and Fairport Tull began to crop up – with good reason.

This was Tull's second official live album and was an almost 'unplugged' type affair, although it didn't quite make it to MTV. Once the album was released and the tour moved to North America, Giddings joined and more titles were added to the set and the tour received the augmented title *A Little Light And Dark Music*.

26

The 25th Anniversary

The 25th Anniversary Box Set – 4CD (1993)
Disc 1: Classic Songs Remixed
My Sunday Feeling / A Song For Jeffrey / Living In The Past / Teacher / Sweet Dream / Cross-eyed Mary / Witch's Promise / Life Is A Long Song / Bungle In The Jungle / Minstrel In The Gallery / Cold Wind To Valhalla / Too Old Too Rock'n'Roll: Too Young To Die / Songs From The Wood / Heavy Horses / Black Sunday / Broadsword

Disc 2: Carnegie Hall N.Y.C. Recorded Live 1970
Nothing Is Easy / My God / With You There To Help Me / A Song For Jeffrey / To Cry You A Song / Sossity; You're A Woman / Reasons For Waiting / We Used To Know / Guitar Solo / For A Thousand Mothers

Disc 3: The Beacons Bottom Tapes – Recorded at Beacons Bottom November 1992
*except where indicated
This was a series of classic Tull songs re-arranged and re-recorded by various members of the band at Beacons Bottom, Ian Anderson's studio, Martin Barre's studio and Dave Pegg's studio.
So Much Trouble* (Anderson's studio) / My Sunday Feeling / Someday The Sun Won't Shine For You* (Anderson's studio) / Living In The Past* (Anderson's studio) / Bourée* (Anderson's studio) / With You There To Help Me / Thick As A Brick / Cheerio* (Pegg's studio) / A New Day Yesterday / Protect And Survive* (Barre's studio) / Jack-A-Lynn / The Whistler / My God / Aqualung

Disc 4: Pot Pourri – Live Across The World & Through The Years
To Be Sad Is A Mad Way To Be / Back To The Family / A Passion Play (Extract) / Wind-up - Locomotive Breath - Land Of Hope And Glory – Medley / Seal Driver

/ Nobody's Car / Pussy Willow / Budapest / Nothing Is Easy / Kissing Willie / Still Loving You Tonight / Beggar's Farm / Passion Jig / A Song For Jeffrey / Living In The Past

The Best Of Jethro Tull: The Anniversary Collection

A double CD of 36 digitally remastered original mixes, this was the fifth official 'Best Of' compilation put out by Chrysalis, but can now be considered the definitive collection.

Disc 1

A Song For Jeffrey / Beggar's Farm / A Christmas Song / A New Day Yesterday / Bourée / Nothing Is Easy / Living In The Past / To Cry You A Song / Teacher / Sweet Dream / Cross-eyed Mary / Mother Goose / Aqualung / Locomotive Breath / Life Is A Long Song / Thick As A Brick (extract) / A Passion Play (extract) / Skating Away ... / Bungle In The Jungle

Disc 2

Minstrel In The Gallery / Too Old To Rock'n'Roll ... / Songs From The Wood / Jack-In-The-Green / The Whistler / Heavy Horses / Dun Ringill / Fylingdale Flyer / Jack-A-Lynn / Pussy Willow / Broadsword / Under Wraps 2 / Steel Monkey / Farm On The Freeway / Jump Start / Kissing Willie / This Is Not Love.

1993 saw Tull celebrate 25 years in style. A world tour without end – well, it seemed to go on forever – saw Doane's return and Dave Pegg's son Matt fill in on bass when dad was away with Fairport. The first of a series of CD collections released for the event was a box set incorporating the now customary lavish booklet and four CDs containing remixed classic oldies, a bouillabaisse of live recordings through the years, new studio arrangements of old favourites, recorded by the 1993 lineup, and the near complete 1970 Carnegie Hall show which had first appeared on the *Living In The Past* compilation.

On The Box Set(s) ...

Anderson: 'To commemorate the 25th anniversary, the record company persuaded me to put together two box sets: a four disc compilation of works ranging from the Carnegie Hall concert of the early '70s to some unreleased TV material. The other is a more commercial two CD package, geared to the first time buyer with a cross section of everything we've recorded to date, remastered for the medium. We have been able to find all of the original stereo master recordings for all of our albums.'

It may have come as a shock to some, particularly those who had been under the impression that Jethro Tull had called it quits years before, that they were about to celebrate their silver anniversary in 1993. Without hits to spotlight their movements, Tull had remained conspicuously absent from the limelight for years. To the average listener / concert goer, it tended to appear that Tull was making yet another comeback, a perennially unfounded accusation against the band.

'At this point in time, I find it very important to continue to perform, I don't want there to be long periods between tours, so that it takes me three weeks to get back into condition. It used to take three days,' bemoaned Anderson.

A Little Light Music – coincidentally, the group's 25th album – should not be seen as a prelude to any silver jubilee celebrations. According to Anderson, that tour was to promote 'Just the new Tull LP, not to commemorate the 25th anniversary.' That tour was, by choice, oriented entirely toward smaller halls and brought the band to cities where they have never performed before. 'We've always played theatre shows in Europe anyway – it's actually a lot of fun on that level,' commented Anderson.

Once a recording group reaches a milestone such as a 25th anniversary, it would probably be easy to compile a fairly lengthy list of past regrets. Anderson, like Frank Sinatra singing 'My Way', has had a few: The band name, for one. 'I would have changed the name if I had the chance, it's always been an embarrassment to me. I also wish critics, even the ones who don't like our little band, would at least credit me for my abilities as a musician, because if somebody asks me about a group, I can say I don't like it, but I can appreciate what they do, particularly if they do it well. I would expect that kind of treatment from a journalist as simply ethical and professional. In fact, when I first left school I headed to the local newspaper to apply to be a journalist. I didn't get the job, of course.'

Shortly after releasing their first album, Tull fell into a pattern of recording and touring every eighteen months which has lasted throughout most of their 44 year history. 'During the twelve months surrounding the 25th anniversary we had been around the world three times and played over 200 shows,' explained Anderson speaking to me at the time. 'That year was a very interesting period of time during which, musically speaking – partly because of the amount of concerts we did and partly because of the amount of time available in hotel rooms and dressing rooms – I came up with a lot of new music, so it was a profitable period of time. It was also an opportunity to visit a lot of countries I've never been to before. The show, which we called *A Little Light Music* after the album of the same name, was a very gentle, acoustic oriented programme, while the current show is a heavier, rock concert with a lot of emphasis on our first few albums featuring songs like "Dharma For One", "For A Thousand Mothers" and "My Sunday Feeling". Many of these songs hadn't been performed for over 20 years.

I rather prefer the mixture of things the way we do them now which is, indeed, more reminiscent of how we did things in '69 –'70 in the sense that, back then, we did play more of an intense performance, although it was a lot shorter since we were usually a support band rather than being expected to play two hours. In fact, even then when you were the headliner you usually only played one hour twenty minutes, so life was kind of easier back then, combined with the fact that at age 23, 24, it was easier still.'

Tull also released *Nightcap*, the third of the trilogy of CD packages commemorating the 25th Anniversary, which featured seventeen unreleased songs and an entire album recorded in the early 1970s between their two Number 1 albums *Thick As A Brick* and *A Passion Play*, which had long been believed lost or destroyed. But the album was not featured in that tour.

At a time when economics hamper the sale of concert tickets for even the most popular bands of the moment, Tull have been able to turn their years of experience in their favour when organising tours, selling out, or at least coming very close to selling out, at the venues they are booked into. There is, of course, some they don't: 'We experienced an embarrassment in Grand Forks, North Dakota where we did not sell out on that tour. But that happens. I remember back in '72 when we were on top of the *Billboard* Chart with *Thick As A Brick* we played in Billings, Montana to about 1,500.'

The fact the band have not had a Number 1 album in 40 years doesn't appear to faze Anderson in the slightest; there is a quiet, calm tone to his voice as he explains the difference in being in a band like Jethro Tull to being a pop star like Phil Collins: 'For bands like us, whose music is more complex and more varied in terms of style and influence, it's quite remarkable that we are relatively popular in almost every country; the only place we are light is South East Asia.

'Someone like Phil Collins, in the day, really was, doubtless, having a real hard time in terms of identity, because he knew he was a lightweight; he knew he sold masses of records and lots of concert tickets, but people perceived him as being middle of the road with nothing really to say. The masses liked him; he was safe; he's a nice guy, a hell of a nice guy. I've met him several times and he's very charming, totally for real. But he knew, just like Paul McCartney, that he was generally perceived by his peer group to be a lightweight and it hurts, because those guys desperately wanted to write some great songs, some positive musical statements, but they're just not fashioned in that mould. Just like I am not able to get up and do some pop songs; I can't sing that stuff anyway.'

During that period, Nirvana, Pearl Jam and The Spin Doctors were being regarded internationally as if they were the next Beatles, or at least the next incarnation of the cutting edge of rock'n'roll. But oh, how quickly times can change and oh, how quickly critics and fans will change their allegiance to something else. Everybody wants to be on the back of something new, just like Jethro Tull enjoyed its time with that sort of popularity.

The enthusiasm a musician has to experience in order to tour constantly over a 40 year period may seem elusive to most, but to Ian Anderson it almost seems a sort of escape: 'I remember I had to perform four nights in a row in a theatre in Sydney, and four nights for me in the same theatre is purgatory. I just hate to go to work in the same place every day, it's like clocking into work. Whereas, when you do one show and drag yourself to another airport the next morning, jump on a plane and go somewhere else ... it has a kind of invigorating feeling of *not* going to work, but going to another place where you happen to be doing your job – but it's all different. I don't even like doing two nights, [laughs] it just doesn't feel right at all.'

Nightcap (1993)

Disc 1: My Round – *Chateau d'Isaster* Tapes
First Post / Animelee / Tiger Toon / Look At The Animals / Law Of The Bungle Parts 1 and 2 / Left Right / Solitaire / Critique Oblique / Post Last / Scenario / Audition / No Rehearsal

Disc 2: Your Round – Unreleased And Rare Tracks
Paradise Steakhouse / Sea Lion 2 / Piece Of Cake / Quartet / Silver River Turning / Crew Nights / The Curse / Rosa On The Factory Floor / A Small Cigar / Man Of Principle / Commons Brawl / No Step / Drive On The Young Side Of Life / I Don't Want To Be Me / Broadford Bazaar / Lights Out / Truck Stop Runner / Hard Liner

Originally, a second two disc box set was to be released after the first two sets of discs for the 25th Anniversary, but Anderson decided it was all getting a little out of hand and that this stuff was going to be costing fans a small fortune – which was true. So rather than squeeze out a four disc set, Anderson got the best of the material that was meant for that set and put it on a double disc set and called it *Nightcap, The Unreleased Masters 1973-1991*. Ironically, this was released with less fanfare than the two selections before it, but contained some of the best Tull material on record, including the entire, supposedly missing, recordings from the *Chateau d'Isaster* sessions. Those recordings took up the first CD and the second was a series of outtakes from 1973-1991. The price of the package was kept low due to the insistence of Anderson, and his mechanical royalties were donated to charity. Anderson has made it quite clear he didn't intend to ever go as far with these Anniversary projects as he had and that there is now nothing left to mine in terms of outtakes for future box sets.

Jethro Tull released a trilogy of recordings marking the band's silver anniversary. The first four CD box has been covered extensively, the second (a two CD set of original master recordings) and the third, the double helping that is *Nightcap*, was released in late fall.

Speaking at the time, Anderson said: 'That package includes the missing album that was recorded between *Thick As A Brick* and *A Passion Play*, plus seventeen unreleased masters recorded between 1973 and 1991. It was originally requested, by a portion of the fan base, that it be a four CD box like the first one, but when it came down to the wire, it seemed more sensible to compress what was really three CDs worth of material onto two CDs. With the carrying time of a CD being 78 minutes, we found we could squash all this stuff onto two CDs and make a much cheaper package.

'I was able to negotiate a deal with Chrysalis and EMI. They, in turn, went out to the retail outlets and have concluded a price which will be fixed in the UK, which will kind of control the European price and forces the hands of the US manufacturers as well, because the four CD box was extravagantly priced. The two CD set is really much too expensive for what it is and, in the end, I was determined that two things were necessary for me to feel right about putting this on the market: that it sells for only 10% or 15% more than the cost of a single CD and I am going to give all the mechanical copyright royalties to charities of my choice because I don't want to be accused of unreasonably dragging out these remnants from the bottom drawer and trying to make capital of it. So it's something I feel must have a charitable element and also a retail price structure which gives people some reasonable value for money.

Left: The band often played the Marquee Club in the early days. This shot is from 1968. Courtesy Glenn Cornick

Below: The band made up in readiness for the *This Was* album shoot. Courtesy Glenn Cornick

JETHRO TULL

THE ELLIS-WRIGHT AGENCY LTD
CARRINGTON HOUSE
130 REGENT STREET
LONDON W.1.
01 734 9233

Top: Early shot from the Ellis-Wright Agency, before they became Chrysalis Records. Courtesy Glenn Cornick

Above: 1968 shot from the *Rock'n'Roll Circus* with Tony Iommi on guitar.
© Unknown

Right: A publicity shot of a young looking Martin Barre.
Courtesy Glenn Cornick

Top left: Promo shot from 1969-1970. Courtesy Glenn Cornick

Top right: Gone fishing. Hampstead Heath. Courtesy Glenn Cornick

Above: The band with Terry Ellis of Chrysalis (far right). Courtesy Glenn Cornick

Top: Stand Up? Cheer up, more like! L–R Martin Barre, Ian Anderson, Glenn Cornick. Clive Bunker in front. Courtesy Glenn Cornick

Above: Terry Ellis took the band to see Elvis in Vegas in 1969, but they had to hire tuxedos to get into the show, hence this photo. Courtesy Glenn Cornick

Top left and above: Two promo shots from the *Thick As A Brick* era. Courtesy Ian Anderson

Top right: The legend that is Jeffrey Hammond-Hammond, long time friend of Ian Anderson from the Blackpool days. © Unknown

Top left: Ian Anderson with Pan's People before the Rainbow concert in 1974. L–R Sue, Dee Dee, Babs. Kneeling, Ruth and Cherry. © Chris Walter

Top right: 'You're my guitar hero' John Evan and Martin Barre. © Heinrich Klaffs

Above: Barrie Barlow, the year before he left the band in 1980. © Rich Galbraith

Left: Tull's musical arranger David Palmer on the 1979 tour. © Rich Galbraith

Top left and top right: John Evan and Ian Anderson on the 1979 US tour. © Rich Galbraith

Above: The late John Glascock (with Martin Barre) a few months before his death.
© Rich Galbraith

Top left: Still from the 1979 BBC TV *Lively Arts* documentary. © Unknown

Above: Ian Anderson pictured in 1982 on *The Broadsword And The Beast* tour. © Brian Rabey

Middle left: Tull's longest serving drummer, Doane Perry. © Patrick Lydon

Left: Ian Anderson, with David Goodier on bass, still working as hard as ever in the new millenium. © Melyviz

'This is, after all, material which was not chosen at the time because it was not representative of being the best of what we could do. That doesn't mean that it was second rate or poor quality, it's just not representative of the albums around which those songs were designed to be a part. As such, there has got to be a question mark over their validity. It was stuff that was unfinished in the recording sense and I added some flutes and whistles and vocals and finally got around to finishing it. There is a bunch of stuff like that, but the box really is the end of it; there is no more, there's nothing else that's any good at all out of all those years of recording.'

When the album finally arrived, it was declared an album of material fans had been waiting for since the *Chateau* tapes went missing after *Thick As A Brick*. Excellent, no weak tracks and almost a jigsaw puzzle of songs that showed the development of what became *A Passion Play* but stripped down and in single songs, allowing the listener to hear more concretely how the recording process took place.

'There is a terrible temptation to see them as rejects, as being second rate material that wasn't worthy of release,' muses Anderson. 'It's easy for me to say that's not the case, but they are songs that I am quite happy to listen to now. They're kind of like bottles of wine or maturing whisky that didn't seem as though it was going to be right at that moment, but let's leave it a few years and check it out again and maybe it will be one of those strange brews that actually matures to be quite a nice tipple, if you happen to be in the right mood. For that reason, this is all being released under the name of *Nightcap*.

'So it's a sort of tippler's dream in the sense that it might be like a glass of slightly flawed, but interesting single malt whiskey or brandy, or perhaps not quite perfect port. For the Jethro Tull fans, I hope, good value for the money, a good kind of Jethro Tull album, but not something that I would expect would be, across the board, to everybody's taste. They are rather idiosyncratic songs.'

On the last Sunday of August 1993, the end of an uncharacteristically hot summer and the mid-point of another North American tour for the band, Ian Anderson spoke about the current Jethro Tull tour (which kept the band on the road until April 1994).

Anderson concedes that putting tours together, even after many years, tends to fall short of expectations in one way or another: 'Somebody should invent a board game where you can actually work things out mathematically, so you can map out availability from places right across the board ... to actually match them up into something that is geographically routable when it comes to organising a tour so that you end up playing three shows on for every one night off.

'If you're dealing with the indoor season in one part of the world, you are in the outdoor season somewhere else. After we finish up in North America, we head to Japan, the UK, South America and then South Africa.'

This tour probably has a name, like most of the tours Tull has been involved with over the last 40 years, but Anderson is not talking about music ... at least he doesn't bring it up until the explanation of this day's events at a local aquacultural facility in Massachusetts have been dealt with. His day off has been spent at a high-tech fish farm. Anderson first made headlines in the late 1970s with a burgeoning fish farm in Scotland. The day we spoke back then, he was visiting a fish farm on a consulting basis. 'This American company is interested in setting up in Europe and are looking for investments – practical, political and social – and advice in terms of countries,' he explained. 'So I looked at their facility and gave them some potential contacts to further their European aims.'

With the amount of work involved in preparing three sets of recordings, Tull did not release a new studio album. However, one band member had found the time to do a solo album. Martin Barre had his first solo album, *A Trick Of Memory*, released in 1994 [though he did put out a limited edition release of live cover tracks called *A Summer Band* in 1992 for *A New Day* magazine].

Although the Lennon/McCartney analogy wouldn't be the most accurate way of describing the recording/performing relationship between Anderson and Barre, it has endured and continues in whatever form it takes, pragmatic or otherwise. A democratic Anderson believes:

> I'm no more Jethro Tull than Martin Barre. Martin and I are close without being close. We have a working relationship which is one that has a healthy respect for the need that both of us feel for our individual privacies. One of the reasons the working relationship has never been allowed to sour as a result of over familiarity or, conversely, becoming too distant ... we sort of maintain a regular degree of discourse and communication without it becoming too intense or personal. We are different people and have very different personalities; it's a sort of enduring relationship because of an ability that both of us have, I guess, to appreciate the positive aspects of that relationship and not let any of the negative ones get to undue proportions. It's a sort of a pragmatic relationship.
>
> I have said this before and would stand by it again: If Martin was no longer part of Jethro Tull, Jethro Tull would definitely cease to exist. I would categorically, emphatically, not go out on the road with a bunch of guys called Jethro Tull that did not include Martin Barre, and I'm sure he would feel the same way.

Over 25 musicians have passed through the ranks of Tull, some having known Anderson as far back as the early 1960s. As they've passed out of the ranks of the band, they have, from a music industry angle, passed from the public eye. But, according to Anderson, several were asked back on an almost regular basis:

Jeffrey Hammond has been re-invited back into the band a couple of times, and every year or so I ask John Evans if he wants to come and play piano on something. The problem is, the guys who had a special role in Jethro Tull, in terms of something kind of characterful and individual, just don't want to do it anymore. They've left that behind and they now do other things with their lives. But the people that maybe you wouldn't choose to say, 'Well, hey, what are you doing next Thursday? Can you come and play on this?' they're the guys who may still be the musicians.

John Evans is in business as a builder and an engineer, which is far removed from music. Jeffrey Hammond is involved in art still, but as a painter. Barrie Barlow is involved in producing and management, and there are guys who, like our first guitar player Mick Abrahams, still do the same things. He's O.K., but he's not a guy that, although I have played with him a few times – I'm sure he'll do something with us when we play in the UK – he's not a guy I'd call in to be part of a Tull album. He's rather more set in a musical style and a musical period that would not make him that easy a guy to find anything useful from in terms of a more contemporary performance.

The people that I would choose to work with again are people who have closed off that period of their life. They will not do it anymore with me, us, you or anybody. They've left that behind and I respect them for that, because music is a bit of a drug – it's all or nothing.

The members of Tull are, essentially, one band people with the exception of bass player Dave Pegg, who did double duty with Tull and Fairport Convention. However, Anderson has guested on several groups' recordings, and although some remain obscure, the impetus to do such sessions has never been anything beyond a respect for the music: 'The last thing I would ever do is ask for money, because if you play on somebody else's record, then either they're so rich and famous that it's an honour to be asked to play, or if they're not rich and famous, they certainly can't afford me, so you do it for other reasons, usually out of respect.'

Respect is something Jethro Tull has earned over the past 40 years. After that amount of time and a stretch of 35 years without what would be categorised 'a hit', to be able to still generate the interest of new and old fan bases is something which can only be equated with a high level of quality. That quality translates to a reverence on the part of the fans that Ian Anderson finds slightly embarrassing to deal with:

'At the end of it, if the music appeals to people, makes them happy or they get on their feet and bounce around and meet the girl of their dreams and have three babies as a result of it, then it's par for the course, because other people have done that to *Living In The Past* and other records – they make babies to our music. I'm not going to complain about that, but I'd like to think they've remained happily married after a few years. I have to take the rap for the downside of human relationships as well. There is probably a person who, on a nightly basis, has to pat little boys on the head who are called Jethro or Ian or what have you, and I understand the sentiments that give rise to that, but it's not a very comfortable thing for me. People who look at me or Jethro Tull or our music as being pivotal in their lives ... I would much rather people just enjoy it the way I would enjoy the next Craig Thomas novel or a Muddy Waters album.'

27

Roots To Branches, A Solo Album And A Live One

Divinities: Twelve Dances With God (1995)

In A Stone Circle / In Sight Of The Minaret / In A Black Box / In the Grip Of Stronger Stuff / In Maternal Grace / In the Moneylender's Temple / In Defence Of Faiths / At Their Father's Knee / En Afrique / In The Olive Garden / In the Pay Of Spain / In the Times Of India [Bombay Valentine]

Released in April 1995, Ian Anderson's second solo album featured twelve instrumentals in an orchestral style based around religious themes and drawing on a variety of world music influences. It was a collaboration with Andy Giddings and was the result of EMI Record's classical division approaching Anderson to record something along classical lines. For this recording, Anderson experimented with a number of bamboo and other flutes:

> They called me to ask me to do an album for EMI classics. Having listened to the request, I decided that I would make a couple of demos and if EMI liked them, then we'd talk about doing an album. They ended up liking them, and they persuaded me to do the album. I wasn't very excited about doing it until I started to write the music. I discovered I was enjoying the challenge of writing a large body of instrumental work, which I'd never done before. I discovered the bamboo flute when I was 20 years old and playing at London's Marquee Club. I got some bamboo flute and a saxophone mouthpiece and the bell end of a plastic children's saxophone and stuck them all together to make an instrument called the claghorn, which I played in the early Jethro Tull.

Roots To Branches (1995)

Roots To Branches / Rare And Precious Chain / Out Of The Noise / This Free Will / Valley / Dangerous Veils / Beside Myself / Wounded, Old And

Treacherous / At Last, Forever / Stuck In The August Rain / Another Harry's Bar.

Roots To Branches is easily one of Tull's best albums in their extensive catalogue. All of the familiar *modus operandi* we have come to expect of a Tull on top form have been incorporated in this album – eclectic musical progressions and shifting time signatures have all been stamped through the work like the name Blackpool in a stick of seaside rock. To draw on an analogy, when I first heard *Benefit*, I could not find one single song on the entire album I didn't find completely satisfying – I still feel the same. Well, *Roots To Branches* does exactly the same thing for me – with only one exception, and that shall remain untold! Anderson acknowledges the influences of the distinctive Asian-Indian feel to tracks like 'Rare And Precious Chain' and 'Beside Myself', probably very much a leftover influence from his previous solo album, but he also says, 'If you go back to albums like *Stand Up*, the European and Middle Eastern music had already crept in way back around the time I was 22.'

The one sad note in the production of this gem was the absence of Dave Pegg, who contributed to only two tracks as he left the band to concentrate on Fairport Convention. Most of the bass parts were played by American session player Steve Bailey. Jonathan Noyce became Pegg's replacement. Peggy hasn't returned to the fold but, like the Ghost of Christmas Past, showed up to play bass and mandolin on some tracks for 2003's *Christmas Album*.

Roots To Branches was recorded in Ian Anderson's recording studio and because of the way the process unravelled, the album turned out to be the 'livest' production of new material from the band since the early 1980s. Doane Perry's enthusiasm for the band he had been keeping the beat for since 1984 has not diminished in the slightest. When asked if this album was recorded live in the studio the answer is obviously yes. 'It's live although there were bits and pieces that got worked on later. There was something special about the recording of that album and I think we all knew that when we were doing it, though I must say that I've always enjoyed making Tull albums for all kinds of different reasons,' Perry says, adding: 'I also think making a record can be a difficult process. I guess I'm always suspicious when people say "Oh, making a record is easy or playing is easy". Music, to me, is a lot of difficult work, not that it's agonising, but it means a lot to me and I take it very personally; how I perform – not to mention how the whole band performs together.'

The end product of the recording sessions that yielded the new album is a collection of songs that rival the quality of anything the band has done in almost fifteen years. 'There were some really wonderful moments,' Perry continued. 'I remember how "Rare And Precious Chain" came together, which was extraordinary in a way, how it sort of started out life as this one piece of music that was more or less straight ahead rock and all of a sudden it just took off in another direction. It had a life of its own and all these parts started presenting themselves like these vaguely East Indian string lines that Andy started playing and then we decided not to play any cymbals on that track. So I came up with this idea which made me think part African drums and Moroccan and sort of Eastern Indian influences, and Martin was playing this wah wah pedal, psychedelic 1960s guitar riff in contrast to all of that, and Ian had all these great lines on top. It was amazing how it became something completely different.'

On *Roots To Branches* ...

Barre: 'I think the idea behind the album was that it was recorded as live as possible, because we went through a whole series of albums where we recorded in Ian's first studio where there was no live room. So *Under Wraps, Walk Into Light, Crest Of A Knave* and *Rock Island* were all recorded with drum machines and either the drum machines stayed or were replaced by drums – Doane or Gerry on drums on *Crest* ... and *Rock* ... so they were all built up from click parts, added guitar, bass etc. It was sort of music by jigsaw method. There's nothing wrong with that, but having moved and obtained a proper live room, Ian was keen to rehearse and record music as we did in the early days. I think the songs are very strong and the playing's very good. It was also different in that we were playing with a new bass player as well.'

On 'Rare and Precious Chain' ...

Anderson: 'I suppose in most cases, perhaps not all, but in most cases, my favourite Jethro Tull songs, whether they're a few months old or a good many years old, will be probably determined not so much by the recorded identity, but rather more by the way I feel about them as live performance songs. Because that is such an important part of making music, there are quite a few songs that I very much like, that are things I've recorded, but never played live. But the majority of my favourite songs would be things that I enjoy playing live and things that we do OK playing live. In regard to the *Roots To Branches* album then, if I was going to single out some songs, I would be surprising myself by picking up on a track called "Rare And Precious Chain." That was one that I really did not think was going to work terribly well live on stage. Indeed, after the first few rehearsals of it I suggested to the other guys that we drop it and they persuaded me that they thought it was one worth working on a bit more to see if it would gel.

'And indeed it turned out, at the end of the tour, to be one of the more enjoyable pieces to play. In fact, we ended up playing it live on TV three or four times. It was one of those songs that really surprised me as being the kind of song that, against some odds, turned out to be not my favourite, but certainly one of the three or four that would spring to mind as being for me, I suppose, the most important songs on the record. It was, incidentally, one on which I played acoustic guitar all the way through. In fact, the song began just with me singing and playing acoustic guitar and the other guys came in and worked over the song. It was just about the only song on the album that was done that way, because everything else was rehearsed by the band and recorded very much as a live arrangement.

'"Rare And Precious Chain" stands almost alone, maybe out of two songs, that were recorded very much at the end of the recording process, and were done in a rather more pedantic way of putting down the identity of the song and the other people coming and hearing it for the first time and having to figure out what to play to this set piece of arrangement. So it was quite an unusual one on the album to be done that way. I was trying to stay within the general terms of rather more eastern scales, but at the same time I am not an academic when it comes to observing the real detail of Indian or Arabic or Spanish or Central European or whatever. I feel about it the same way I feel about folk music: I don't really like folk music; I don't really like Arabic music; I don't really like classical music; I don't really like jazz. But there are little elements of the construction of all those kinds of music that intrigue me and are very seductive and very sexy. From that point of view, I try to introduce those elements into the way that I write music as a very eclectic thing that, to me, is both fun, but is not purist.

'I hope that it is not just pastiche. I hope that it is a vigorous hybrid and not merely some disastrous genetic mix up, but the elements work for me and I try to stay reasonably close to what I feel is that kind of stylistic *modus operandi* for a certain song. I think it's important that you don't just drift within the same song and then, suddenly, one minute you've got the Middle East and then you find yourself playing a line stolen from Muddy Waters in 1960 – that would not be a pleasant mix.

'I feel that, to me, it tends to relate as it relates to other things; it tends to retain some of the influences as on the album *Stand Up*, which is going back to the first collection of music that I wrote, which was a sort of original and eclectic mix. On *Stand Up*, there were mandolins and balalaikas and references to more eastern and African and European sort of ethnic noises, instrumental sounds and instrumental structures. To me it's [*Roots To Branches*] a kind of grownups version of the *Stand Up* album, in a way, and that didn't occur to me. It was somebody else who made that comparison. When I thought about it I said "Yes, it is, it's the 40-something-year-old version of *Stand Up* which was done when I was 22."

'The profound influences that affected me when I was 16-21 … that's when most of what I work from got into my head. From hearing a lot of different things at that time, when you are very susceptible to the powerful emotional and, perhaps, even intellectual messages that music is there to give you. Those are the things I think you work with for the rest of your life. You may redefine them, but they are there and they don't fundamentally change a great deal. I think, really, they haven't from Jethro Tull's second album on. Most people, from their second album on, are going to find it much, much harder to be spontaneously creative as they were with their first couple of records and thereafter you tend to be working, to some extent, on the redefining, the refocusing of those few influences.

'And some people only have one thing that they do. Not to be mean about it, but some great rock and rollers like Bo Diddley or Chuck Berry are pretty one dimensional. Somebody like Muddy Waters … it's one and a half tricks. In the case of Beethoven it's more like four, five or six that he knew, but if you're fortunate enough to have more than one or two good ideas in your lifetime, especially that are halfway original, then you're a very fortunate musician indeed. Most people don't have any really good ideas and are forced to make a living by imitating and emulating their peers or their predecessors in terms of musical heroes. Some actually bring something new to the scene and those are very special.

'That's what painters do, that's what playwrights do. Kerouac had one idea and he flogged it to death – and he was a pretty crap writer to begin with – and as soon as he hit on *On The Road* he hit his stride and he stayed with that for a bunch of novels and that was his one idea and we remember him and we revere him for that very excellent idea – not entirely original – but he put it into that context … that made it special.'

Barre: 'It's off-the-wall and it worked probably for the opposite reasons that anything else on the album worked, because everything else was precision plus and very rehearsed and very much scrutinised. Whereas this one was done at the end of the album and there was more attention to feel and getting something off the wall than getting something that was spot on, played metronomically perfect.

'So it was quite nice and quick and off the top of everybody's head and it came together quite well and it was different; a departure from a lot of other styles and it had something about it that a lot of other music elsewhere doesn't.

'I think we were looking for phrases that didn't sit in the obvious place, hence most of the songs on the album started on beat two of the bar. I think Ian wanted it to all sound a bit different, strange, without it being bars of fives and sevens and nines so, although it's strictly in fours, it doesn't have the appearance of being so, because things do start in a strange place within the bar, which is nice. I like things like that in music. It's a neat way of creating something that's off beat without being difficult for the listener, so you can tap your foot through it and you don't have to worry where one is in the bar. But then if you do scrutinise it, it is clever and it's different if you want to do such a thing with the music. I used a Manson on that song which is the guitar I used on the recent US tour, but it was built for me later on in the album, so I only used it on a couple of tracks. It was made by Andy Manson's brother who makes acoustic guitars – one makes electric, the other makes acoustic.'

Jethro Tull In Concert (1995)
Minstrel In The Gallery-Cross Eyed Mary / This Is Not Love / Rocks On The Road / Heavy Horses / Tall Thin Girl / Still Loving You / Thick As A Brick / A New Day Yesterday / Blues Jam / Jump Start

This album wrapped up a busy 1995 for Tull releases, although it was actually taken from a Hammersmith Odeon concert from four years earlier. It was put out by Windsong International and was only the second album since Chrysalis' formation not to be put out on the label. Funnily enough, the other record not on Chrysalis was also recorded at the Hammy Odeon – *Live at Hammersmith '84* on Rare Fruit records.

28

Tull's Unique Place In Progressive Rock

By the time Jethro Tull had recorded *Benefit*, the band's style was already loosely being referred to as 'Elizabethan Rock'. It's no mistake or coincidence that this music came from England; the root of any musical style will tell, no matter how broad the branches of its tree. Though the term 'Progressive Rock' was applied indiscriminately, each group ploughing that furrow had its own little niche under the catch-all term.

Sgt Pepper was still fresh when the progressive rock bands took off to develop the most important and exciting genre of the early 1970s. It was a sign of the times that by the late 1970s, the nihilistic punk movement was doing its level best to send this relatively new music, now seemingly prehistoric, into extinction.

But progressive rock refuses to do the decent thing and die, thankfully. 'Over the past few years there has been a rise in popularity for progressive music,' according to John Wetton, who played the bass and sang with King Crimson, Asia, UK and Family and has seen it all. 'The message is that there is a quite healthy, forward going movement toward progressive music, and I mean that as a generic term,' Wetton continues. 'Progressive, to me, when we started, meant it had to be really adventurous, always pushing forward.'

'I think the term "Progressive" really said what it meant, which was music moving forward,' agrees Anderson. 'And I think when progressive music became less popular and faded into the background, so did a great deal of the originality. Consequently, music has become a marketing tool, to a large extent, instead of something that is art-based.'

'I have never had a problem with the [term], because I have always felt that's what we were and still are: a progressive band. Progressive rock – I actually can't remember the origin of the title – I don't think I had a point of disagreement with it because that, in a sense, was arguably, for a lot of us, our intent – to take what was established as a music form distinct from commercial pop music, but to take it into areas beyond its obvious North American roots and in some ways the important thing was it didn't matter where you went, as long as you went somewhere. What was really important was the opportunity to do things with that music.

'It was in an era when ELP, Genesis, Yes, Jethro Tull, etc. had the opportunity to integrate some very fundamental musical roots with a kind of low art form in terms of trying to develop things that were ... that had some intellectual argument behind them. Most of it was a lot of pretty ropey music that came out of that era, but not without its charm. It had to be done, people had to play around with it, and clearly today there is, as always, a contingent of folk out there who have quite a soft spot or liking for that sort of grandiose music, like *Tarkus* or *Topographic Oceans*.'

Progressive music seemed to come out of nowhere at a time when three chord rock ruled the day, and many of the musicians from that era have opinions about the genre's seemingly spontaneous genesis. 'I think there can't have been anybody around back then, any of the bands, who were not really aware that we were all, in our own little way, writing the book of rock music,' says Anderson. 'Of course, we were well aware of the fact that we were all so different. That's why it was so exciting. Many of those bands were true originators, and were coming out with something that had never been done before and, in lots of cases, has not been done again.

'There were also quite a few important American bands that many of us could not fail to be impressed by and, in some ways, moved and influenced if not by the music, at least by the stance musically, politically and socially by the Frank Zappas, the Captain Beefhearts and others who were very much a part of what was going on.'

Yes, but where did all of this originality come from? What were its resources, I wonder?

'I think, for those of us who were interested in the music, on the one hand it was the relatively recent awareness of the huge legacy of the 1950s and 1960s urban black American blues artists that began to finally shower around our heads, in the form of import records in the mid-1960s; and then that spearhead of American rock music, from The Doors to The Grateful Dead to Zappa to the anarchic charm of Captain Beefheart,' responds Anderson. 'I do feel that Britain did play a very vital role in providing a point of reference for all of that American creativity, whether it was blues, jazz, or rock. Britain always had a way of feeding back another angle on it, another way of relating to it, another point of reference.'

According to Steve Hackett, formerly guitarist with Genesis and now a successful solo artist, "'Progressive' was a term that came out of jazz in the 1950s, and it was a term that really applied to people like Roland Kirk. It meant free form, abandoning tones and scales as we know it – abstract music that was coming up through jazz. In a way it was a misnomer [in rock]. [Then] it was the jazz platform that was allowing all that stuff to come through. But progressive music now can embrace all of that, and all of the classical and orchestral influences. What would you call Gershwin? He was the first great progressive artist. [For both genres], what really comes through are the great melodic moments, although there might seem to be an enormous difference between, say, Jethro Tull and Weather Report. You've got something quintessentially British, and something American'.

'There's definitely an element of jazz in progressive,' John Wetton says. 'I see that progression, because I think that jazz influenced progressive music. After a while, listening to progressive is going to be like "Jazz-Lite", so you may as well go all the way. I can see how you could enter music at the progressive level and want to go all the way to jazz – or go all the way to rock – because I think progressive music sits somewhere in the middle. I think it took elements from both.'

Greg Lake, ex-King Crimson and ELP, concurs. 'I think a lot of the underlying principle of jazz is freedom,' he says, 'and that same principle was carried by the progressive rock genre. So I think that's where the identity of progressive rock and jazz share a common playing field. Where people find it easy to make the journey from one to the other, because both musics are the same, where a certain element of freedom is the underpinning of the music.'

'I think that's what some people will do, whether it's mellowing, maturing, boredom or just the need for change,' Ian Anderson says, with a more sceptical eye on the sojourn from prog to jazz. 'I'm sure it's all sorts of different things. It's very difficult to generalise, but quite clearly some people progress. I am told some people progress from cannabis to heroin. There will be some people who will progress from Bon Jovi to Ornette Coleman, given time (or vice versa), but the majority of people have predictable and set tastes. My opinion is that most people don't change their tastes that much.'

Whatever progressive means today, it is probably safe to assume that it will mean something completely different and absolutely the same tomorrow, just as it did ten and twenty years ago. Something as complex and diverse as a genre of music that goes beyond the standard three chord progression cannot be pinned down or explained away over a cup of coffee. There will always be the Tulls and their own internal evolutions, and there will always be the so called pretenders to their thrones. Progressive rock is here to stay.

29

The End Of Tull?

The world and his wife know at least some of the lyrics to 'Aqualung'. Since the song was first introduced to the world in the summer of 1971, the band has had to live down the success the song and the album brought them. It's not that success was a burden for Tull, it's just a bit perplexing that so many albums have followed and people still insist on requesting that one song.

That's not to say Tull's other LPs were relegated to the bargain bin five minutes after they were released. On the contrary, Jethro Tull's musical integrity has remained intact, even though radio has virtually ignored them since the mid-1970s. Part of the reason, may have been their attitude towards the 'star-maker machinery'. One of the original groups to have profited from the underground band phenomenon, Tull always skirted the glitz and glam of the spotlight, letting word of mouth advertise forthcoming albums and tours, which it did (and still does) very successfully. In September 1987, Chrysalis Records in New York said their office had been flooded with calls requesting information on a new LP and/or tour. Both were on their way. *Crest of a Knave* was released in mid-September in the States and in early October in Canada. To promote the release, Anderson, flew into New York for two days for interviews and a guest VJ spot on MTV.

Anderson was 40 at the time and played down the fact that the band was about to celebrate its 20th anniversary, saying he was there to promote 'Just the new Jethro Tull album'. With what sounded like a grin behind the words, he set aside the milestone with 'I've always thought that 25 years would be more impressive.'

Of the band members at this time, only Anderson and Barre date back to the days of *Aqualung*, and Anderson is the only original member left. Anderson's attitude toward nostalgia, in keeping with the fact he's been leader of the band for so many years, is that it (nostalgia) should be a very personal thing. Yes, it's nice, but could we please keep it in perspective?

'We, as a group, indulge in nostalgia all the time.' Anderson says, 'After a concert or recording session, we sit around and swap fishing stories from ten-twenty years ago, which is a very private and personal thing. We are just like a bunch of old cronies drinking beer in a cabin somewhere [laughs]. We are very, very boring people, socially.

'People will come to a concert and a certain song will remind them of their first date in the back of some car with a Jethro Tull song playing on the radio. It will mean something deeply personal and very moving to some people, but I can't share that from my end. I sometimes think that if you try to share it [nostalgia] in a global sense and make a big deal out of it, it sort of loses the meaning it usually has. I'm a bit reluctant to bring nostalgia conspicuously to the fore in terms of commemorating something on any large scale. However, I do think from the number of letters I get on the subject, there are a lot of people aware of anniversaries'

During their first two years together, the group enlisted a firm following in the UK, and then turned their sights towards the other side of the Atlantic. They invaded and conquered with bestselling albums *Benefit*, *Thick As A Brick*, *A Passion Play*, *War Child* and *Aqualung*. The UK lost interest and abandoned Tull shortly thereafter. Times and attitudes have changed since the early 1970s and, today, European audiences have been replenished with younger blood, smoothing things out a bit in terms of fanbase.

'Our strength in the European market has actually increased or stayed the same over the last few years,' Anderson explained. 'It's now popular in the UK to not knock Jethro Tull. If you were to go to a Tull concert in the North of England you would see what certainly seems to be a good 50% of the audience around ages 17 to 18. We have replaced, or are in the process of replacing our audience. Have been for years.'

During the 1970s, music journalists had a field day, frantically searching for new ways to describe the prancing, Toscanini-with-St Vitus-Dance-flamingo-on-speed who evinced a mad-dog Fagin stance. When it came to media interviews it was Anderson, the maniacal front man, who was most sought after. He became Jethro Tull.

Journalists have been asking Anderson the same tired question: 'When do you think you'll call it a day for Tull?' ever since they released the prophetically titled *Too Old To Rock'n'Roll...* back in the late 1970s. When the question first made its rounds, it caused some consternation, but nowadays Anderson hardly reacts: 'When the audience decides it's time for us to stop. I think they will have some subtle way of letting us know that maybe we should call it a day. As far as our careers are concerned, health permitting, there's a few years left to go and a few albums. But there will be a time to stop. I certainly wouldn't want to go on by coming out once in awhile and doing some nostalgia concert and screech my way through *Aqualung* – that would be sad.

'I've always had the feeling that I would continue to do it, to a much lesser degree than in the past, for several years yet. Certainly, every 18 months or so, I should think we'll come out with something,' he reckons. 'I don't do music any longer because I need the money. Doing music now is kind of, back to the slightly romantic idea of playing music for fun and for the slightly crazy enjoyment of being on the road. That's not something I could ever stop doing. The whole point of recording an album is to be able to get up and play those songs in front of real people in a real environment. I suppose you might think that there isn't any real end to it, but there must be some upper limit, some point where, because of physical limitations, it might become absurd to be on stage dancing around.

'I've seen Eric Clapton play and I've thought ... I wish that's all the energy I had to put into a show. So I'll probably end up playing very polite acoustic music as I head toward 70. But for the moment we have dates set up as far in advance as November 2013, so we'll be around for some time to come.'

[Author's Note: At the time of writing, the 2013 tour features two different sets: one is the *Thick As A Brick* Tour featuring both *TAAB* albums, the other is the 'Best Of Jethro Tull' (*sans* any original Tull members, though David Goodier and John O'Hara are playing) billed as Ian Anderson. The length of the tour would daunt a man half Anderson's age, so clearly he is showing no signs of slowing down, thankfully. However, there are equally no signs of a Tull reunion on the horizon.]

Part 2

The Thoughts Of
Ian Anderson

30

Ian Anderson's
Time Bomb Theory

When Anderson spoke of this Time Bomb thing, it was in answer to the question 'What was the effect of doing the *Thick As A Brick* album like on a young musician?' It squarely sat alone in the history of rock music as a one of a kind album. Although it wasn't really written as one song in one fell swoop, it was presented that way and did get edited for release on 45rpm and radio air play, so it was the first of its kind from various angles.

ANDERSON:

> Whether you're John McEnroe and you've just lost the last point, or you're on stage doing that sort of a thing, you are like a time bomb. If somebody touches you, or somebody gets on the stage who shouldn't be there, or something happens, you really would kill at that moment. I wouldn't make a good bank manager, for example, because I'd be exploding quietly twelve hours a day and probably would have died of a heart attack or some evil cancer years ago. At least I think being lucky enough to get on a stage and explode in a controlled environment is a fortunate occupation to have

That statement probably caught a few of you off guard, but for anybody who has ever been a performance artist, the analogy is extremely real. If there's one thing that I feel keeps Ian Anderson on the road as opposed to being a quiet, sit at home and record polite albums once a year, type of artist it's that Time Bomb Theory.

ANDERSON:

> I think there are two sides to it. To a lot of people who have pent-up emotions or surplus physical energy – the going on stage is an outlet, it's a safety valve. I guess the same could be said for professional and competitive sports as well.

A lot of people who are drawn to that sort of life are people who do have this tremendous excess of energy. I think people who, on a quieter level, have an excess of creative energy might become obsessive landscape painters or novelists or whatever. Essentially it is quite a healthy thing to do if you are lucky enough to have that outlet.

It's the people who don't have the kind of outlet who perhaps get a little bit screwed up in their lives if these energies have nowhere to be constructively channelled. There's nothing really to do then but get into crack cocaine or whatever it might be. Those of us who have something to do with our lives are quite lucky, but there's another side to it which I think, in a sense it almost fuels that thing within you. It makes it bigger than it might have otherwise been. So I'm not sure which one comes first. I suspect the need to express, the need to have something to do comes first and once you start doing it you find you're putting some pretty high octane fuel in the fuel tank and it needs somewhere to burn. It's feeding back on itself all the time with this need to do even more. I think that's why it's very difficult if you've been on tour to get back to a (by most people's standards) more normal, domestic way of life. It's quite difficult.

According to Anderson, it takes two or three weeks just to change your whole physical and mental daily routine, just to get back to living in a home again and after you've been at home for a week or two, you start to feel very restless and begin to feel the need to go out and do this thing again. He feels it's a bit of a mixed blessing. A kind of strange, creative wanderlust that afflicts the sort of people who do the thing he does. The Rolling Stones don't need the money, but they're out doing what they do again.

'Well, maybe they do need the money and they are out doing what they do again, but I'm sure in all cases there is this sort of balance between wanting to do it and it's also nice to get paid for it,' Anderson reflects. 'That is part of the human condition that we all like to have a job, and we like to feel that we get paid for it. We're quite proud of it and it earns us our daily bread. I think you only have to look around at most of the people who have been professionally engaged in making music since the dawn of contemporary music, let's say since the '50s and '60s. There are not many people who have chosen to give up. Most people probably go through a time in their careers when they think they want to give up for whatever reason but most of them don't really choose to quit, it gets under your skin.'

Anderson thinks one of the reasons that he finds it possible to go on in terms of doing live concerts, as well as making records, is because his musical interests are a lot broader and his musical skills are not in any particular area. Sometimes he wishes they were, because he might be better served by concentrating on one or two things other than having such a broad musical palette with which he insists on working. But, at the same time, he would rather be free to move across the border lines that exist between different musical styles and different kinds of musical contexts in which Jethro Tull has been placed over the years.

'I was thinking about this earlier today,' says Anderson. 'Most people tend to lock into a certain point in Jethro Tull's history or certain kind of music or a favourite album. I think most people would find that they only like 25% of what we do and I think that's one of the reasons we have such a broad following. People are, perhaps, not as emphatic in their liking of our material as in the case of other bands like maybe Status Quo in the UK or ZZ Top, for example.

'But for me, on the other hand, the creative viability of Jethro Tull is that it is very broad, it is always evolving, album to album, year to year. It isn't just about doing the same thing year to year, although there are a lot of songs that I am fortunate to have written that I do enjoy playing and, for the most part, can enjoy playing them in the way in which they were originally written and performed. For some of the audience I think it's perhaps a little bit too much like hard work to sit through all the kinds of things we throw at them.'

The fact he and Tull are part of music history is pleasing to Anderson; especially the variety of what they've done over the years and part of the reason that he personally finds it not just possible to do what we does, but something that he dearly looks forward to doing.

31

Singing

Anderson has an uncanny ability to know when he has trod on his own Achilles Heel and deftly moves to another part of his foot when weaknesses emerge. This means he has always been able to take advantage of unexpected calamities and turned them in his favour.

'Absolutely correct,' Anderson agrees. 'I think everybody, as they get older, has to do that to some extent. Luckily, I didn't make my name as a singer. I've never been a natural singer. I never found it easy to sing, it's always been a struggle for me in the studio and in concert. I don't feel it's something I am born to do. I just feel that I was the guy who had to do it and since I started doing it, it would be difficult now to stop and have somebody else get up and sing my songs. So I have to do the best I can, but it's never been my forte.'

When it comes to how he ended up as vocalist, Anderson remembers: 'I was in John Evans' living room with my cheap guitar and John had his first drum kit and Jeffrey Hammond with his first bass. We had these old radio amplifiers without any case, and we used to have a loose speaker in a cardboard box. That's when we first attempted to play music. When it came to getting a guy to sing, it was me. If we could get a guy who could be the singer, that would have been fine. In fact we did try out one guy, but he didn't work out. So, I ended up being the one who tried to sing the songs until we could find another singer. I just ended up doing it.'

So Anderson began to sing by default, because the other members of the band, he claims, were even worse than he was. It would be hard to dispute Anderson's claim, because no one else has ever taken the microphone and tried. Anybody who has heard Anderson sing, recognises the depth of his self-deprecation. Oh sure, he's no Tony Bennett, but from the way he explains his vocal abilities, one would expect something almost unlistenable. In fact, in the very early days of The John Evan Band, after a particular performance, a journalist or friend of one of the band members – the story isn't completely straight as to who the person was – came back stage and made reference to Anderson by asking, 'Who is that singer? He's great, he sounds just like Elvis Presley.' To the rest of the band, the comment went over rather well, and it earned Anderson the nickname Elvo!

Anderson, on the other hand, immediately altered his singing style to deliberately not sound anything like that. When asked about the incident, Anderson shrugged it off: 'That Elvo thing was a reference from our saxophone player, Tony Wilkinson, who dubbed me Elvo, because something I had been singing apparently came across with baritone richness like a latter day Elvis Presley.'

Anderson has never been a comfortable singer. It was not something, he says, that he was born with a talent for. He admits he has always been envious of those people who are naturals, who never have to work hard at it and for whom the quality and the expression of voice is something that is just largely a genetic thing. Some are born with it. What to do with it is important too. Anderson says:

> I would probably find it difficult to sing the material on some of my solo albums, it would be quite daunting for me just because there's a lot of it, vocals, that is, and it covers more or less the range of the music I've always done. My voice is a natural baritone; I'm in the Bing Crosby territory. I am not your Lou Gramm or your Robert Plant, I've always had a voice that was pitched at least a fifth, if not more, below the average male rock vocalist, so I'm kind of struggling when I get up around an E or an F. That's what most guys go up to.
>
> On the other hand, the folks who just sing with a more throw away style, which I would have to say Mick Jagger is an example of – he's never been a technical singer, he just throws it around and he can get out there and more or less do what he's always done – are still completely convincing at what they do now as they ever were. And that's because they didn't start off by electing to go for the limits. There are those folks who, I think, make a very difficult bed to lie in for themselves, because they decided straight off they were going to try to soar to those dizzy heights that are maybe scalable in your 20s, barely reachable in your 30s, and by the time you're in your 40s, it's got to be a very good night before you get there.
>
> And those are just the guys who are the singers. When you move on to the instrumentalists who really go for broke, again, age is going to bring its limitations. Somebody like myself: I have the best and the worst of both worlds; I have something I can do that I think I can always manage to do okay, but I also have some stuff which is pretty hard for me to do.
>
> These days, there are some nights when I find it very much a strain to sing, particularly certain pieces. I'm O.K. on most material, but there's certain things

163

that do cause me considerable difficulty and have always done so. To be absolutely realistic about it, there have always been certain things that have never been easy for me to do.

I either have to make some allowances by changing the way in which I do it or not doing it at all. I try and make the right choices. I think it would be true to say for the average vocalist, throughout their professional career, they're going to find they will have to drop the key of their songs from the beginning to the end of their career by a full tone. It is inevitable. It's not a case of making excuses.

In my case it was more difficult, because as a singer you breathe a certain way and as a flute player you breathe in an entirely different way, so I've had a difficult time of it as the two have contradictory requirements. As a flute player, it's not made it easy for me to continue developing my voice and, indeed, my attempt to extend my vocal abilities in '82, '83 and '84 was probably a bad choice. I should probably have gone through a voice teacher, or somebody, to try and better conserve my abilities, because that was when I began to have great difficulty with my voice and, indeed, did not sing for an entire year.

He goes on to add, rather mischievously:

My singing style was something that I worked quite desperately hard on in the early days. I tried to deliberately make my voice sound rather flat and aggressive. Anything that would just not sound smooth; it's just never been a natural thing for me. I'm much more comfortable singing in a voice that doesn't attempt to imitate black American origins or American accents.

It always sounds patently ridiculous to me when I hear such talents as Elton John singing in this fake sort of North American accent. It's not a regional thing it's just a sort of a peculiar mixture of American. I find it kind of absurd that Mick Jagger sang that way. I've always preferred bands that sang in their natural voices which is why, bottom line for me, I would rather hear Johnny Rotten sing than Elton John. Another is David Bowie, although he's very much a put on with a sort of adopted slightly Cockney accent. You might call that a sort of Cockney-pop vocal style, but he tended to stay much closer to his origins rather than do the American stuff. Take the singer who used to sing with Foreigner, for example, as being a classic great-to-middle-of-the-road American rock vocalist. I mean, he's got a brilliant voice and a brilliant sound to his voice. That's something that I don't think you can fake, you either have it or you don't. Unfortunately he doesn't either [laughs].

We played some concerts together recently in Germany. He started off rather well, but by the fourth song he was going for those high notes and he wasn't making it anymore. That's a difficult thing to have to deal with; to create this impossible cross to bear in the studio when there's 23 takes or something and when it comes to having to do that live on stage every night, it's a whole different ball game these days. I've tended to learn my lesson in the studio. I don't go for certain vowel sounds, certain constructions that are going to cause me difficulties.

32

Band Tensions

Questions of discontent within the band have been there since Mick Abrahams was the first member to leave. The answers are simple on one level, yet complicated on another: what band doesn't have its share of discontent?

ANDERSON:

I think that the majority of discontent that comes around between members of any band just has to do with the fact that you are not always compatible people in the first place. Part of the spark that comes out in the music is very often because of conflicting personalities and slightly volatile relationships. I think that was very much the case in the original Jethro Tull. Everybody got along with Clive Bunker, he was an easy going guy. I played on a track of one of his albums and I was thinking, he doesn't have any enemies, everybody thinks Clive's a nice guy. But he was the only guy in the original four piece Jethro Tull who was easy going. Everybody else, in different ways, was hard work with each other.

Mick and Glenn just did not hit it off; never liked each other. I felt, up to a point, that I was O.K. with them, but I didn't really feel, for different reasons, that either were my sort of person. But musically, and in terms of the kind of on-stage identity that the band put across as a group, I think that was, in part, a product of what was a slightly volatile intense relationship between three quarters of the band off stage.

And other bands like The Who, The Kinks and The Rolling Stones – these very volatile relationships are legendary and I'm sure have their quirky insidious part to play and why such great and dangerous music came out of so many people like that. But at the end of the day it doesn't mean that you all find it easy to sit in a bar together and have a drink at night at the end of the show.

I think within Jethro Tull, the personalities of the band have probably become a little bit more ... they've been pulled together, I guess, just by a matter of getting older, maturing, being a little bit more philosophical, a little less demanding and also just because the people who are in the band now probably do get on and have more to talk about – more things that we do have in common, although I guess we are still fairly different from each other. But I don't think it's a good or a bad thing. I think having those tensions is part of what makes the thing come alive. But at their worst they're very destructive and quite bad for people ... bad for their health and some people just have chips on their shoulders and are never very happy.

John Evans and Barrie Barlow are two people that I never got the impression were very happy doing what they were doing. I'm not necessarily being critical, and Barrie would be the first to admit that he wasn't happy. That just happens to be part of his character and he's always been one of the most professional people you'd ever meet in the music business. He would always give 100% of what he could do and very passionately cared about doing his best. In a sense, that made Barrie a perfectionist and, like most perfectionists, they get upset when things aren't the way they're supposed to be. So Barrie himself would be a very hard task master in regard to his own work as well as other people's. And in the years since Jethro Tull he's tried to play music with other people, to manage bands, to produce bands, and I get the impression that he's probably trying to see a level of professionalism that's not attainable. I don't talk to Barrie very often. He's probably the one person that I know would probably be least likely to call me or me to call him unless it was something we had to talk to each other about, whereas the other guys are pretty much ... well, I see them fairly often.

33

Inspiration

Here's one of those big subjects, the kind that every Tull fan has wanted to know since they were first blown away by a Tull song – when, where and how do the ideas for songs arrive? At the gate without much fanfare or through long, arduous sessions of soul searching and gazing through a window for hours, trying desperately to come up with a line?

ANDERSON:

> I wish there was a simple kind of, entertaining, anecdotal response to that, but there isn't. It just really is anytime, anywhere and the one key element which you should always have with you is the means to record that notion whether it's pen and paper or a tape recorder. So I always have something with me, because there is nothing worse than having an idea come to you and no way to put it down for later recall and development. If you wake up in the middle of the night and you say 'I'll remember that in the morning' you know you won't, so it really can happen anytime. I think that's the right way for it to be, so that you don't have to find yourself in a particular mental state in order to create those moments when they present themselves.

> I think there are two kinds of composition frames of mind that you can be in: you just get a lucky break and something lands on your lap; or you have to rely on your expertise, your art as an approach to the job to conjure something if there isn't an inspiration moment going on. You sit down and work at it.

> But generally speaking, my creative efforts tend to be in the first part of the day. I think if I were a writer or a painter I would do it in the morning. I would try to finish by lunch time, but the morning is the better time for me to get things happening. But never look a gift horse in the mouth, if you get a good idea at midnight – go for it too.

> There was a time when I used to come back to a hotel room after a concert with my guitar and work on some songs. But I think that was more when we were a support act. Then we would be finished by 8:30 – 8:45p.m. and then back at the hotel rather early with some time to kill, and I would sit in my hotel room and

work on some ideas. But normally speaking, now, as the headline, by the time we get back to the hotel room it's midnight and time to go to sleep. I sometimes get a bit of time around soundcheck as well.

'Budapest' was originally recorded at about nineteen minutes. That was in rehearsal and demo form. And in the end, I think we just whittled away the stuff that was the weakest and decided to make it a ten minute song. But the thing about pop and rock songs is, it always seems to me, that there's a great temptation to put everything into the realm of the three to four minutes. Normally, in the Jethro Tull context, we like to think that we do songs on most of our albums that do vary from the couple of minute quickie acoustic things to things that have been, typically, six, seven or eight minutes long. On occasions, even longer than that but, in an ideal world, I think that six or seven minutes is a pretty good length for the kind of music we like to write in a band context.

If you're going to explore the ideas of setting something up, getting a theme, reiterating that theme, developing it, have some sort of secondary theme that comes into play, and then an improvisational area, the return to the principal theme again, add some outro material and you put it altogether – you're looking at six or seven minutes. And that seems to me to have happened quite a lot. If you listen to a lot of classical music you'll find that recognisable chunks of music – six, seven and eight minutes is the length of time people tend to like to work with.

34

The Writing Process

I like the idea that this previous bit of information could well be described as 'The Beginner's Guide To How A Tull Song Is Born'. This next section goes further, exploring what actually goes on at the time of the creation of a song and from where Anderson draws his inspiration. It's one thing to talk about where and when and how long a song can be, but here's the real meat and potatoes of the matter. Therefore, I bring you: Ian Anderson, musical landscape painter:

ANDERSON:

Generally speaking, things are either up or down in life. There tends to be happiness and sadness and they tend to be the two real forces behind making music. I operate on another plane as well. I also write in a way that is a bit more like painting pictures, setting a scene, telling a story. It is not just necessarily reflective of the human emotion as sung in the first person – most popular music is sung in that way. People who do work in more descriptive terms, who are the landscape painters of music – settings scenes, describing something to you, perhaps still in a very personal way, nonetheless, it is an observation, it is more objective, not just purely subjective as an emotional outpouring and I tend to do that as well. That's the middle ground that stops me from being either one thing or the other. I can also create things that are more descriptive and objective and I present them as any good presenter on CNN or BBC World News would. I try to do it in an unbiased way and not try and force the issue in terms of telling people how they should react to it. But like any human reporter on CNN or BBC I kind of slip in the odd nuance that kind of directs people as to how to respond. But there's a bit of editorial censorship which goes on in writing that kind of music. You don't really want to go out and preach when you're doing the descriptive piece, you slip it in but it's got to be subtle.

So I do try and find this bit of balance. I don't have to try too hard, it usually just works out that way. But if I find the balance has drifted a bit in one particular year of making music, perhaps too much towards something, again without having to sit and work it out, the natural tendency is to redress that balance by letting the pendulum swing back the other way. I don't like it wildly oscillating, I think there's just that slight shift which is better than just black and white and light and dark; there is a lot of middle ground in my music that keeps it from being too emotionally flaky

I'm very fond of descriptive pieces. I began really by having an interest in the visual arts rather than the musical arts, so my almost natural way of thinking is to see things in terms of very visual images and they are very often not only the route to descriptive songs, but at the root of more personal subjective pieces as well. I still think very strongly in terms of images rather than just gut reactions.

I love instrumental music because you're free, to a large extent, of the obvious need of lyrics. The bottom line is, however much I like instrumental music, and however much I would like to be an instrumental musician rather than to have the chore of singing (because it certainly wasn't what I wanted to do when I first started, I hated the idea of having to sing), I had to because none of the other guys could or would. So you realise that lyrics are part of it too. But in general, I think music can, and should, be more challenging than it sometimes it is.

For me, on the other hand, the creative viability of Jethro Tull is that it is very broad. It is always evolving, album to album, year to year. It isn't just about doing the same thing year after year, although there are a lot of songs that I am fortunate to have written that I do enjoy playing. For the most part, I can enjoy playing them in the way in which they were originally written and performed, but it does certainly take me as well as the audience, whether they like it or not, through a whole lot of different musical moments in a live concert. For me it's interesting and I have to have it that way. For some of the audience I think it's, perhaps, a little bit too much like hard work to sit through all the kinds of things we throw at them. I'm pleased that the variety of the music we do is part of rock history, and part of the reason that I find it something that I dearly look forward to doing.

How many famous musicians/composers get quizzed on the ever-evolving nature of their muse, of their way of creating and how they, rather than Joe Public, ended up with the constant and, seemingly, endless supply of ideas and references for songs, music or lyrics? All of them, is the quick answer. It makes for good journalistic fodder, good copy, sells magazines and makes folk heroes and subscribes to the power of genius within the common people.

Sometimes we are confounded by the answers we are supplied when we ask an artist where they get their ideas, and sometimes it bores the pants off of us.

The problem with putting this question to Ian Anderson is that I've rehearsed it for thirty years and for thirty years – we're talking about interviews for magazines that span that period and each successive album under the Jethro Tull banner – I've only received cursory answers, bits and pieces to a puzzle I knew had to be finished within a given period (who knew it would take thirty years?).

When this book finally became a reality to Ian Anderson, and I say that with a reconciling sort of notion rather than a notification that a book would be printed, I believe he actually decided to let the answers out. The problem with that is that once the answer(s) started, they flowed. Answers that I, as a writer and fan, have been seeking for thirty years came out in a very recent interview, and it's not the sort of reply you interrupt. You'll see what I mean. This first part probably asks more questions than actually answers them, but it's been worth the wait.

ANDERSON:

When it comes to writing the songs, it's not always the music first, I would always be the first to recognise that it's easier to write music for me than to write lyrics, but probably something less than 50% of the time it's not the music first: it may be a lyrical idea it, could be a line of lyrics, it could be a title, it could be something that's a reference in prose terms that you haven't quite put into song/lyrical context. At least it's some words and that can be, in my case, less than 50% of the time. Let's say it's 35% or 40% of the time there's something lyrical that pre-dates the musical idea, or more than 50% of the time it is the music first.

I think that somewhere in the subconscious, even with any kind of musical line, for me, it's not absolute. I very rarely write an instrumental piece of music consciously. It's more often the case that I write something and I know, behind it, there is some idea; there is something just waiting to pop to the surface. And in terms of some word references, even if they haven't quite arrived yet, I know it's just a very small step away. So I think there's quite a strong relationship between lyrics and music in my case. Although, as I reiterate, for the third or fourth time in this long sentence [laughs] it's likely to be more often than not that it's the music that comes first to mind.

Moving on from that notion: I think there's a point that does deserve mention, not regarding my lyrical or musical input, but the genre of British rock music of the '60s, '70s, '80s, or whatever, might be that a whole lot of us folks didn't come out of music college. We didn't go to the London College of Music, or wherever. We actually came out of art school; we came out of the painting pursuits. And I don't know if it's the same in America, because I don't really know enough about the individuals concerned, but it must be more than coincidence that almost everybody that springs to mind came out of the British art school tradition.

Anderson cites everybody from Eric Clapton and Jimmy Page, to Eric Burdon as people he believes were part of this phenomenon:

You know we all went to art college to learn music and those who went to music college were never heard of again. I like to think there's something in there; the translation of the visual ideas to musical ideas. It's not such a big step, especially if you grow up with the very broad view that we have of painting when we learn about these decades ... of these centuries; we have so much to look back on from prehistoric cave paintings on through what is the jazz of painting and which is the loosening up of art at the end of the 19th century when people like Manet and Monet started shifting the boundaries and became the forerunners of what is Impressionism, subsequently, a much more abstracted approach to it. But all of that ties in so much with the musical evolution as well. If you look at classical music loosening up, and the ethnic influences of blues music and other ethnic music forms into the 20th century, it all parallels what happened in the visual arts.

So it's kind of natural that a lot of us folks that went to art school in our late teenage years, found a very obvious outlet in pop and rock music as alternatives to the slowness of the visual arts (and the very solitary nature of expression of which that tends to be) for those of us who enjoyed the speed and the improvisation of live performance and the idea of performing in front of other people.

Music was such a natural extension of the thing that we were principally interested in, which was the visual arts. I guess there is a serious piece of writing to be written by someone sometime drawing the parallels between the British pop and rock music of the '60s, '70s, '80s and '90s and the art school tradition that seems to have been, not exclusively, but surprisingly, largely responsible for such an incredible amount of talent.

In my case, I have all these visual references that all the time spring to mind. Above and beyond everything else, I can go back to the very early songs of Jethro Tull on the *Aqualung* album; things like 'Mother Goose', for example; it's a visual reference. Right now I can see the picture in my head from which those words came. I think that's very much the case, even now.

It's a very, very visual picture; sometimes it's narrative, sometimes it's telling a story, sometimes it's a picture postcard, sometimes it's a snapshot of some alternative realities whether it's a holiday memory or something you'd seen on your travels while you were working. Whether it's a poignant moment to something you've seen on CNN or whatever, it's very, very visual and putting that into words is a very natural extension for me.

The idea of the written word, of the musical flow of that very abstract form, that music, in the visual reference of the picture, is like the three corners of a triangle – you've got to bring them together. Happily, it's not too difficult a job;

they almost seemed to gravitate to each other, they draw into almost certain feelings that that's what you should be doing and if one of those three elements proves not to be right then it's easy to scrap the song and start again. To try and find another picture and to try and write a new set of lyrics and to try changing the music are things that are very, very difficult. Once you've started down that path you throw away the song and start again, you can't change one of those elements or all of them – it doesn't seem to work.

Part two of Anderson's reconciling is more naturalistic and predominantly in the standard musical circles as to what makes a composer (notice I say composer, rather than musician) tick. And that's where you would expect most 'musicians' to draw their ideas from. I call this 'Music From Everyday'.

ANDERSON:

The most principal reference I have is I write about pictures, although I do think in terms of subject material as well, which is probably another part of that question of the majority of pop and rock music over the ages being about the 'boy meets girl, boy loses the girl' nature. It's pretty simple and is usually about the kind of love won, love lost, love lack of, phenomenon. It's on that level.

There's another kind of pop and rock music which is more about things, not so much intellectual, but about circumstances, about conditions. And I suppose, for me, the first time I started to really notice that was when I was about 16 and I first heard the music of Bob Dylan. I'd never been a really great fan of his, but at least for a generation of people he probably brought to pop music the idea that you could sing about something other than the kind of lovey-dovey stuff that seemed to be the stock material from which most songs originated.

Growing up as a teenager, I was listening to black American blues, but that was almost universally all about 'rolling and tumbling all night long'. It was a variation on the theme: 'I woke up this morning, my baby left me,' or euphemisms – basically sexual in orientation – and, apart from rare exceptions, that seems to sum up most of black American music.

So I'm fairly pleased that I've used the language with which I was blessed, because I think the English language is particularly good for pop and rock music writing and I'd rather try and stretch, at least, my own boundaries by not settling into a comfortable easy, limited vocabulary and limited style. But lyrics always remained the difficult thing. Writing music is so much easier. You can be ambiguous, when you're abstracted to that degree. Once you start saying words, then it gets awfully tense, because you are either misunderstood or, God forbid, you're understood all too clearly! If I were to throw some real admiration in the direction of a couple of lyrical writers it would be for some of the work of Mark Knopfler who, I think, has written some of the really fine pop and rock lyrics. In a more abstract fashion, Don Van Vliet, better known as Captain Beefheart, managed to evoke – sometimes in a quite blatant and fraudulent fashion – some jazz-like approach to the avant-garde 'Jazz-Lite' approach to music and lyrical writing. I say that very respectfully, because the poor man is dead now. Any time I listened to his music it always amazed me that he's never received more recognition than he has for producing something that's a whole lot closer to pop music as an art form than just about anything else that has ever come out.

That brings Part Two of Ian Anderson's reconciling the differences of where music and lyrics come from, for him, to a close, for the moment. It doesn't, however, mean that the conversation has come to an end or that we stopped speaking. Once certain ideas that have been sought after for thirty years have been uncovered, and names like Captain Beefheart spring into a conversation, the temptation to pursue an unusual avenue becomes, to say the least, irresistible. The conversation, of course, branched off in another direction completely, and that was the subject of two of America's more interesting and gifted composers – Captain Beefheart (Don Van Vliet) and Frank Zappa. As it turned out, he had a lot to say about both, most of which was quite complimentary.

35

The Captain And Zappa

On Beefheart:

Captain Beefheart never really had bands that were competent musically in the broad sense. What he did was, he managed to raise the level of internal anarchy to where it produced a spark, quite often a very naive one, but nonetheless a very purposeful one, and a very strong sense of something that nobody else could really do unless they were as anarchic and as deeply, fundamentally principled as Captain Beefheart himself was. And, indeed, it was instilled in his musicians. But ultimately, they were all disillusioned. They got upset with him, because he was a tyrant and he could be very cruel and hard on his guys and I know this, because we worked together. It was one of those illustrations of how someone can go from being a band leader to being quite a ruthless and cruel dictator in a nanosecond. Everybody knows that Don was a very gifted, eccentric character, but he played upon that eccentricity and became something too much larger than life, and forced himself on his guys in a way that was far too manipulative and sometimes quite cruel.

Surely he must have known the bottom line is that he was still responsible for bringing out of his musicians something that they never ever would have reached on their own and, however painful the process was, it leaves us all enriched and better off in the hearing. But boy, he was a tough cookie. You wouldn't want to be the bass player in his band.

He once said to me, 'Look, I can take that Hammond-Hammond guy away from you just like that,' snapping his fingers. 'I can control people, I can do this, I can do that, and Hammond-Hammond will do anything for me.' And I said 'Maybe he will [laughs] and maybe he won't. But look, the point is, you already have a bass player, who is a perfectly nice chap. And you made him cry last night because you were really cruel to him. Hopefully he'll still be at the gig tomorrow night and hopefully Jeffrey Hammond will still be there playing for Jethro Tull tomorrow night. Why do you have to make it a blood sport?'

That's kind of how Don saw things; that manipulation was part of it. I think it was, in turn, because he felt manipulated by record companies and industry and all the rest. He carried this perpetual giant chip on his shoulder that he was being put upon and sat upon by the music industry. Back then, those guys were pussy cats compared to what we have now. Back then, record companies, and particularly the one Don was with, were nice guys compared to today. Poor old Don wouldn't last five minutes now.

We were both with Warner Brothers at the time. Word got back to him that I had an appreciation for his music and he phoned me up, and invited himself onto the tour. I tried to talk him out of it because I didn't think they were going to have an easy ride in the US, because they were cult status in the UK. And, indeed, they did have an awful time in the US. People just did not like them – this was around the time of *Thick As A Brick* – the audience didn't like him and they gave him a really rough ride. He was getting booed off the stage opening for us in the US, but selling out at the Albert Hall in the UK – which is no mean feat, then or now, as it's a 5,000 seat hall.

On Zappa:

I never met Frank Zappa and I always wish that I had. I often had a sense of guilt that, when he was dying, I found it very difficult to pick up the phone and call him, even though, according to one of his children, he would quite like to have heard from me and other people. But not being someone I knew, I just found it very difficult, knowing the situation. What do you say to someone who's got just weeks or months to live? So it's a very difficult thing to just pick up the phone and call someone you've never spoken to before. I always wished that I had. I couldn't find the words to make that conversation happen.

At any rate, he was a much different kind of guy, much more of a cerebral person, and for me, one of the two all time great American creative folks, but very dark and sometimes a rather sad kind of person. Beefheart and Zappa were two totally different types of people: Beefheart had a natural, comic ability about him and Zappa seemed to have to work very hard at it – but in a rather bitter and cynical way, which is not always enjoyable. In spite of which, he did some of the best pop music of the 20th century. He was not so immediately likable; he was a man struggling with his own identity and obsessive about what he did. In fact, I thought about him only last night, in the sense that I was doing a mix, and I was thinking, I've listened to this music a hundred times, now I'm trying to mix this thing, trying to bring it all alive. I've played three quarters of the notes that are on it, I've written it, I've recorded it, I have sung it, I've produced it, I've engineered it. I'm mixing it and now I am, yet again, having to go through and refine it and redefine it in terms of the very final part of the process. And I thought, boy, poor old Frank Zappa. He was still remixing his earlier catalogue up until the moment he died. He must have really been obsessive about his material to have to feel it necessary to get it right after all these years.

I'm sure that he would have been delighted to have known of the peer group acceptance that he had over such a long career. But for him, I guess, things seemed very frustrating, seemed like a personal battle of one sort or other. To a lot of the rest of us, I guess, Frank Zappa was one of those people ... one of those very few people that you would say, 'Well, they only ever made one of those.' And in many ways, thank goodness they did, because more than one Frank Zappa would have been too much for this world.

That's the really important thing to me: the individual, the creative spark; whether it's pure, whether it's pompous, whether it's humble. All of that fades into unimportance compared to originality. It's so hard, particularly in this day and age, to come up with something that is truly original and, in Frank Zappa's case, he was in the particular place where he may not have been the most original musically, but he put together all the ingredients that were available to him and the end result is something that nobody else did and nobody else probably ever will. Which is why I think he will be remembered in a hundred years' time and The Spice Girls won't.

36

The Recording Process And More On Writing

In the recording studio today, Anderson rules supreme – that's because the recording studio is no longer the domain of the octopus-armed engineers of the past who had a plethora of dials and tape machines to run, necessitating the graft of an arm or two extra. It seems that the larger and more sophisticated the quality of the recording equipment, the less need there is for outside intervention. The home studio has grown up to the point where it is no longer for demos only; digital technology ushered in the professional home recording studio.

ANDERSON:

I can walk a few yards to my studio and do everything that needs to be done without having to call on any assistance. As far as being producer of the Jethro Tull 'sound', that's a different story, and we always needed outside help with engineering, etc. But if you go right back to the beginning to the recording of *This Was*, it was made in the studio with just the band members and an engineer. Terry Ellis, who was credited as producer on the early albums had, honestly, little or no creative input at all. He was producer in the sense that his father, in the case of the first album, or his father's banker, and later his company, were bankrolling the sessions. That's the producer in the movie sense, the person who is paying for the production. But in the creative sense, Terry didn't have anything to do with any of the albums. He would be in the studio from time to time and I'm sure he made some, what he hoped were, creative suggestions. Some of them, I'm sure, were taken notice of. But he wasn't a producer in the sense of creative producers in rock music who are very much, perhaps, an equal part in producing the final results in the artistic sense.

So right from the beginning it was pretty much the band, the studio, the studio engineer and Anderson's inclination and background. Anderson was able to assimilate the technical side of music making; he took that mantle on early.

Certainly, by the time they were doing *Stand Up* he felt he was controlling the sessions pretty much. It was pretty well his job by then and Terry's role as producer, and then as executive producer, was a way of making him feel comfortable with his management role in the band. So it started off pretty much that way and it's been that way ever since.

⟡⟡⟡⟡⟡⟡

It's an intentional decision to have the writing process appear twice, as it does here. Many of you will have picked up on the reason already. If not, the writing process takes place in distinct places, areas, or a specific domain. Earlier, Ian Anderson explained the generalities of what his process of bringing ideas to life entailed. In the following section he will deal with relating the writing process directly within the confines of the studio where, without wishing to sound too precious, magic can happen.

The subject of which came first, the lyric or the music, was quite well documented. Here we continue the subject, but within that holy realm of knob twiddling.

ANDERSON:

Putting lyrics on a song after it has been completed is not peculiar to me. A lot of people work that way. They are, perhaps, very reluctant to commit themselves to something as personal as a song lyric in the early periods of rehearsal or recording and, because of recording technology being what it has been for many, many years, you tended to add vocals last, because they're the most upfront and obvious thing. That is, of course, until the digital age came along. Until then, you really didn't want to put your vocals on and have them run across the tape heads hundreds of times unnecessarily. You want to have those vocals go on there as much near the end as possible, so there is still plenty of oxide left on the tape. Having said that, there are albums we've made where I can look back to rehearsals with the band doing vocals in the studio, or in the rehearsal room, prior to recording.

Equally, there are a lot of occasions when we had been doing some very detailed rehearsals with the music, and while we always have a pretty good idea of the vocal and the tune and I usually had some lines for the vocals, I don't necessarily have the whole thing written at that stage, because I like to feel the song is progressing musically down what looks like a profitable route before I commit myself to writing the lyrics and doing the vocals.

But there are occasions where I've done the opposite. I go out with just a guitar and do the basic track and put my vocals on at the very beginning and then everybody has to come in and overdub to that, but sometimes that leaves them with little choices. They are having to work with something that's already formatted and laid out.

According to Anderson, on the occasions when they are working in a more fluid way with just the bones of the tune and sketchy ideas of lyrics, at that stage, the band are able to make more contributions. They are, on the one hand, free to do stuff that's less constructed by knowing exactly what the lyrics are about before or, indeed, the way they have to be. But at the same time they don't have the same points of reference that a good idea of the lyrics would produce, that might help them with their creative input into the song.

But he can see their frustration, sometimes not knowing where a certain song is going and having to feel around in the dark. In the recording process, someone has to go for it. Somebody has always got to lay their stuff down so, at the end of the day, somebody's got to be going in there and making the commitment on tape. It may be everybody at the same time or, more often, it's one, two or three people and the folks who add their stuff later have a little bit more head room. Their options are reduced too, because they have to work within the format that has been laid down.

Each person reacts in a different way to the recording process and none live that close to each other, so it's not the same as it was when they were younger. They could just get together on the spur of the moment and make music. Every one lives in a different part of the country. Martin, for example, hates recording in the studio; he hates to be put on the spot. He has to deliver the goods, and Anderson understands why, especially having made a couple of solo albums on his own, it must have really been quite scary for him to make that commitment. It's quite daunting to know that you're going to put something down that day and you're going to be judged on it for the rest of your life. And it's always been like that. Sometimes you just don't feel up to doing it, but you do it anyway, because that's what you are paid to do. Then you end up having to live with it.

ANDERSON:

Just take any band of five guys together in a studio one day and you can be sure that one of those five there would rather be fishing, or something, or someone has a cold or stayed up too late last night. To have everybody at their best all the time is impossible.

Essentially, the song is there and then you go back and decide what to do. That would apply to a lot of Jethro Tull songs as well as pieces on the solo album. I think I prefer the approach, the idea of constructing a piece of music as a more abstract arrangement and then doing whatever you have to do to put that into the recorded form ... it's interesting and it's satisfying, but I don't think it quite has, for me, the excitement of the more off the wall approach, which is whether the very first thing you do is the vocal and then musical accompaniment. I think, probably, that would, for me, always remain the most reliable, satisfying way to make music. It would, at least, have the first statement, be something which, in itself, encapsulates what that song is about. It's hard to do if you're an instrumentalist, because if you're playing the flute, you're dealing with the top line only, so you have to think in more abstract and complete terms and then you go to construct an arrangement around that top melodic line. So as an instrumentalist, for me, it's harder to write music in that kind of way, but as a songwriter, dealing with lyrics and music, I derive the most pleasure from making the initial statement, which is essentially the song, the vocal, lyrics, that top line and the essential musical accompaniment all in one hit – that's always got to be the big prize.

37

Light And Dark

In 1992, Jethro Tull recorded the live album *A Little Light Music*. By the time that tour reached North America, Anderson knew from experience that audiences just don't sit still, they want to boogie to heavier, louder music. The show was augmented by the inclusion of so called dark music and renamed *The Light And Dark Tour ('92)*. This was, to some, an odd approach for the band to take, particularly because they also chose to play in smaller venues at the same time, which made for a double shift in the *modus operandi* of a Tull concert: there wasn't a set of new music at the beginning of the show to showcase a new album and they weren't playing in hockey rink size halls.

But that *Light And Dark* moniker was something that had been alluded to for many years, Anderson making most of those allusions. You've heard, as well, that Anderson has always referred to the Tull catalogue as having light albums and dark albums and that one usually followed the other.

ANDERSON:

It occurred to me a few years ago it tended to be that Jethro Tull albums fell into a pattern where a bright album seemed to always be followed by a dark album, not for any obvious purpose, but on balance you find one album tends to be a little up and smiling and the next one is a little bit darker, brooding and contemplative. It's not infallible, but it's a general tendency.

I would say the album *Roots To Branches* was a little reflective and on the darker side. My guess is it's a natural instinctive thing that the next time I started writing a bunch of songs, there is a little bit more of a balance, a little warmer and a little more optimistic, sunny air about them. Of course, there are contemplative moments and more serious kinds of heavier subject matter songs. But, on balance, I would say, yes, it's kind of lighter. Again, it's just an inevitable swing on the pendulum; I don't think there's anything more to it or less to it than that. As far as that having any bearing on record sales is concerned, I don't think it has much to do with anything, because I would always contend that the *Aqualung* album was rather dark. It has a few light moments on it, but, obviously, did pretty well. *Thick As A Brick*, on the other hand, which followed it, was, to me, overall, a brighter and lighter sounding record and that sold pretty well. So I honestly don't think it has much bearing on it. You can write wherever you want; write and play in whatever way you want to play but, ultimately, commercially speaking it will survive or fail on its intrinsic, commercial, musical qualities. In the case of Jethro Tull, we're not a very commercially obvious band, so our sales have tended to not be spectacular, but relatively reliable over the longer-term.

38

Instruments

Playing an instrument can be a lifelong dream, ambition or vocation, but usually it's one instrument and it takes years and years of practice and brow-beating from a parent or two, along with some grey-haired music teacher who would count out beats while you squirmed in your seat waiting for the allotted practice time to come to an end. The following statement is a bit like turning on one's own peer group, but it's a theory I've looked at quite closely, and it is this: many critics, particularly the ones who are most acerbic and unrelenting in their bashing of certain bands or styles of music, are failed musicians. It's not a new notion and I'm sure there are some who also hide their true bias quite convincingly. Further to that notion, is the idea that the more complex and intricate the style, the more acerbic – how's 'jealous' as a word to slip in here? – the criticism, while the more simplistic and working class the act, the easier the critics seem to be. Think about it.

I still remember hearing rumours about Ian Anderson having been part of an orchestra and having taken formal flute lessons – it wasn't too far-fetched an idea when you consider how young he and the rest of Tull were when he was blowing 'Serenade To A Cuckoo' etc. Pondering just how hard a task it was for Anderson to acquire abilities on so many instruments, including the flute, soprano sax, sopranino sax, etc. is something you may have done to some small degree over the years. So, just how difficult was becoming a multi-instrumentalist (and before the idea of Jack-of-all-trades sets in, we're not even considering that)?

ANDERSON:

I would say, in most cases, it's not too much of a struggle to get something happening on most instruments, personally. But the worst of them was the flute! For me that was the harder instrument to get any kind of a useful contribution from. The saxophone from my point of view as a non-sax player is just a bit of fun to try and translate the fingering of the flute. It's an instrument I never really much enjoyed. I always enjoyed the idea of it more than the actual playing of it and the commitment has to be there with an instrument like the saxophone, because you're not just making the noise, your having to control the pitch as well. And unless you really do play a lot and keep yourself in shape, then you'll just find it really difficult to play in tune without hurting your lip. It's not an instrument I would ever want to invest that time in, in order to play it properly.

I just have to admit that I don't think I'll ever play saxophone again. I actually really came to dislike the instrument from the few occasions I've tried to pick it up again and get to some basic level of proficiency. I find it's just not worth the effort for me. I have actually gone off the sound of it. I can't really think of many players outside of the notable jazz Be Bop players who I particularly enjoy.

I particularly dislike sax players like the ones who play on the works of Bruce Springsteen or that Gerry Rafferty sax player guy. It's fairly good playing, but I actually find it an irritating sound. I always found Charlie Parker was quite brilliant; his improvisation was brilliant and not in terms of impeccable tone or impeccable technique, which I don't think he had, but what he did have was this incredibly fertile imagination. He had a real ability for thinking ahead all the time, harmonically. Roland Kirk I actually knew as a sax player before I noticed him playing the flute. Back at the time when I was in my late teens I listened to a few of those guys, but kind of lost interest with Ornette Coleman at that point; it just got a little too avant-garde for me.

The time when we were using saxophones in the band was a while ago. I don't even own those saxophones anymore, I sold off the soprano and sopranino. I think I still have an alto in the music room. I don't think it is in any way a great asset to be a multi-instrumentalist. I can pick something up and then maybe get a tune out of it. If you are a multi-instrumentalist, almost certainly, you gloss around the finer points of those instruments and you have a shallow and probably rather unsatisfactory technique and, so, I certainly don't think it's anything to be proud of. My excuse would be that I'm really sticking to the three broad areas I have always done: playing acoustic guitar, mandolin and the bouzouki; they are all sort of the same kind of thing. The flute is the instrument I'm associated with. The flute-like instruments and the other stuff, again, which I have always played with Jethro Tull, has been various odd bits of percussion and that extends to playing those instruments on this album. I have played bass on several Jethro Tull tracks in the past and, indeed, on the *Stormwatch* album, because John Glascock was in the hospital. So I'm basically sticking with the things that are in the guitar family and the flute family. Those are what I really concentrate on and I'm not terribly interested in the challenge of picking up totally alien instruments.

Anderson actually thinks that most of the reed instruments and other woodwinds are so different to the flute it would be like starting again. He doesn't think he wants to make that effort just to become a very second rate clarinet player or oboe player or for that matter, saxophone player:

I don't think I want to mess around with those things. I play a bit of keyboards now and then, but it's not something I feel I'm likely to want to do very much again. It gets to the point where you know it's not something terribly rewarding and not something to be proud of if you're just doing an average job. I prefer to stick with the things that I feel I have something a little more special to offer, which is the flute family and guitar family.

Anderson has stated that one of the most important aspects of being in a band like Jethro Tull has been that he has been able to call himself a musician, rather than a pop or recording star. And over the years his flute playing has improved to the point where his style today is light years ahead of where it was in 1968.

'I think it's like anything you do a lot, you just get better at it. But you can lose touch with other aspects of playing. It is a determination of mine, in the final years, to try and improve my flute playing in terms of the range of what I can play,' Anderson says.

39

Mastering The Acoustic Guitar

ANDERSON:

Before I left the north of England to travel south with the John Evan Band, where we were going to base ourselves in the Luton area, just north of London, I sold my guitar. Actually, I traded it in for a microphone and, on impulse, a flute. I arrived down south, minus guitar, with harmonica and the flute. The microphone made sense because Mick Abrahams was an accomplished guitar player. There seemed little point in me being in the background as a rhythm guitarist, because in the John Evan Band, there were keyboards, two saxophone players with plenty of different tonalities and textures which wouldn't involve any assets if a rhythm guitar were added. So I sold the stuff and I didn't pick up playing guitar again until the second Jethro Tull album when Mick left the band and Martin joined.

I picked up the acoustic and started playing guitar again and I kind of just picked up where I left off, but using acoustic rather than electric. I would play some electric guitar on albums like *Benefit*, a little bit on *Aqualung*, but it's always been an occasional thing, it's always been when there was something there that I just kind of knew, a simple riff or something where I thought 'I can do that' and just run out and do it, borrow one of Martin's guitars and play that bit just to push things along. Basically, I just started playing around again at the end of 1968, beginning of 1969.

I suppose I learned a little bit about it by listening to people like Bert Jansch and Roy Harper, people who are part of the English and American modern folk tradition. They, as self accompanists, brought something a little more interesting into the world of guitar, not just merely strumming along. They would actually be picking notes and adding little passages within a sort of chordal context; that rubbed off on me around the time I was writing songs for the *Aqualung* album. I tried to incorporate some of those ideas into my songwriting and later on *Thick As A Brick* and later albums, *War Child*, right up to today.

I tend to try to create a guitar part which is not just the question of always playing strummed chords with a pick, but as a combination of picking single notes within the chordal structure and sometimes using a couple of fingers to pick grace notes and parts of the melody or harmonies to the melody around a chordal structure. I try and do something I think is my style, but it is a style that certainly I would not have developed if it hadn't been for hearing people like Bert Jansch or Roy Harper. And Roy Harper wouldn't have developed his style if he hadn't been listening to Bert Jansch's stuff.

40

The Changing Business

Since the beginning of the modern music era – we might be inclined to call it the rock era were it not for the fact there have been a lot of other styles of music co-existing, but for our purposes, either will do – much has changed. Not only has much changed, but a plethora of adjectives might easily fall into a category of how it's changed; most will agree it's been for the worse. How often do you find yourself asking 'How in God's name could a song like that get on record, or radio?' I suppose that question has been asked by amateur critics since music began, or at least since it got its own little industry.

Mediocrity tends to be a catch-all phrase that dispels the magic of there being a logical explanation as to why we hear the bottom of the barrel when what's at the top gets lost. In this kind of environment the music business wants hits from its employees and, make no mistake about it, musicians are employed, in one sense or another. So how has a band like Tull been able to remain 'employed' for 40 years without being pink-slipped [US term for getting fired]?

ANDERSON:

There has never been any tour, since the first time we got on the plane, that didn't mean you got on the case and worked hard to sell records or concert tickets. So far in all my predictions that I do before and during a tour, I write on the ticket sales sheets the actual update on ticket sales to date that I get every three or four days from our agents. I do my predictions and last night I was 23 seats out. I have a wealth of experience to draw upon in terms of the way sales go, and a wealth of predictive experiences based on anything from the weather, religious holidays, the day of the week and all the other factors.

But as far as the balance of North American dates, the promoters and the band will make money. That's my dedicated position and always has been. I don't take dates from promoters based on the highest offers. I accept dates from promoters based on loyalty and based on sensible offers, whereby the promoter is obliged to work for his living; he doesn't just go to sleep on the job because he only has a low guarantee to meet. At the same time, I refuse and often ask promoters to re-negotiate their guarantees to me if they offer us too much money, because I don't want to be proverbially always the good guy who if the promoter doesn't cover his guarantee gives him a break. I always want a promoter to be in a situation where, even if he makes a $1,000, at least he went into percentage and that makes everybody happy. I'm sure it's become even more obvious lately, that the concert business is in definite decline and that everybody falls substantially short of, if not expectations, their hopeful anticipations of what they might sell.

I once received a fax from one of the biggest promoters in the US asking us to tour with Genesis. It's very flattering to be given equal billing on a tour like that, but I had to say no, because they were doing the exact same places as we had just done – which we call the sheds. So from a business stand point, it wasn't a very viable thing for us to do. We had been at those same venues so much over the past years. Offers like this come in quite often. We recently received two other offers of a similar type and it would be all too easy to just say, 'Yes let's go do it' but common sense had to intervene. You have to realise that you can't do everything and put yourself in position of overexposure.

That is me, if you like, having an interest and expertise in administration and the business side of my music business, as opposed to the Music Business in capital letters, which is something that has always been there. I've always had this interest in both sides of the business and it comes in handy to know what's going where because, in the end, you don't have to worry about somebody ripping you off. So that's always been, from my point of view, my idea: to have those two sides of your character is kind of fun and kind of important. When I went to art school all those years ago and started developing the serious interest in music that was always tempered by an ongoing interest in science and technology, essentially, quite opposite disciplines. I see that as being contradictory and I see it as being a nice equal balance in my life.

A lot of older people attending Jethro Tull concerts now are going for nostalgic reasons. It has something to do with their growing up period, that they want to cling on to something for whatever reason, but looking at the audience that's not all that's there; a lot of younger punters are now going to shows. They're not there because of nostalgia, they're there because of some other reason and it's fascinating as to what that reason might be.

ANDERSON:

For the most part, I'm just glad that they're there and they're enjoying it and they're wide-eyed about it, so it's good to see that the audience is as broad and varied as the average Jethro Tull album.

We are touring, but The Doors aren't and Jimi Hendrix is not, nor Muddy Waters and, however macabre it may sound for some folks, it's always going to be a case of going to see these guys while we still can, because you never know if The Rolling Stones are still going to be touring, because Keith Richards might die next year. I'm using them as an example, but the same thing applies to us.

41

The Move To Solo Work – Anderson And Barre

Martin Barre's guitar playing has kept heady company with Ian Anderson's flute up front in the mix on every Jethro Tull album since 1969. But when Barre approached the record label originally created in the early 1970s as an outlet for Tull's music, asking them to release his debut solo album, he was turned down. 'Chrysalis asked me if I intended recording a guitar album,' Barre explained from his home in Devon, England, 'which, of course, I didn't, and when I said no, they asked who would be singing. I said, "Me". They turned me down.'

Being the second longest serving member of Jethro Tull, the negative move on the record company's part was perplexing. 'I'm very, very pleased with my solo album in a way that I never normally am with Tull albums,' he explained. 'I'm very critical of things I do on Tull albums – I don't know why. In some regards, I find them very hard to listen to after we've recorded them, but with mine, when I hear a track, I still get a positive reaction from it and I think "Oh yeah, I did that right and I'm pleased with that". I think I did my very best and I don't think I could take any of those songs and do them better. I can listen to them and honestly think that they're the best I could have done them.'

For those interested in the nuts and bolts side of things, Barre recorded that first solo album, 1994's *A Trick Of Memory*, in his home studio with his arsenal of Tom Anderson electric guitars, GHS .010 to .046 Boomers strings, an array of old 1970's Marshall 50-watt amplifiers, and an old 15-watt Ampeg run through Vox, Fender or Marshall 2x12 and 4x12 cabinets.

Barre's acoustic guitars were made closer to home in England, and include a Manson and a Fylde – both small-bodied, which he claims sound great through Shure M-57 mics. Rather than rely on signal processors, he used various mics placed in strategic locations in the recording room and mixed down to one channel.

After recording side by side with Ian Anderson for 25 years, being flung into the face of recording studio mayhem all alone, Barre recorded an album that bears little resemblance to any of the Tull albums he's contributed to. Styles range from electric and acoustic jazz and R&B to Elizabethan madrigals, with a heavy rocker or two for good measure.

'Working without Ian on board was very exciting,' he explained, 'because you're in at the deep end and there's only you to answer to. When you're in that situation, you come up with the best of you, or you just collapse and you can't do it, and thankfully, I coped and I enjoyed coping with it, and I liked working with other musicians.

'I also liked being responsible for coming up with all the music; it's nice after having 25 years of sharing responsibility, where you can easily duck out of a decision or just pass the buck to somebody else, particularly to Ian, who's obviously got vast resources as far as music goes.'

Although there had been a lot of pressure on Barre to do an album like most 'name' guitarists and to turn out a disc of guitar histrionics, he decided to record with a band instead of producing an entirely solo effort. 'I've got dozens of recordings of guitar albums: Joe Satriani, Steve Vai, Scott Henderson, Jeff Beck – there's so many great guitar players – I've got them all,' he continued, 'but I just didn't want to be another one of those, and I also wanted a band that I could tour with.'

In keeping with his approach to maintaining a good band spirit and a high level of musicianship, the album was recorded live without any editing; all of the backing tracks were played live and he went with the original arrangements. 'I didn't really want to change them. At the time I thought "That's the song I wrote and I don't want to change it". We didn't even use a click track, sequencers, or drum machines. No musician is perfect, and it's the imperfections that make them different.'

With the obvious left of centre material the album comprises, radio, predictably, ignored it for the most part, but Barre was not fazed: 'I am sure records like that won't get airplay, particularly when you send a package off in the mail and hope it falls into the right hands. But when I've rung up a few stations in America on the spur of the moment and asked if I could come over and talk and play the album, the response has been great.'

When a group has been around as long as Tull have, they're questioned continually about how long they intend to carry on recording and touring: 'In many ways it's more fun to tour and record now with everything a bit more laid back and under control,' Barre reflected. 'We would really love a Number 1 album, but it would be unbelievably difficult for us to get something like that at this stage of the game.'

Divinities And Roots To Branches

The nature of Ian Anderson's solo album, 1995's *Divinities: Twelve Dances With God*, was a tad left field compared to recent Jethro Tull projects. Anderson explains how it came into being:

> About a year and a half before, EMI Records' classical division started to try to make contact with me to discuss doing an album for them. I assumed in some classical context, and it took some months before I agreed to have a meeting with them to explain to them why I didn't want to do that sort of thing. But they explained, what they had in mind was not for me to play with an orchestra, doing Mozart, not for there to be an orchestra-meets-Jethro Tull kind of album, but that they wanted me to write some original music for the flute and orchestral instruments. [Author's note: Quite right too Ian! The hardcore Tull fans will, no doubt, have noticed that I am not even discussing 1985's *A Classic Case* – the classical arrangements of Tull songs with the London Symphony Orchestra]
>
> They suggested some sort of religious theme and we got talking, and I agreed to do some demos which they liked and then went on to do a whole album. This was challenging for me, because I have never written a body of instrumental work on, and for, the instrument that I'm best known for playing. So it was quite a challenge to have to think in terms of melody, in terms of structure of what I could do on the flute, and actually extend my flute playing technique to accommodate the need to make it carry the whole tune, as it were. So it wasn't easy, I really had to work pretty hard, but I think it was worth it in the end.
>
> It's gratifying when a record company comes up with that sort of enthusiasm and that sort of commitment to support an artist in something that is obviously not, primarily, a commercial venture. So it was nice for EMI to have made that effort. I suggested to them, subsequently, that they should probably be in contact now with George Michael and with Prince, because they're such nice guys at EMI Classical Music Division I feel they should meet some of these other artists who seem to have a little problem getting along with their record company!

The tour for the album was wrapped up that June in time for Anderson to head back to England in order to finish the art work and mastering for the new Tull album, which had been recorded and mixed in the spring. There had been speculation that Anderson might have prolonged the *Divinities* tour, but he was already lining up the itinerary for the Tull project. 'We rehearsed for the Jethro Tull tour during that August, so something pretty special would have to come up to take me away from that for the remainder of the summer,' he said at the time.

While speaking with Anderson that year – 1995 – the idea of a sequel to *Thick As A Brick* was showing up in conversation, or at least rumour. There had been some information leaked that the up and coming Tull album was to have been a sequel to *Thick As A Brick* .

'That's not the case,' he said emphatically. 'It was a possibility that we might produce an album that was a little bit more presented as a whole rather than a series of individual songs but, inevitably, when you start working on things, you realise there are a number of different directions which, if they should turn out in the rehearsal period to be leading down the same track, then fine. But if they are actually representing different directions both lyrically and melodically ... to cobble things together to sort of sit together isn't a good idea, you know, they've got to be part of a whole or not. What we have are nine or ten substantial songs, some of which have some thematic bonding, but nonetheless do not deserve to be linked into some grandiose master plan. What we have is a Jethro Tull rock album – most of it is fairly up sounding music; in fact I still want to record one more piece of music for it, because quite often I like to get close to the end of an album and then come up with some final piece or pieces that fit the last little bits into the jigsaw puzzle.'

This was a conversation we had immediately preceding what became *Roots To Branches* and the idea of a *TAAB2* album might have been considered something of a gamble coming at a time when progressive rock was going through a rough patch, compared to today.

42

Tull Trends

The days of seeing Jethro Tull at the 20,000 [seat] arenas in Canada will not return but, if you pop into many countries of Europe, 10,000 seaters are not uncommon. There were years from about '72 to '75, when Jethro Tull did the indoor arenas and that was within the 10,000 to 25,000 seater venues from Madison Square Garden to Maple Leaf Gardens, or whatever, and that was something we did and we still, from time to time, find ourselves in those kind of environments. But Jethro Tull has always been, and has never left at any time, the theatre tour circuit. Playing theatres, like in London, is a classic example. The fans were vociferous in their dislike of going to see Jethro Tull at Wembley Arena. Jethro Tull, in London, having learned their lesson in the early '70s, always played theatre dates, because that's where the British audiences expected to see Jethro Tull and we play exactly the same circuit now in the UK as we played back in the late '60s and early '70s. And they are the same venues that everybody plays if they are not playing Wembley, Earl's Court or the NEC. We're talking major bands doing the UK tours and the majority of them are playing places like Wolverhampton Civic Centre, which is a 2,000 capacity crowd in a rather dingy place in a town near Birmingham.

Yet, miraculously, and surprisingly, you find multi-platinum artists from the USA actually playing at Wolverhampton Civic Centre and playing virtually nowhere else in the UK. I went to see The Spin Doctors there once and although they were very good, the audience pretty much rejected them. You can't equate size of venue with popularity, you have to equate your chart status in *Billboard* with the underlying popularity and there's no better example of that than The Grateful Dead and, in the '70s, Led Zeppelin, who never had any singles. They had a lot of lead tracks that were given a very serious amount of airing on rock radio, as did Jethro Tull, but they weren't a singles band, didn't have any pop hits and, to my knowledge, were not ever an AM radio act in the US. But their record sales would be close to about 100 million.

Jethro Tull today probably earns for EMI somewhere in the region of a million and a half to two million dollars a year. What Anderson has said to EMI, not unreasonably, is that Tull are the kind of act that most record companies, although many of them don't realise it, would love to have, because Tull are the guys that actually pay for the cleaning ladies to clean the toilets and the offices in every EMI office in the world. And there are many of them. As a contribution to overhead, Jethro Tull is the kind of band most people would love to have if their accountancy office pointed it out to them that this is what keeps the record company going.

Of course, every record company likes to be visible and every record company likes to see itself with two or three acts in the *Billboard* Top 40 at any one time, and get at least half a dozen multi-platinum sales per year. It's visibility, but it isn't what makes the world go round. What makes the world go round for EMI, is the Pink Floyd catalogue and The Beatles catalogue and the vast amount of artist catalogues which are continuing to sell. The marketing potential for catalogues are in a pretty similar category as to marketing opportunities that exist for Beethoven, Mozart and other guys.

ANDERSON:

I tend to joke about nicking a song from Bach's box set for Jethro Tull but, all joking aside, that is the position I think pop and rock music is in and, in a very small way, Jethro Tull is a part of the phenomena and the ongoing, 'just simmering' level of popularity is something which I don't think is varied. In a very obvious way in the last fifteen years the catalogue is holding up very well.

When Chrysalis had an office in New York, they had a particular guy who was the AOR radio guy and it was his first year working with them and I think he was only there two years; his name was Kevin Sutter. He was a relatively new employee and most anxious to make his mark, and we were kind of the first act in town that he got his teeth into. He worked hard on the band, but importantly, rock radio in the US had recently done an about turn back to the AOR format. Many of the stations in the early '80s had gone into what was termed 'alternative' or whatever. It was their way to play to the 16 to 24 demographic and they stopped playing bands like Tull. Jethro Tull suffered in 1982 with *Broadsword And The Beast* because it didn't get any radio play. All the radio stations had gone into this mass move seeking a different audience.

The last time Jethro Tull had an album, KNEW apologised and said 'Sorry for the irony because although we play Jethro Tull, we now play classic rock, the cut-off point is 1978, so we only play Jethro Tull music up to 1978.'

New artists get a tremendous amount of support from their record company, where someone is really carrying the flag for them and is working their balls off for them. But it's true to say for bands like Tull, and I expect the same thing applies for the Moody Blues and a whole bunch of other bands that have been around as long as we have, that it's not ever going to be the same. A member of Pink Floyd voiced a complaint to me just a couple of weeks ago that seemed to suggest that they didn't find it particularly easy to deal with either the men in suits, you know, the record company, or, indeed, the hip young things who are the folks who they deal with in television and radio. But that's the way things are for Jethro Tull.

To have a hit album and gold or platinum record in the US could not be done without a major breakthrough in television and I don't think that would be a possibility with the kind of music that I write, and the kind of profile the band has, as far as MTV is concerned. Sure, we can wander in, maybe get a few minutes of time on *Much Music*, or something else if we visit Canada, but if you're looking at the global picture, Jethro Tull does not get asked to play on German television and yet some of the bands being played on German TV – and I watch them on satellite TV in Europe – I wonder how on earth do these folks get on German television? And yet, Jethro Tull, who outsell them in concert and outsell them in record sales by ten to one, must not be deemed right for television.

It's just a fact of life that people have this sort of view that Jethro Tull is basically a live act and not oriented toward television. Tull are not going to go out of their way to seek those possibilities even when they do occur. Anderson is quite happy with that. He also has this theory that if the band ever had that sort of PR person, the type who never stops working for them, they would just have burned themselves out a long time ago in terms of overstayed welcome.

ANDERSON [SPEAKING AFTER EMI BOUGHT CHRYSALIS]:
I think our reputation is based on live performance and relatively low advertising. We do what is necessary to sell concert tickets, we do what is necessary to sell what is a reasonable amount of records, but beyond that it's just not worth going to town in terms of the level of publicity and promotion that would be appropriate or expected as a first or second time out contemporary young rock act. I think Jethro Tull is different. Our rather low key way still requires a lot of effort on my part, because records don't sell themselves and concert tickets don't sell themselves. I actually put in a few hours of work most days for six weeks before major tours and virtually every day while on the tour. There's a lot of great folks that I've worked with over the years who have made a great effort for

Jethro Tull. Unfortunately, the average person is only around for two or three years before they either get fired, or perhaps they get an offer of a better job elsewhere, and so there's very little chance to build that loyalty.

A particular occurrence a few years ago at Chrysalis Records in the UK, was a more obvious example when the international department was closed and they fired everyone. EMI bought out Chrysalis after that and I knew that was the beginning of the end, because without an international department you cannot be a proper record company. After that, people just dropped like flies and amongst those folks were a lot of people who, not just for Jethro Tull, but for many other acts, were great supporters and crusaders.

And when I write *my* book [laughs] I will be most anxious to point out the names of the folks who really, I think, deserve that long term credit for having supported Jethro Tull when we were not always a great payoff for them. I have a great deal of loyalty for the idea of Chrysalis Records, but I don't own any stock in Chrysalis or EMI Records. My loyalty actually has to be transferred to EMI Records and, within that, a big and very global and somewhat mixed operation, because as far as the US is concerned it is a mess.

I've had to learn to live with the fact that the people I developed my early musical career along side are no longer there, and I have to accept that there are few people at Chrysalis that I know any longer and even fewer at EMI, but at least it's a start. If I were to go to another record company I doubt if I would enjoy the same tenuous relationship that I have with Chrysalis or EMI, so [laughs] after some considerable re-negotiating, I am literally signing another contract with Chrysalis right now for a new Jethro Tull pair of albums and Chrysalis Music as publishers after a relationship of over 20 years. So, one way or another we find our way through it all. They still want to represent me and I am still happy, ultimately, to be with them.

My job during these next few months is really to try to establish the best rapport with the record company as possible, so you can be critical about them and they can be critical about us, that we're not – and never have been – a mainstream commercial act. So we have to accept each other for what we are and make the best of the arrangement. So I now have to find the new Cindy Redmond [Cindy Redmond was a publicist for Chrysalis New York at the time of *Crest Of A Knave* who worked very hard for the band] and I have to try and find the folks within the record company who make that little bit of extra effort on the basis of, hopefully, striking a cordial personal relationship with key individuals.

There was also a press person in the Chrysalis International department in the UK during the preparation of this book who was tireless in her work for Tull and we became good friends, but she was one who lost her job when the department closed. Sadly, I have misplaced her details in a lost set of boxes. I was planning to visit her while in England, she had been so helpful with my connection to Tull as a writer and journalist. It was not a happy time for the label, and the artists losing employees of such worth was a blow to the workings of the company.

This interview was conducted back in 1995 and some things did change down the road. There is an old saying that goes: 'Big fleas have little fleas upon their backs to bite them, and little fleas have lesser fleas, and so *ad infinitum'* After acquiring Chrysalis, EMI Records themselves were recently bought out by Universal.

More than just the names of record companies have changed though; the face of the entire industry has gone through a few facelifts since the days of the one track per side from the group of six major progressive bands in the early and late 1970s.

'The degree of business reality, the pragmatic approach towards rock and pop music as a commodity now as opposed to the late '60s and early '70s, when there was a cheerful and amateurish enthusiasm from people like Richard Branson, and Ellis and Wright at Chrysalis, or any one of quite a few of the smaller labels that existed back then that enjoyed a fair degree of commercial success doing what, to them, was fun,' reflects Anderson. 'Since then things have changed a great deal.

'The Bransons, the Ellis' and Wrights have had to admit that, ultimately, they were better off taking the money and getting out and leaving it to the hard-nosed professionals to run their businesses for them. Quite frankly, in this day and age, I am much happier to be part of an EMI-controlled operation than to be subject to the whims and occasional excesses of the likes of Terry Ellis or Chris Wright who are not cut out to be businessmen, certainly not capable of calling the shots in the way they might have done in years gone by. I say that not with any sense of wishing to do them down, but it is just the reality of it.'

With the advances that have been made in technology from all angles, it's surprising to learn that Tull use very little of that technology to get music across, apart from several of the 1980s albums, when synthesisers were *de rigueur*.

ANDERSON:
I don't rely on the technology that much. Increasingly over the years I've been drawn away from that stuff. When it first appeared in '82 -'83, when the first

sequencers, primitive though they were, and the first so-called drum machines and samplers arrived, it was very interesting to understand how they worked and what might be done with them. It can be very useful to have sequenced music available when you're doing demos as it makes it easy to present them to someone else but, as a form of finished music, it becomes rather sterile. I don't have a problem playing with sampled acoustic sounds, but I feel that they've got to be played in real time. The nuances and the subtleties of programming are such that dynamic control, tempo sensitivity is much better than it was before – you still have something that is fundamentally at its best when it is kept at its simplest. It can never have that variety of unbelievably complex and obscure levels of human interaction.

The charm and the vitality of the best of American rock music is something which is basically a one off performance, live, real and something unapologetic, not within the realms of replication via computer technology. Since we first heard that thing which was Grunge, it has already moved on geographically and moved on musically. That's not to say that bands like Pearl Jam are not in their own way still flying the flag, they are the vanguard of something that was very special and very peculiarly North American, at a certain point in time when it was good to see American rock music coming back to the forefront of the world's attention.

Personally, I infinitely prefer that kind of music than the latest offerings from most of the British pop groups. I personally do not enjoy the music of Blur and Oasis. Similarly, it's bands like Bon Jovi that are filling the stadiums over here and Bon Jovi are the sort of show biz, sanitised, middle-of-the-road schlock rock of America. To me they are a large scale cabaret band.

43

Learning

Ian Anderson is his own harshest critic at times and can also be disarmingly modest. His insistence that his guitar playing was second, maybe third-rate, is well documented, and led to his decision to trade his electric guitar in for a microphone and flute. That, of course, doesn't explain how this 'second rate' guitarist emerged on the *Stand Up* album as almost a virtuoso acoustic guitarist. Certainly, within a few years he had mastered the instrument to the point where many accomplished guitarists would have difficulty replicating many of the Tull acoustic ballads.

'In the beginning, I didn't tend to spend a lot of time learning to play the guitar,' Anderson explained. 'I began by playing black American based music with urban country blues; people like Muddy Waters and John Lee Hooker. It was pretty basic stuff and I was O.K. doing that, until I heard Eric Clapton in his John Mayall days. I realised this was a guy taking a big step forward, he had a much more rhythmic and precise way of playing, which I felt was really beyond me and, because at that moment as you'll recall, we were about to work with Mick Abrahams. It seemed to me that rather than just be a strummer or a second guitarist, that Mick was a much better guitar player, much closer to the style of, if you like, an Eric Clapton. So it seemed much more appropriate for me to try and switch to something a little different. Maybe it was more than a subconscious move on my part to pick a reed instrument.'

So having sold off his guitar equipment, Anderson went to the local music shop just to browse and see if anything would take his fancy. In fact, he ended up trading in his guitar for a microphone and a flute. 'It was actually a few months before I got to grips with playing the instrument,' he states matter of factly.

About the time Jethro Tull effectively began in February of 1968, Anderson was already playing the flute on stage and finding that he was getting a more than a little attention for not being a guitar hero. The first complete piece of music that he learned was 'Serenade To A Cuckoo' by Roland Kirk. The reason for that was when Jeffrey Hammond heard that Anderson was learning to play flute, he played him an album of Roland Kirk's.

'I guess I probably heard this particular track two or three times and it stuck in my head,' remembers Anderson. 'I had an immediate affinity for that kind of music which was not jazz. That particular piece was more blues based and it was simple. The improvisation element, which is mine more than Roland Kirk's, owed more to Eric Clapton than to Roland Kirk, whose background was far more real and almost academic jazz. My approach to it was much more simplified and more naive, and the scat style of singing stuff while playing, singing over the instrument, is something that's not Roland Kirk's property or mine, or Mose Allison's; it goes back to the beginning of music – it's got to be 10,000 years old. It's just that people started singing along with their instruments. Many piano players have adopted little things like singing along with what they're playing, you know that kind of thing Mose Allison does?

I actually met Roland Kirk in America because we were booked to play at a jazz festival. Roland Kirk was appearing there and he was a perfect gentleman, who offered some supportive words for doing his piece of music. I have heard that he could be very abrasive, very difficult to deal with. He could very easily have torn me up for wrecking his song, but instead he was very polite.'

44

Technology

ANDERSON:

My working relationship with Mobile Fidelity [the sound lab that remastered many of Tull's albums] goes back a long way and, of course, in order for a company to do the sort of specialised work like Mobile Fidelity does is more economical for a smaller outfit than for a company like EMI. To produce that kind of quality product when you're dealing with something like 40,000, 50,000, 60,000 units, EMI wouldn't bother with that.

Of course, to make sure that the fan gets a higher quality product, I have as my listening reference my remastered *Aqualung* and my remastered *Thick As A Brick* and I also have the digital clones of all the original masters kept up in my studio to ensure that what I listen to is top, not second, quality multi-generational copies, and not something that comes from Hong Kong.

One of the projects I'm working on is the full cataloguing of Jethro Tull masters and I'm not just talking about two-track masters but the complete multi-track masters. For example, I had the original sixteen-track master of *Aqualung* and the digitally remastered version of the CD and the multi-track playing simultaneously and was switching back and forth to make sure that I wasn't dealing with an outtake but the original. I noticed that the multi-track which was over twenty years old sounded better. The studio that we recorded the album in was new then and wasn't giving us the kind of quality we had hoped for at the time. I've always maintained that the *Aqualung* album suffered from more problems technically than any other album. So when the time came to mix and cut the album, we ended up compensating for the technical problems and ending up with an inferior product, and it's amazing to me that the multi-track still sounds so good today. Eventually, I'll get around to re-doing that album because of the advances in technology and rather than it being a simple two-track mix it will probably end up being a five-track surround sound recording.

I feel very possessive about the catalogue and I think you have to be ethical as far as offering quality for reasonable money. But that side of me is a very a different animal to the side of me that has to go into the studio and play instruments or write music, because there's nothing wrong with being two-dimensional as a professional rather than perhaps [laughs] simply one dimensional. Although it's, perhaps, relatively rare in pop music and the rock world that you find people who can actually understand about finances, or understand anything about the way it works; how to put together records.

Since 1974, Jethro Tull has, effectively, not had a manager and Anderson always tried to understand, since he first walked into a studio, what was going on. And since the first time he was actually in the receipt of any money he has always tried to understand something about taxation and basic accounting.

ANDERSON:

So I realise these days, that had I ever considered letting myself just follow whatever the status quo was and just made music and let everybody else simply manipulate and control and ultimately market the thing that I do, without me really understanding what was going on, would have been very foolish and that is a classic situation for most artists to be in.

It's fairly easy to decide which members of the band from the past and the present receive particular royalties; there is a clear cut contract and it just happens, because of the outside activities that I have been included in, like fish farming, that I have an accounting department as part of my head office in Scotland. These days there's a computer programme which we, in fact, inherited from Chrysalis Records when EMI bought them out and twice a year the right payments are made. Then there's a programme that analyses every track on every album and calculates what every individual in the more than twenty earning members of Jethro Tull is due.

That process happens twice yearly and it's actually down now to a few hours work. It used to take a couple of weeks [laughs]. The most arduous part of the operation, and least cost-effective part, is sticking the stamps on the envelopes because everything else is on computers. There are guys who played for Jethro Tull for whom those royalty cheques are actually, if not the only money they make, very important for them to get. It has always been a principle of mine that no one has ever had to wait for more than one or two weeks to get their share of the money. In these days, it's an even more important operation, because a lot of the guys who left Jethro Tull, left to do other things outside music. In some cases, I think those royalty cheques are really very important, not the size so much, but more importantly, the regularity and the predictability of something they can actually almost budget for.

Looking back, it's within about a 10% difference on a six month basis, and so it is actually important. And these are people I speak to on the phone, for the most part, on a pretty regular basis; many of whom I see fairly regularly as well. So the last thing you really want to have to speak to somebody about is money or business or financial relationships. You effectively put that to bed and it really doesn't have to enter into conversations.

45

Picking The Team

Once all of the people within the Tull circle who had been friends of Anderson's back in Blackpool (Evans, Hammond and Barlow) had left for the last time, a new criteria for finding the right musicians for the band had to be found. It's no secret that the magic of the 1970s band, which was made up of friends, produced the biggest and most long lasting of the group's music. So how did Ian Anderson make the leap from a band of friends to branching out with unknowns?

ANDERSON:

Early on, it was a question of people that I knew, because I didn't really know anybody else. When Glenn was asked to leave, or fired from the band – not out of any kind of malice or disagreement, he'd just wasn't cutting it musically or socially with the rest of us – we felt that it really had run its course and there really wasn't anybody else to ask, it was either go back and ask Jeffrey, or we would be looking around in the dark for someone new.

When Jeffrey left in his turn, and we had to find somebody to replace him, we asked John Glascock to join – somebody we had been working with for some weeks on tour in the US, who played with a support band called Carmen which had disbanded by then. When he left the band and subsequently died, he was first replaced by a fellow we knew from Blackpool named Tony Williams. After John died, we actually had to look around for the first time for somebody who was a bass player in the music world. The name Dave Pegg came up because, by then, Fairport Convention had pretty well disbanded. I would say it's never very easy; it's never really a case of sitting down and saying 'This guy would be really good to play with so we'll get rid of the one we've got and go with this one instead.' That's never been the reason for doing it, it's only ever been that someone has gone for whatever reason and then you have to look around and you tend to pick people you already know rather than go out and look for someone completely different.

That has happened in the case of Andy Giddings, for example, who was one of many keyboard players that we worked with in 1990-1991. When he joined the band we had been working with probably three or four other keyboard players trying to find someone who would click musically and personally. It wasn't particularly easy to find someone that time. Drummers have usually been someone we knew from some other context, people you would play with as a support band. So it's not easy and the worst possible thing to have to do is to go out into the wide world and do auditions. I've had to go out and look for some percussionists in a particular field of music and having to get in touch with a lot of people and going through tapes to find a couple of guys who will probably be able to do the job.

I must admit, I don't ever like to have to work with strangers, because it really is hard work to forge the relationship, musically as well as personally. On the other hand, when it works out and you've got some new fellows there that you get on with, it's very inspiring, musically and personally to have some new faces around. A lot of times I'm asked to play with other people. I genuinely just don't terribly feel in the mood for coping with that. It's very flattering, to part of me, but the other part of me can't be bothered to do that show or, socially becoming part of somebody else's world, because I don't do drugs and I don't do parties. I don't have quite the same lifestyle as the average musician, so I'm not really at home with most other musicians (or at least I don't think I am). I haven't known enough of them to be sure, but the one thing that would worry me is that I'm not really part of their world – to live that sort of lifestyle.

46

Family Matters

Ian Anderson has been very careful to keep his private and public life separate. There are no scandals in his world and he has had the foresight and intelligence to not bring his family and their private lives into the open. The result is that very little is known about that part of his life beyond what he will obviously talk about, or what may have slipped out over the years. Were more of the pop and rock personalities of the era able to maintain that level of privacy, they might not be constantly fighting with the tabloids. But when asked about his family and private life, it just seems there isn't much to tell – or he's only telling a bit. But certainly at this point in time it's a very small aspect of the Tull story, so the following piece is quite short.

ANDERSON:

> Now that our children are sufficiently grown, my wife, Shona, travels around with me most of the time. She was originally in the PR department at EMI Records and then went to work for Chrysalis, which is where I first met her. Eventually, she left there and then came to work as Jethro Tull's secretary. She is subsequently working again for the band in the sense of doing the PR with various people in different countries. More importantly, she is doing the job that most people ascribe to tour managers, that is, travel arrangements and hotels and keeping tabs on the interviews and the promo stuff and actually doing the settlements with the promoters every night – which is a couple of hours of work with computers and calculators – and going through the financial stuff. So she's out there doing that stuff. In recent years, the fans have got to know her and who she is. I think people who are close to the band are well aware of what my wife does but, on the other hand, we just kind of do what needs to be done, it's no big deal, it's not the sort of stuff that makes the press, if you know what I mean. We've had a couple of children, they've gone to university and she is working for Jethro Tull again.
>
> My children have always had music around them, they know what it is, they've always had fairly broad tastes in music, both of them, because they had

access to it. A lot of children don't, because they only see a very narrow world of what's on television or the local radio stations and it's very driven by peer group likes and dislikes as well. I think our children, because music has been part of their life, have witnessed it in a lot more variety, they've had broader tastes. My son is more personally involved in music than my daughter who likes music, but doesn't particularly play music. My son plays mostly drums these days – not in a band but for his own amusement. He's been in school bands and things, but he's quite serious about playing music and has a very broad taste.

They both studied television and radio; you know, broadcasting and sort of media type stuff; it's a very competitive field. It's kind of like how everybody wanted to work in a recording studio or record company 30 years ago; everybody wanted that job. The area is so competitive that the engineer at my studio, a few years ago, turned down a fellow who wanted to work so bad that he was willing to just make the tea. A while later it turned out that he was the engineer and co-producer of the most successful album by The Police and we didn't even give him a job making that tea. So it's a tough world out there; it would probably be easier to be a dentist or doctor.

I mentioned to you in an earlier interview, that my brother had emigrated to Canada. What I neglected to say was that he only was in Canada for about three years, when he first got married, then came back to Scotland to work for a big company connected with the oil industry; he was a marine engineer, you see. He came back to the UK when things began to happen in terms of oil exploration and he's now retired, so actually both my brothers are retired and we still don't really see them because they live up in the Glasgow area.

My Scottish activities have always been in other parts of Scotland. Glasgow is not an area I usually go to. I'll see them once in a while, maybe once a year, if that. We're really not a very close family. My brothers are much older than me. We have a different kind of lifestyle, different kind of careers, different backgrounds all together. We're respectful of each other as siblings, but we don't have much in common. They're more similar in age and they live in the same area and see each other quite often. They fool around in boats and do the same sort of things they did as teenagers. They are in their late 70s, which makes me the kid brother. I never was part of their growing up and they were never part of my growing up – they left home, so we're not really close at all. I remember when I was young they were at home, but they were going off to college and, after that, they went their separate ways. While I was growing up it was, more or less, like being an only child. Basically, they were never home and by the time I got to my teenage years, they were settled down in far away parts of the country, so I didn't witness their growing and they didn't witnessed my growing, and that's probably the most profound time when people get bonded together, in those formative years.

The conversation about Anderson's family was actually part of a spin-off conversation from the formative years of what Jeffrey Hammond referred to as 'The Blackpool Mafia', which were Ian John Evans and Jeffrey. Talking about his family is either uncomfortable or uninteresting to Anderson, and so the conversation quickly reverted back to friends as opposed to family.

ANDERSON:

Going back to what I was talking about before and Jeffrey; those are the years when you form friendships and that's when we knew each other best, as teenagers. We're very different people, but there's a bond between us, it's always been there and always will be there. It's a very important part of your life and if you miss out, even with your own brothers, even with your own blood kin, I think you miss it, it's gone, you can't go back. Fortunately blood is only slightly thicker than water, I think. My oldest brother's name is Robin and the other is Alister. Alister was the marine engineer and Robin was involved with the Scottish Ballet, although he was originally a pharmaceutical chemist. Before that he was an ice skater; he got badly run over when he was a kid and he got very seriously crippled and as a therapy, when he was learning to walk again, they put skates on him and towed him around the ice, and he was able to skate a little bit before he could walk.

Then he carried on with skating as a therapy and he became quite a good skater. By the age of 21 he was the Scottish Figure Skating Champion, turned professional and that was the end of it. The first week of skating for a living he collapsed on the ice and was told he would never skate again. He didn't have the stamina from the damage of the early injuries – it would never allow him to skate professionally. So he went back and finished his pharmaceutical degree, became a pharmacist and he did that until he was 40.

[Author's note: Since conducting this interview, Ian's middle brother, Alister, passed away recently and we offer sincere condolences to the family for their sad loss]

Anderson likes to think, perhaps, it was the fact that he had not toed the line and was, by then, becoming successful as a musician and had done his own thing, as it were, that influenced Robin to quit his job and to go off to work for the Arts Council as a trainee theatre manager at an arts theatre in England.

From there he reached the heights of theatre manager and administrator for the Scottish Ballet, which he did for about twenty years. When he retired from that, he returned to being a pharmaceutical chemist in his spare time and went back to college to catch up on what he missed on earlier in life.

While we were on the topic of his brothers and Robin's involvement with the Scottish Ballet, the old story of how Ian Anderson and Jon Anderson of Yes had collaborated on a project for the ballet came up.

ANDERSON:

When Jon Anderson and I got involved in that project together, the contact was actually the artistic director, who was also the house choreographer. He wanted to do something away from the mainstream, the main sort of crowd-pleasing ballet that most people are accustomed to. He wanted to do something a bit broader in terms of bringing in some other musical forces to the thing. The idea of commissioning some work from contemporary musicians was my brother's. I don't know where the original suggestions came from and whether somebody else was involved. At any rate, we did this stuff and I don't think it was terribly successful, because the trouble with writing music for ballet is that it's very demanding on the orchestra as far as rehearsal time and performance time.

I have always found working with orchestras very frustrating, which is why, at this late stage in the game, I'm determined to try and write some orchestral music, or music that an orchestra can play in support of what I do, which is actually, largely, easy for them to play. Let me do the difficult stuff and give them fairly easy stuff to do; maybe just limit the things you really have to rehearse with them just to the few tricky bits that they do have. It's not really fair on them when they know that they need more time to rehearse to do their best, and they just don't have it because no one can afford to pay an orchestra that kind of money to do the amount of rehearsal that a rock band has to do.

47

Success And Failure And
Living In The Future

I like the reference to the Blackpool Mafia; it has a certain, almost surrealistic warmth to it when you realise it was a nickname for a group of friends in school who grew up to be, at one time, the most popular rock band in the world, with an underlying friendship on the part of some that will outlive the musical entity. Therefore, the subtitle to this next, section is: 'The Blackpool Mafia'.

ANDERSON:

When you're growing up and you're 15 or 16 years old, you connect with the guys you're growing up with. There is a camaraderie between you when you're growing up in all its nuances, so the people that you meet and make friends with form a very special time in your life – you know, those magical moments in everybody's life from puberty until the end of your college life when you're in your early 20s. It's a really special time, everything is just so exciting, everything is happening, everything is written in terms of personality, in terms of your experiences. Everything is so profound, you never forget those moments as a vital part. Most of us, whether we make movies, make music, paint or whatever, do live off those moments for the rest of our lives and they are the vital five to ten years where most of our real life experiences are born.

Those relationships are very, very special, and they're also pretty volatile, but I think they're pretty special in a sense that you shared something at the time, or when you were all virgins, in the sense of this deep practical amalgamation that you make with other people for some creative purpose. Whether it's your first girlfriend or getting together with your buddies and forming your first garage band, it's something very intense and a very special period of time. In the case of John Evans, Barrie Barlow, Jeffrey Hammond and me, these were our first experiences at playing music, our first experiences of getting in front of an audience. I think those moments are special and they're always there and

I would like to think that those guys remember those moments with fondness, not regret.

I'm sure that Jeffrey and I are still quite close. We don't see each other that much, maybe three times a year and we talk on the phone and stuff, like real buddies, because we don't live that close, maybe an hour and a half from each other. It's not very convenient because of families, but I guess we've remained on close terms and there is a special bond that exists between me and Jeffrey that is not between me and a bunch of other ex-Jethro Tull members. Jeffrey is a very creative, a very off-the-wall and genuinely eccentric character and is one those people who I deeply regret is no longer with the band.

Anderson was pretty angry with him at the time he wanted to leave, because he felt he had a lot more to offer Jethro Tull as a musician. Jeffrey never saw himself as a musician, he always felt that he was a sham, he didn't feel that he was the real thing and Anderson would say 'That doesn't matter, it doesn't matter how you get there, it's the end result that's important.'

ANDERSON:

I still think, listening to Jeffrey's contribution, a lot of it may have been taught to him parrot-fashion, but there is stuff that he played of his own invention and, in a way, he played it with a level of performance that was unique. So for me, it doesn't matter how you get there. Jeffrey is a much better musician than the average bass player or cellist in the average symphony orchestra, who is just reading the music that is given to him. Jeffrey did that, and more, given that he had no musical education. I think he did a great job and you don't have to excuse yourself for having done what you did without the benefit of it necessarily coming naturally to you. I've made the same disclaimers with regard to my vocal abilities. The bottom line is: once you've done it and are recognised for it, well that's it. It's too late to change what you've done, you now actually have to live up to that reputation and I always felt that Jeffrey bowed out too early.

He still had a lot to offer the band and it was a great shame that he decided that he'd gone down that road far enough. He always did make it clear that he was only going to be in it for three or four years, or whatever, and if he could make some money and never have to work again that was good. And that's what he achieved and now, seemingly, it's too late to change his mind to get him to come back. We actually had Jeffrey lined up to come to do a TV show in Vienna with us. His wife was ill and he couldn't make it last minute, but it would have been great to have Jeffrey on stage again.

Epilogue
All The World's A Stage –
Wrapping Things Up

J-Tull Dot Com (1999)
Spiral / Dot Com / AWOL / Nothing @ All / Wicked Windows / Hunt By Numbers / Hot Mango Flush / El Niño / Black Mamba / Mango Surprise / Bends Like A Willow / Far Alaska / The Dog-Ear Years / A Gift Of Roses

As the new millennium drew near, Tull pre-empted it with 1999's *J-T Dot Com* which not only ushered in the internet age, but was also their URL [however, they seem to have the stronger www.jethrotull.com as their web address now]. It had a number of great songs, the Ian Anderson solo material was not evident and orchestral musings had not yet arrived. *Dot Com* was a solid album that was a celebration and could have been a continuation of new, great Tull offerings. It wasn't, but was a swansong to the Tull recording careers of Andy Giddings and Jon Noyce, which, for the latter, had only just begun. They did stay with the touring band for a few more years though. To date, it is the last real Tull rock album. It probably wasn't intended to be anything like that, but with the material that followed it being mainly Ian Anderson's solo work, that is the way things panned out. A good marketing ploy on this album was the secret bonus track that was to introduce Anderson's solo album *The Secret Language Of Birds*.

The Secret Language Of Birds (2000)
The Secret Language Of Birds / The Little Flower Girl / Montserrat / Postcard Day / The Water Carrier / Set-Aside / A Better Moon / Sanctuary / The Jasmine Corridor / The Habanero Reel / Panama Freighter / The Secret Language Of Birds, Part II / Boris Dancing / Circular Breathing / The Stormont Shuffle / Extra Track Intro / In the Grip Of Stronger Stuff / Thick As A Brick

Rupi's Dance (**2003**)
Calliandra Shade (The Cappuccino Song) / Rupi's Dance / Lost In Crowds / A Raft Of Penguins / A Week Of Moments / A Hand Of Thumbs / Eurology / Old Black Cat / Photo Shop / Pigeon Flying Over Berlin Zoo / Griminelli's Lament / Not Ralitsa Vassileva / Two Short Planks / Extra Track: Birthday Card At Christmas

An interesting project was Anderson's third solo album, 2000's *The Secret Language Of Birds* which came five years after *Divinities*. It was not dissimilar to the preceding album, although showed his interests moving further and further away from rock (as was evidenced by the orchestra album and tour in 2005). In the same way that Tull started the brash 1980s with synthesizers on *A*, Anderson captured the more naturalistic multi-ethnic zeitgeist of the new millennium. What fans and record companies alike have wanted from Anderson is an acoustic album representing the type of material such as 'Look Into The Sun' from *Stand Up*. *Rupi's Dance* was supposedly that album at long last, but so much time has passed since those acoustic ballads of old, that *Rupi* just didn't seem to fall in that zone. It is perplexing in that it is a departure from *Divinities* and *The Secret Language Of Birds* in style, but doesn't fall into anything from the Tull of old either. Perhaps had this material been brought to the band, and sparkled up with some heavy lead lines and the full Tull treatment, it might have been a fairly enjoyable Tull album. As it is, I never know how to look at it and I recall listening frequently to come to some sort of final comment – I never found one.

The bonus track of 'Birthday Card At Christmas' was an early Xmas present, which also opened the Christmas album which came hot on the heels of *Rupi's Dance*.

The Jethro Tull Christmas Album (**2003**)
Birthday Card At Christmas / Holly Herald - Hark! The Herald Angels Sing - The Holly And The Ivy / A Christmas Song / Another Christmas Song / God Rest Ye Merry Gentleman / Jack Frost And The Hooded Crow / Last Man At The Party / Weathercock / Pavane / First Snow On Brooklyn / Greensleeved / Fire At Midnight / We Five Kings / Ring Out Solstice Bells / Bourée / A Winter Snowscape

Whilst this Yuletide offering didn't exactly pull up any Xmas trees, it offered some old and new songs, some re-recorded even and proved that not all Christmas albums have to be produced by middle of the road acts. Inevitably it contained

'Ring Out Solstice Bells' the Christmas hit from 1976, which is still dragged out to this day on compilation shows of Christmas hits. One has to say, it has stood the test of time better than many other festive offerings from other acts. The album was updated in 2008 to include a charity concert from the atmospheric St Bride's Church in Fleet Street, London.

The lack of availability of DVDs of past and present material was rectified with the new millennium and continues to this day with a new 4 disc set just released in the summer of 2013 called *Around The World Live*, featuring material from the Isle of Wight festival in 1970 up to 2005.

In 2001, a DVD and CD called *Living With The Past* was released, with appearances from various band lineups. The DVD was a welcome addition at the time due to the lack of availability of Tull things to watch. This release seemed to fire off a slew of DVDs which had been available on older formats, including the long format rock video *Slipstream* available as VHS and Laserdisc from the 1980s. Anderson never was satisfied with *Slipstream* and, he claims, it was that which held them back from producing further video products. However, it was released with the remastered *A* album in much better quality.

The 25th Anniversary video, filmed mostly in a pub in the UK, brought a number of former Tull band members together for the evening and the original line-up performed. This was originally only on VHS, but was later released on DVD. A copy of the Madison Square Garden satellite show, also a VHS release, made it to disc, as did the 1970 Isle of Wight show; Tull were finally catching up with their video catalogue. Included with the Ian Anderson Orchestra CD release was a DVD of the same. We also saw a release of the Montreux Jazz festival show from 2003, not so far back as most of these releases, however, it is worthwhile mentioning for the completist collector.

Ian Anderson Plays The Orchestral Jethro Tull (2005)
Disc 1
Eurology / Calliandra Shade (The Cappuccino Song) / Skating Away (On The Thin Ice Of The New Day) / Up the 'Pool / We Five Kings / Life Is A Long Song / In the Grip Of Stronger Stuff / Wond'ring Aloud / Griminelli's Lament / Cheap Day Return / Mother Goose / Bourée / Boris Dancing / Living In The Past

Disc 2
Pavane / Aqualung / God Rest Ye Merry Gentlemen / My God / Budapest / Locomotive Breath

Never one to stand still, Anderson founded The Ian Anderson Orchestra and in 2004 recorded *Ian Anderson Plays The Orchestral Jethro Tull*, which, as the name implies, was orchestral versions of Tull classics with the mighty Frankfurt Neue Philharmonic Orchestra. David Goodier on bass and John O'Hara on keyboards were retained from *Rupi's Dance*. A DVD and double CD album ensued with a tour to promote it.

To be honest, this period was a stretch in too many directions. I lost my copy and I don't miss it. Anderson had wanted to do an orchestral version of Tull songs, but it came and went. This project came close to the *Rubbing Elbows With Ian* tour which had Anderson playing story teller and musician 'inter-reacting' with the audience. The tour got its name because Anderson does not like shaking hands in person, preferring to rub elbows. Whether this is a fear of germs and having to cancel gigs, we don't know. Certainly, he has cited the insurance on cancelled concerts due to illness and poked fun at Pavarotti for missing so many concerts. The first time I was aware was in 1995 when he wore a placard around his neck saying 'Cannot shake hands, sore wrists' – it was a chuckle to say the least.

He also had son James Duncan on drums (who didn't stay for the newer projects) and Florian Opahle was also featured on guitar. Goodier became the permanent replacement for Giddings and John O'Hara took Jon Noyce's spot on bass, leaving Doane Perry and Martin Barre as the only remaining Tullites. This was until the mid-2000s when Anderson put two line ups together touring as Jethro Tull, with Martin and Doane in their places – and The Ian Anderson Band with Florian and new drummer Scott Hammond (a name most will recognise, he has worked with everybody from Bruce Dickinson to Gilbert O'Sullivan – the mind boggles!) in for the Ian shows. These two separate entities played entirely different set lists.

Proving that the work ethic was alive and well and manifesting itself in Ian Anderson, not only were all these new projects crammed into a little over a decade, they were all coupled with tours. It told on some of the band's faces as in 2007 here in Montreal, the show ended abruptly with Ian disappearing almost by magic, and back stage, Martin walked out looking exhausted, while Ian disappeared out a side door. A 'Meet and Greet' which had been put together quickly never happened. This was the last tour by Tull to Canada and no one looked happy. The next show, in 2009, was an Ian show and the itinerary was much more interesting, the flare had returned, but we never saw Martin and Doane again.

Then came the news of the 40th anniversary catalogue. This mammoth undertaking to celebrate the event by enhancing each album with extras, started, logically enough, at the beginning with *This Was*, which featured a second disc of unreleased materials including BBC radio sessions. It has to be said, that many of the so called unreleased songs from any period have shown up both on the 20th Anniversary five album/three disc set and on remastered single discs.

Stand Up featured two versions of the Carnegie Hall concert from *Living In The Past*; one in stereo, the other a DVD 5.1 version. The spatial renderings were excellent. *Benefit* (as we've seen, not Anderson's favourite album) was ignored. I have heard a rumour that something is being prepared, but the people at the record company are saying nothing. Then, of course, after skipping *Benefit* we saw the two offerings of *Aqualung*. *Aqualung* appeared in a two CD package and a deluxe box set with a book, a vinyl 180 gram pressing, two CDs, a DVD and Blu Ray all full of extras and the 5.1 re-mixes and a book, all housed in a hard case. It should be pointed out that being 5.1, the album is remixed – it has to be, as it could not have the extra three tracks and subwoofer track or no change in mix, hence the original album on the CD and the extras on the second. It is a box for the *Aqualung* fanatic. A double album on vinyl of both TAAB 1 and 2 has also been released on 180 gram vinyl and mixed by Steven Wilson (the remix King, in addition to his other many talents, he has also worked with King Crimson and ELP remixing some of their back catalogue). *Thick As A Brick* also showed up as a double disc release coinciding with the 2 vinyl box set. So that is where the 40th anniversaries are up to this point.

Another project, in the can for 30 years, was the idea to improve on the *Aqualung* album. Anderson had never been happy with the end product, as Island Studios on Basing Street was new and full of technical glitches. Tull and Led Zeppelin both recorded their landmark albums, *Aqualung* and *Led Zeppelin IV* there at the same time, although Zeppelin only began their album there and headed out to other parts to complete it, whilst Tull stayed for the duration. The band, while still the Tull of the 1990s rather than the original lineup that made the original, recorded the entire album live for an invited Washington DC audience in 2005 and called it, logically enough, *Aqualung Live*. This is the sort of project it's best for the listener to comment on. Anderson had told me he had listened to the multi-track of *Aqualung* not long before and was quite surprised how good it sounded – interesting how time will change some ideas.

TAAB 2 (2012)

From A Pebble Thrown / Pebbles Instrumental / Might-Have-Beens / Upper Sixth Loan Shark / Banker Bets, Banker Wins / Swing It Far / Adrift And Dumbfounded / Old School Song / Wootton Bassett Town / Power And Spirit / Give Till It Hurts / Cosy Corner / Shunt And Shuffle / A Change Of Horses / Confessional / Kismet In Surburbia / What-Ifs, Maybes And Might-Have-Beens

TAAB 2, Whatever happened To Gerald Bostock? was a tongue firmly in cheek revisit to the past and a catching up with the supposed writer of the original volume, namely a, by now, grown up Gerald Bostock. It's a fun, interesting album and concept which has garnered great press. It has been touring for months with Ian's band, the concerts featuring the entire two *Thick as a Brick 1 & 2* in concert. Anderson, knowing full well that two 43 minute songs back to back is a wee bit much for his vocal chords, has brought along a second singer to keep strain to a minimum. The album – *TAAB2* – came as a pleasant surprise to those of us old enough to remember *Thick As A Brick* when it was first released back in 1972. And it arrived in time for the 40th anniversary of the original.

Tull were not the only members of the prog rock aristocracy to be celebrating the big 40th anniversary of their catalogue with 5.1 remixing and remastering. King Crimson produced a mammoth fifteen disc box set to commemorate *Larks' Tongues In Aspic* (which many fans still consider their best album) turning 40.

TAAB2 does pay homage to the original with lyrical and musical references to its predecessor. This time there are individual songs instead of the single one song being stretched out over 2 full LP sides. *TAAB2* did well and seemed to satiate the hard core pack, but it made more sense to those who were here when the first was released and the band presented it in its full length in 1972.

The current tour has been a success, but with only Anderson up on stage from previous band incarnations, this is not Jethro Tull. This may be causing some strife with Martin Barre as he was actually involved in the first *TAAB* and was left out of both this album and tour. What can you say about the album except it is enticing, some songs much better than others, and the comments on Gerald's 40 years are fun. For my money, the original album was musically stronger. It is best said that it is what it is and I think after taking the concept and putting the tongue in the cheek by doing this, most fans are now wondering what next? Will there be another instalment of another hit album?

A Passion Play is presumably next in line for enhancement, we hope. *A Passion Play* was played in its entirety in June 1973. Here in Canada, I had the privilege of witnessing it firsthand. The lead in was almost 40 minutes of a small dot growing with a heartbeat which led to a video until the band burst onto stage – best theatrics ever.

It has never been performed in a twenty minute version as *TAAB* has been for the past 40 years, so do we get a proper reworking of *A Passion Play*, do we get an *APP2* as well, or do we just get a quick nod and move on to *War Child*?

And does Tull have a reprieve too, or is that it and the future is The Ian Anderson band or what? Certainly enough pressure has been placed on Anderson since *Too Old To Rock'n'Roll* over how much longer he could keep the band going. Well, it would appear that answer is finally peeking out from behind the CD racks.

As to whether Tull will return as we knew it, that remains to be seen. I heard a rumour that some time back Ian took Martin and Doane into a room and said, 'I can't do this anymore.' And that is as far as it goes until another chapter opens, but this one is closed. Goodnight and good listening.

Sources

The content of this book was derived through a series of interviews that took place with the past and present members of Jethro Tull and their associates in an eight month period and including interviews from past talks with Ian Anderson dating to the late 1970s. Also, for the record, the interview with Jeffrey Hammond that spanned two days in two three hour chunks, was only the third time Jeffrey had ever been interviewed – thank you Jeffrey, I'm sure that was not an easy task.

The opportunity to make this a much better book presented itself by placing me in the position to carry out interviews to the nth degree. To all of the participants and to anyone who has submitted photographs, a very hearty and warm thank you. To Mrs Evans, whom I had promised to get in touch with, but couldn't, thank you for the offer. To Jethro Tull, the entity, musicians, legacy and Ian Anderson – thank you for the opportunity to spend countless hours in front of a stereo and a live band and enjoy the fruits of your labour.

Band Members Interviewed

Mick Abrahams, Ian Anderson, Martin Barre, Clive Bunker, Glenn Cornick, John Evans, Andy Giddings, Jeffrey Hammond, Eddie Jobson, Dave Pegg, Doane Perry, Peter-John Vettese, Tony Williams

Also Chris Wright, co-founder Chrysalis Records.

About The Author

Brian Rabey never expected to write about music and home theatre for 30 years. Having studied music from age 5, he discovered Tull at 15, bought a flute at 16 and learned the Tull repertoire. Originally writing an album review on a Tull album, while studying and working in professional theatre, as a one off reply to a predictably negative concert review, he was drawn in and has published for up to 60 markets and was pulled away from work as an actor and theatre technician. The publishing of *A Passion Play: Ian Anderson And The Story Of Jethro Tull* arrives in year 31 and is his first published book. He continues to write and record from his studio in Montreal, Canada.